Gulf
Capital
&Islamic
Finance

Gulf Capital &Islamic Finance

The Rise of the New Global Players

Aamir A. Rehman

New York   Chicago   San Francisco   Lisbon
London   Madrid   Mexico City   Milan   New Delhi
San Juan   Seoul   Singapore   Sydney   Toronto

1 2 3 4 5 6 7 8 9 0   DOC/DOC   0 1 6 5 4 3 2 1 0 9

ISBN   978-0-07-162198-4
MHID   0-07-162198-9

This work is based upon the author's experience, research, and individual perspective. The views expressed in this work are the author's and do not necessarily reflect those of Fajr Capital or any other firm. The book is not sponsored or approved by the author's employer or any other entity. It does not include any confidential or proprietary information of Fajr Capital, its shareholders and counterparties, or any other firm.

This publication is designed to provide accurate and authoritative information in regard to the subject matter covered. It is sold with the understanding that neither the author nor the publisher is engaged in rendering legal, accounting, futures/securities trading, or other professional service. If legal advice or other expert assistance is required, the services of a competent professional person should be sought.

—From a Declaration of Principles jointly adopted by a Committee of the American Bar Association and a Committee of Publishers

McGraw-Hill books are available at special quantity discounts to use as premiums and sales promotions, or for use in corporate training programs. To contact a representative please e-mail us at bulksales@mcgraw-hill.com.

This book is printed on acid-free paper.

Library of Congress Cataloging-in-Publication Data

Rehman, Aamir A.
    Gulf capital and Islamic finance : the rise of the new global players / by Aamir A. Rehman.

        p. cm.

    ISBN 978-0-07-162198-4 (alk. paper)

    1. Finance—Persian Gulf States.   2. Finance—Religious aspects—Islam.   3. Investments, Foreign—Persian Gulf States.   4. Persian Gulf States—Economic conditions—21st century. I. Title.

    HG187.3.R44 2010

    332.09536—dc22

                                                                    2009042346

To Drs. Razia and Abdul Rehman, for the countless sacrifices, gifts, and blessings of parents, for which I will be eternally indebted; and to my wife, Hina Ghory, for bearing untold burdens with warmth and grace to enable my pursuit of a passion.

C O N T E N T S

ACKNOWLEDGMENTS

This book represents a collective effort. The analysis was supported by a superb research team, led by Faisal Ghori. As research director for the book, Faisal recruited and managed a strong team of researchers, overseeing the research for all chapters while providing valuable input for the book overall. Faisal also provided significant drafting support for Chapter 9. His efforts were at the core of this endeavor and were pivotal to its completion.

Angel Leu, in addition to leading the research for Chapter 1, also provided comprehensive support in preparing the full manuscript and managing its finalization. Her contributions have been critical to completing this project on time. Andrew Goodman provided outstanding research for Chapters 2 and 5, and also provided strong drafting support for Chapters 5 and 10. Hisham Mabrook supported the research for Chapter 3 and provided a thorough review of the Islamic finance sector. Alex Campbell supported Chapter 4, contributing helpful overall research as well as transaction-specific information.

Andreea Ursu provided thorough research for Chapter 6, exploring Gulf investments in emerging markets in detail. Chapter 7 benefited from research support by Farhan Abbasi and Marjan Tabari, who compiled a comprehensive memo on Islamic investments. Chapter 8 was supported by Chris Blauvelt, who researched the challenging topic of disclosure practices. Alper Gokgoz provided a thorough research memo on sourcing Gulf capital for Chapter 9. Chapter 10, on the implications of Gulf activities for global investment strategies, was insightfully researched by Adil Syed. Victoria Zyp provided robust research for Chapter 11, exploring approaches for regulating Gulf investments. Chapter 12, on Islamic finance capabilities in global financial institutions, was well researched by Sabrina Siddiqui.

Rafi-uddin Shikoh, in addition to providing general input, supported the drafting of Chapter 6. Shira Mazor assisted in the formatting of the manuscript. Abdur-Rahman Syed, Imran Javaid, and Zohaib Patel provided general input and support. Munir Zilanawala, who masterfully managed the research process for my first book, *Dubai & Co.*, provided immensely valuable input on this second work and helped to enforce a strict timeline for producing the manuscript. Andrew Bartles provided valuable administrative support between the release of *Dubai & Co.* and the start of work on *Gulf Capital and Islamic Finance*.

I am immensely grateful for the support and love of my family in producing this book and in countless other ways. My parents, Drs. Razia and Abdul Rehman, have made sacrifices and provided blessings that can never be repaid. My wife, Hina Ghory, has borne—with grace—the burden of tolerating my hectic and travel-filled schedule, giving from our scarce time together while encouraging me throughout this effort. I am likewise grateful to my sister, Naheed Abbasi, and to my extended family and relatives for their inspiring encouragement.

Iqbal Khan, CEO of Fajr Capital Limited and former founding CEO of HSBC Amanah, has been a close mentor and dear colleague for over a decade. His values-based leadership and vision remain a constant inspiration, and I am grateful for his enthusiastic support of this project. I wish also to recognize my colleagues on the Fajr Capital management committee—Javed Ahmad, Dato' Noorazman Aziz, Kamran Faridi, Rafe Haneef, Saud Hashimi, and Rizwan Kherati—for their warm collegiality and unwavering support for this effort.

In addition, I am grateful to the Middle East Institute—and, in particular, Ambassador Wendy Chamberlain, Dr. Michael Ryan, J. F. Hulston, and Stephanie Swierczek—for the encouragement, resources, and opportunities it has provided me as an adjunct scholar since 2008. The Harvard Islamic Finance Project, its staff, and its affiliates—including Dr. S. Nazim Ali, Prof. Baber Johansen, Prof. Samuel L. Hayes III, Taha Abdul-Basser, and many others—have provided me with an invaluable perspective on the Islamic finance sector since 1995. Additionally, I wish to recognize instructors at leading universities—and first among them, Prof. Salah Hassan of George Washington University—for drawing on *Dubai & Co.* for use in their curricula and for providing me with direct access to their students. Trevor Lloyd-Jones of the publication *Business Intelligence Middle East* is also to be recognized for his enthusiastic distribution of my commentary.

I thank the research team for *Dubai & Co.* and all who contributed to its worldwide success. I am further grateful to dear colleagues from HSBC Amanah and the Boston Consulting Group, through whom I was privileged to explore global corporate strategy, the Gulf region, and Islamic finance. The guidance and observations of innumerable colleagues have helped to shape the perspectives articulated in this work.

The publishing and editorial team at McGraw-Hill has been a true partner in this project. Senior editor Leah Spiro has been an understanding and supportive colleague, as has editorial director Mary Glenn. Leah and Mary are to be commended for their strong transition in taking over from Jeanne Glasser and Herb Schaffner, their respective predecessors, who warmly launched this project. I am grateful to Janice Race, Tania Loghmani, Jane Palmieri, and other colleagues at McGraw-Hill for their stellar contributions to the manuscript. I take responsibility for any errors or shortcomings in the manuscript, and I thank all who have contributed to its preparation.

Despite their increased importance for global markets, Gulf capital and Islamic finance remain unfamiliar to many senior executives and financiers. A deeper understanding of these phenomena can, I believe, help foster the trade flows, investment ties, and commercial relationships that are the cement of mutual respect and harmony. It is my hope that this book may be a modest contribution toward that end.

Gulf Capital & Islamic Finance

Introducing the New Global Players

The world of finance is being transformed before our eyes. Many of the long-established "rules" of capital markets face fundamental questions and rapid change. Long-revered multinational banks have been deeply shaken by a global financial crisis, in which Wall Street giants like Citigroup and Goldman Sachs participated in massive "troubled asset" programs. Recognizing the regulatory lapses that contributed to the financial crisis, regulators around the world have taken more activist positions and increased their intervention in capital markets. At the height of a credit crunch fueled by the spread of misrated and opaque "toxic paper," money markets in the United States faced unprecedented pressure—in an extreme episode, even money market funds briefly slipped into negative returns.

This transformation of financial markets—which was still under-way at the time of this writing—reflects the changing topography of the global economy. Large, developed economies such as the United States and the United Kingdom have taken on unprecedented levels of public debt to stimulate their domestic economies and stabilize key economic sectors. These measures, which were considered essential for economic recovery, have set the stage for long and protracted deficits. Companies and individuals in the world's leading economies find themselves facing a painful process of "deleveraging," seeking to recover from the burdens of high debt levels in recent years. For many economies, generating fresh capital for investment may be a multi-year challenge.

At the same time, in contrast, a number of economies, mainly in emerging markets, are continuing to grow. A handful of countries (a fortunate few) enjoy large capital reserves, continue to generate budget surpluses, and act as next exporters of capital. As many economies are slipping deeper into debt, others are busily accumulating savings. Our long-held belief that capital naturally flows from developed economies to emerging markets no longer holds—today, saver nations in the developing world provide much-needed capital to the world's largest economies. This shift in topography is fundamentally changing global markets.

In the evolving financial topography, the economies of the Gulf region—the six countries that make up the Gulf Cooperation Council (GCC)—are new and increasingly important peaks. Individually and in aggregate, the member states of the GCC—Saudi Arabia, the United Arab Emirates (UAE), Qatar, Kuwait, Bahrain, and Oman—are playing an increasingly pivotal role in global markets. At the same time, Islamic finance, a phenomenon that is distinct from but deeply linked to the rise of the Gulf, has evolved from a niche, regional sector to an increasingly integral part of the world's financial system.

ON THE WORLD STAGE

When General Electric (GE), one of the world's most admired companies and a titan of US business, resolved to sell its plastics business in 2007, the most attractive buyer was not a midwestern chemical company or even a European conglomerate. It was the Saudi Basic Industries Corporation (SABIC), a leading industrial conglomerate. SABIC, by the way, had once reached a market capitalization of $135 billion—a shade under those of Google and Honda, and greater than that of Coca-Cola.[1]

As Citigroup—at the time, the world's largest bank—began to buckle under the pressure of the credit crisis in 2008, the first waves of relief did not come from Wall Street or from Washington. They came from the Abu Dhabi Investment Authority (ADIA, a Gulf sovereign wealth fund) and Prince Alwaleed Bin Talal (a Gulf-based private investor). ADIA, typically discreet in its investment activities, is widely viewed as one of the world's largest institutional investors. Prince Alwaleed, individually or through his firm Kingdom Holding Company, is also a major shareholder in Apple, the Four Seasons Hotels, and a host of other multinational firms whose total customer base worldwide is in the hundreds of millions.

When Ford sold off its business line Aston Martin—world-famous as James Bond's preferred vehicle—the principal buyers were two investment companies not from Detroit or Tokyo, but from Kuwait. Further, the transaction was an Islamic one, structured to conform to the guidelines of Shariah to meet the preferences of Aston Martin's new owners. The Aston Martin transaction was by no means the first Islamic acquisition of a prominent US firm; for example, Caribou Coffee (America's second-largest coffeehouse chain) is owned by a Bahrain-based Islamic investment firm.

Such high-profile investments by Gulf-based and Islamic institutions are not surprising when one considers the following facts:

- Collectively, the Gulf states control over 40 percent of the world's known oil reserves and nearly a quarter of global natural gas reserves.[2]
- By the end of 2006, the GCC states' foreign assets reached an estimated $1.9 trillion.[3] No doubt, these grew substantially in 2007 and early 2008 before suffering losses in the subsequent financial crisis.
- Gulf-based investors either currently hold or historically have held major stakes in prominent global companies. Both Gucci and Tiffany & Co., for example, have been owned by Bahrain-based Investcorp in the past.[4]
- In 2006 alone, the net capital outflows from the Gulf were above $200 billion—a figure surpassed only by China.[5]
- In the same year, GDP per capita in the GCC reached $19,000—nearly three times that of China and more than five times that of India.[6]
- In the auto industry alone, Gulf investors hold major stakes in Daimler, Ferrari, and (as mentioned previously) Aston Martin.[7]
- The GDP per capita of Qatar is astonishing—it was nearly $86,000 in 2008. That's 1.8 times the US figure of about $47,000, 2.6 times the figure for the EU, a whopping 14 times

that of China, and 31 times that of India.[8] Some are
forecasting that by 2011, the small, resource-rich Gulf state
will have the highest GDP per capita in the world.[9]

- According to the McKinsey Global Institute, the Gulf's total
  foreign wealth could reach $8.3 trillion by 2020. This would
  correspond to about $270,000 per GCC citizen at that time.[10]

- Nearly all leading global financial institutions, including
  HSBC, Citigroup, Standard Chartered, and Deutsche Bank,
  among others, now offer Islamic financial services and view
  Islamic finance as a significant opportunity.

- In 2008, the *Harvard Business Review* featured a piece on the
  rise of Islamic finance as a new global player in its issue on
  "Breakthrough Ideas" for the year.[11]

The global financial crisis and economic recession—which are still
underway at the time of this writing—have deeply affected the Gulf
region and its investment activity. The credit crisis and the subsequent
global fall in investor confidence rocked GCC stock markets, wiping
away billions of dollars of market capitalization in 2008 alone. The
drying up of global debt markets has brought many capital projects—
especially a number of Dubai real estate initiatives—to a screeching
halt. Perhaps most fundamental, however, has been the steep decline in
oil prices as a result of the global recession. Trading at around $150 per
barrel at its peak in 2008, oil fell more than two-thirds in value before
settling again at around the $50 per barrel mark. This fall in oil prices
slashed government surpluses in the Gulf and severely reduced the
supply of new surplus capital available for investment. Some
observers, therefore, have questioned whether Gulf capital will remain
as important to global markets as it has been in recent years.

In assessing the ongoing importance of Gulf capital despite the
dip in oil prices, consider the following four facts:

1. If no additional surpluses were generated in the Gulf, the
   region would nonetheless still have substantial reserves that
   have been built up over the past years. According to a
   McKinsey forecast, the returns on GCC foreign assets would
   exceed $1.6 trillion over a 14-year period even "if the GCC
   never invested another penny."[12]

2. Gulf-based investors, like institutional investors worldwide,
   have no doubt suffered losses as a result of the financial

crisis and global recession. Unlike many other institutions, however, Gulf investors (especially in the UAE, Qatar, and Kuwait) can expect fresh infusions of capital as a result of their ongoing budget surpluses.

3. Even at modest oil prices, key Gulf economies will accumulate new capital. Assuming an oil price of $50, GCC economies would gather $4.7 trillion between now and 2020.[13]

4. Gulf investors enjoy sizable reserves and "dry powder" for acquisitions in an environment of lower asset values worldwide. In an increasingly capital-constrained world, Gulf investors are a rare source of liquidity. Thus, they could remain central to global investment markets for the foreseeable future.

GAPS IN UNDERSTANDING

Despite the growing importance of Gulf capital and Islamic finance, most business and finance leaders today have little understanding of these areas. They acknowledge that these phenomena are influencing the shape of global finance, but the drivers, forms, and implications of Gulf capital and Islamic finance tend to be only partly understood through headlines and news flashes.

These gaps in understanding are natural. The rise of the Gulf as a business and financial center is, after all, a recent phenomenon. Islamic finance, although present in its modern form since the 1970s, came to the attention of global financial institutions in a serious way only in the 1990s. In the corporate worlds in which most senior executives spent their formative years, the Gulf region and Islamic finance were not central to global corporate or financial strategies. Senior executives' exposure to these topics tends, therefore, to be quite limited. Schools of management have historically had little in their curricula on these fields, although this is changing fast. Leading institutions have been steadily increasing their focus on this area through initiatives such as the Islamic Finance Program at the Harvard Law School and the Cass Business School's MBA program with a focus on Islamic finance.

At the same time, public information on these topics has often been piecemeal, anecdotal, or hard for international audiences to access. As with most emerging fields, participants have generally had little time to analyze these phenomena holistically. In the field of

Islamic finance, much of the foundational literature—with notable exceptions[14]—has focused more on economic theory, legal principles, and instrument structures than on the evolution and relevance of the industry. In discussions with financial professionals worldwide, I have often heard readers express interest in work reviewing the rise of the Islamic finance sector from a commercial and strategic perspective.

Additionally, international discussions on Gulf capital and Islamic finance often take a geopolitical perspective rather than offering an empirical analysis of the opportunities. Some observers, whose perspectives are often rooted in misconceptions about the Middle East region and its institutional investors, view these phenomena with suspicion. The controversy in the United States regarding Dubai Ports World's acquisition of the British firm P&O (operator of several US ports)—dubbed a "debacle" in a Harvard Business School case—was a prime example of such suspicion.[15] Members of Congress raised objections to the acquisition (which had the support of the security-sensitive Bush administration), and the transaction was ultimately restructured so as to avoid the controversy. A common perception of Gulf investors as a potential threat prompted *BusinessWeek* magazine to run a cover story in 2008 entitled "Who's Afraid of Mideast Money?"[16]

As sovereign wealth funds have gained prominence in recent years, fundamental questions have been raised about their intentions and the potential impact of their role on the global stage. Such questions are only fair, and warrant exploration. An accurate assessment, however, must be guided by a robust and fact-based review rather than colored by fear and hostility. Fear-based assessments can lead to many missed opportunities for mutually beneficial investment flows, potentially derailing otherwise promising financial and business collaboration.

The time is right for a holistic analysis of Gulf capital, Islamic finance, and their impact on global markets. In crafting their global strategies, financial professionals worldwide increasingly wonder

- Is the wealth of the Gulf here to stay, or is it a short-term phenomenon?
- What institutions in the Gulf are making investments, and what are their objectives?
- In what regions, countries, and sectors are Gulf institutions investing?

- How can international firms tap into Gulf capital?
- What makes Islamic finance "Islamic"?
- What is driving the growth of Islamic finance, and will this growth continue?
- What does it take to serve Islamic finance customers?
- How is Shariah compliance affecting capital flows?
- Should the world be afraid of Islamic finance?
- How is the rise of Gulf capital affecting financial markets?
- Should the world fear or welcome Gulf investors?
- What role might the Gulf play in capital markets in the long term?

This book addresses these questions and more, serving as a strategic guide for financial professionals assessing the opportunities, strategies, and markets that have been affected by the rise of Gulf investors and Islamic finance as new global players. The themes discussed hold relevance for investment professionals, corporate finance advisors, investment bankers, CFOs, regulators, analysts, researchers, and others whose work depends on a nuanced understanding of the changing topography of global financial markets.

YOUR GUIDE TO THE NEW GLOBAL PLAYERS

This book—your guide to the rise of new global players—has four sections. Part I provides background and context on the rise of Gulf capital and Islamic finance, addressing the origins and drivers of these phenomena. Part II discusses developments and trends related to these areas, providing insight into how they are evolving and what directions their future evolution is likely to take. Part III focuses on the global implications of the rise of these new players— what their increased importance means for investors, bankers, regulators, and international markets broadly. The book's Conclusion, envisions the role of Gulf capital in an emerging, multipolar financial order. We explore how Gulf capital and Islamic finance are changing the landscape, and whether they should be seen as opportunities or as threats. Overall, the book is designed both to give you a firm grounding in these emerging areas and to help frame your thinking on how to incorporate them into your organization's strategy and daily business.

Part I: Background and Context

The first chapter of this book discusses the origins and sources of Gulf prosperity, as well as the outlook for the region's wealth in an uncertain future. Though they are known today for their sleek buildings and visible wealth, the countries of the GCC have modest origins as merchant societies and cross-regional traders. The principal source of Gulf wealth, the area's oil and gas resources, has experienced remarkable volatility over the decades, marked by tremendous booms in the 1970s and 2000s with steep corrections in between. Healthy surpluses, especially in recent years, have enabled the region to amass trillions of dollars in invested wealth. The current financial crisis and global recession have certainly affected the value of Gulf investments, reducing portfolio values significantly. A more fundamental effect, however, has been the steep decline in oil prices from their 2008 peaks. Still, even with this decline, key Gulf states—particularly the UAE, Qatar, and Kuwait—may continue to enjoy significant surpluses and to generate income from their substantial reserves. In fact, the environment of cheaper asset values worldwide may encourage Gulf investors to expand their portfolios in the current period.

As Gulf wealth is inextricably linked to energy markets, any forecast of GCC investments must consider various scenarios for oil and gas prices in the years ahead. We therefore discuss potential upward and downward pressures on oil prices, as well as systemic shifts (such as the momentum of renewable-energy initiatives) that have the potential to fundamentally shape oil and gas markets going forward.

Having reviewed the drivers, scale, and outlook for Gulf capital, we turn our attention to the landscape of Gulf-based investors. The GCC investor base is not a monolith, and Chapter 2 classifies and describes the various types of Gulf-based investors. The best known among them are the "generalist" sovereign wealth funds (SWFs) such as the Abu Dhabi Investment Authority (ADIA) and the Qatar Investment Authority (QIA). These funds, some of which were established decades ago, exist principally to preserve and grow the wealth of Gulf nations through prudent international investment. We will discuss the stated objectives and activities of these SWFs, and also explore how the term *fund* is often a misnomer for Gulf SWFs, which might better be understood as "trusts."

A second category of Gulf investors that we shall explore is "specialist" government-funded investment vehicles such as Mubadala

Development Company of Abu Dhabi and the Saudi Industrial Development Fund (SIDF). Though also government-supported, these vehicles have narrower (and often more aggressive) objectives and operate more like private investment firms than like public agencies. The past decade has seen dramatic growth in these specialist institutions. As GCC governments respond to the current financial crisis and economic recession, additional specialist entities, such as an $800 million Saudi vehicle for agricultural investment,[17] are being launched for both investment and overall economic objectives.

In the Gulf private sector, there are also multiple key categories of investors. Some GCC families have long been sophisticated global investors, holding significant portfolios worldwide and participating in private equity, hedge funds, and managed accounts with multinational financial institutions. Though they are often underestimated, some of these investors have frequently shown themselves to be as savvy as their international counterparts when it comes to investment decisions and negotiations.

Since the boom of the 1970s, there have also been a number of private investment houses (such as Investcorp of Bahrain) through which Gulf investors have invested internationally. The 2000s have witnessed an expansion in the number and type of these companies, with firms such as Abraaj Capital of the UAE and Global Investment House of Kuwait tapping into regional liquidity and developing targeted funds and investment vehicles. The appearance and expansion of these private investment houses represent an important stage in the development of Gulf capital markets.

Chapter 3 reviews the rise of Islamic finance in the Gulf and beyond. Islamic finance is rooted in a set of basic principles with universal relevance. While the technical aspects of the Shariah are themselves a sophisticated science, the core principles of Islamic finance are largely accessible and relevant far beyond the Muslim world. For example, the principle that a person should not profit from activities that he believes to be immoral—a core tenet of Islamic investment—is shared by ethical investors of all traditions.

In discussing the origins of modern Islamic finance, we note that its pioneers have largely been from outside the Gulf region. Groundbreaking institutions were founded in a range of countries, including Egypt and Malaysia. Today, however, the GCC region represents the bulk of the accessible Islamic finance market.[18] A majority of the industry's leading institutions—for example, the Saudi bank Al Rajhi and the regional conglomerate the Al Baraka Banking Group—are based in the Gulf and owned by Gulf shareholders. We review the principal drivers of the growth in Islamic finance's overall market share, including the expansion of product offerings and strong Shariah affinity among GCC youth. As the sector has expanded, it faces key strategic challenges related to regulation, human capital, standardization, and other such areas. In particular, we will probe a perceived trade-off between gaining market share and retaining Shariah authenticity—a trade-off that will have fundamental conse- quences for the Islamic finance sector in the coming years.

In the global financial crisis, many observers—including the Vatican[19]—have pointed to Islamic finance as a potential source of ideas and solutions. Our discussion of the sector will touch on the rel- evance of Islamic finance principles to the crisis, while noting that the sector's application of these principles has been incomplete. The crisis can, therefore, both highlight the relevance of certain ethical princi- ples found in Islamic finance and act as a reminder to the Islamic finance sector of the importance of these principles.

Part II: Developments and Trends

After Part I of the book describes who these new global players are, Part II discusses where the players are going. Having laid the ground- work of context and background, we turn to a discussion of key developments and trends related to Gulf capital and Islamic finance.

Chapter 4 highlights the increased sophistication of Gulf investors. In the oil boom of the 1970s, Gulf investments (beyond the development of core infrastructure at home) flowed into traditional asset classes and "plain vanilla" investment products such as US Treasury bills. Investments were largely managed by foreign institu- tions, and in-market investment organizations were scarce. In a num- ber of ways, the scale of Gulf investments exceeded the sophistication of Gulf investment strategies.

In the boom of the 2000s, GCC investors have expanded to a far broader range of asset classes. While US Treasuries, fixed-income products, and large-cap equity positions still make up a large part of Gulf portfolios, GCC investors have also given increased attention to real estate, private equity, hedge funds, and other "alternative" asset classes. This increased sophistication has largely been enabled by enhanced human capital and organizational capabilities within Gulf institutions. GCC-based investment bodies and firms have, especially over the past decade, had greater access to world-class talent and have built solid investment teams with diverse backgrounds and global expertise. At the same time, the world's leading investment management firms have largely "discovered" the Gulf and are clamoring for access to the region's capital.

While raising the overall return prospects for Gulf investors, the increased sophistication of investment portfolios has also exposed GCC investors to more financial risk and raised these investors' visibility profile. Buyouts and large equity stakes are, by their very nature, high-profile forms of investing. A number of Gulf-based investment firms have positioned themselves—through prominent acquisitions, co-investment alongside leading global firms, published research and thought leadership, and other public relations activity—as world-class institutions. Kingdom Holding Company's stakes in prominent brands like Apple, as well as Prince Alwaleed Bin Talal's investment in the Four Seasons Hotels alongside Bill Gates,[20] build an image of Kingdom as a serious global investment institution.

The global financial crisis is likely to affect the sophistication of Gulf investors in a number of ways. Investors who were highly speculative and leveraged have experienced massive losses, and some firms may shift their strategies, scale back, consolidate, or even disappear. In the buildup to the crisis, a number of high-profile assets (including Citigroup and, according to some reports, Lehman Brothers)[21] were marketed to Gulf investors, who were seen as potential providers of lifesaving capital. This experience is likely to cause Gulf investors to be more discerning in future investment reviews and more confident in the outside world's need for their capital infusions.

Another key trend—explored in Chapter 5—has been the increased interest by Gulf investors in domestic and regional (GCC) investments. Whereas the local investments of the 1970s built the region's "hard" infrastructure—airports, roads, utilities, and the like—the boom of the 2000s has enabled investments in "soft" economic infrastructure. Investment in the diversification of local economies, the creation of free zones (most notably in the UAE), and the human capital investments needed for knowledge-based economies have been made in earnest over the past decade. These investments, while also generating a financial return, enhance the fundamental competitiveness of the region and are part of longer-term development strategies put in place by Gulf governments.

Although all GCC states are members of the WTO, the process of opening Gulf markets to foreign investors has been a gradual one. Foreign ownership stakes are generally limited by regulation. Free zones in which full foreign ownership is allowed have thrived in the UAE, setting an example that Qatar, Bahrain, and others have begun adopting in targeted ways. Intra-GCC investment is a growing trend that is not limited to free zones, and the expansion of Gulf businesses into adjacent GCC markets is becoming more common. That said, the GCC is far from fully integrated as an economic unit, and significant progress in opening markets still needs to be made.

Listed equity markets in the region have experienced a number of booms and busts, including two cycles over the past eight years. From 2001 to 2006, a swell in liquidity and an increased regional/domestic focus led to a tremendous boom in stock prices. The market capitalization of key Gulf companies reached meteoric heights—UAE-based property developer Emaar, for example, became the highest-valued developer in the world.[22] Then a sharp correction in 2006 wiped out more than half of the total market capitalization in the UAE, Saudi Arabia, and Qatar, and over a third of the value in other GCC markets.[23] This decline, although painful, brought valuations closer in line with emerging-market standards. Stock prices rose again in 2007 and much of 2008 before the global financial crisis led to another severe downturn and "bust." Gulf equity markets remain largely sentiment-driven, with retail investors contributing the bulk of invested capital and typically trading more on confidence than on the fundamental analysis of companies. This was particularly evident in the bust of 2006, in which many companies lost more than half of their market capitalization despite achieving earnings growth and solid fundamental results.

Macroeconomic trends in the region—including sustained prosperity, demographic shifts, and regulatory reform—suggest a promising outlook for investment in the region. Furthermore, expansionary budgets in the region in the wake of the global recession suggest that strategic sectors may experience fast growth. That said, the best investment opportunities are generally *not* on the public markets and are accessible only through private equity and joint-venture vehicles.

In recent years, Gulf-based investors have significantly increased their interest in emerging-market investments. This trend, discussed in Chapter 6, is of great significance for those who are seeking to attract Gulf capital or to advise investors based in the region. While the "typical" Gulf portfolio remains heavily oriented toward investment in the United States and other Organisation for Economic Co-operation and Development (OECD) markets, investments in the broader Middle East—the Levant region, Egypt, and North Africa—are sizable and growing. Leaders and companies in the broader Middle East are actively courting Gulf capital, and GCC companies find expansion to other Middle East markets to be a natural path for growth.

At the same time, Gulf investments in China and India have also been increasing. For example, the Kuwait Investment Authority was the single largest subscriber in the Industrial and Commercial Bank of China's 2006 public offering—at the time, the largest IPO in world history.[24] Gulf investments in China and India have been high-profile and warmly welcomed, encouraging ongoing capital flows to complement existing trade flows. Africa represents a new frontier for Gulf investors, and investment flows have begun. In 2005, for example, the Gulf African Bank was established as Kenya's first Shariah-compliant bank, with major GCC investors from the UAE, Oman, and Saudi Arabia as shareholders.[25] As postcrisis valuations have made emerging markets more accessible than before, Gulf investments in high-growth parts of Asia and Africa are likely to continue in earnest.

Investment by GCC-based investors in Southeast Asia has been significant and has been supported in part by the presence of Islamic finance in both regions. Two of the Gulf's leading Islamic banks—Al Rajhi of Saudi Arabia and Kuwait Finance House—have expanded into Malaysia as a key growth market for their businesses. Dubai Islamic Investment Group (part of the emirate's Dubai Group) has taken a 40 percent equity stake in Bank Islam Malaysia, Malaysia's leading stand-alone Islamic bank.[26] Singapore, too, has attracted Gulf investment for an Islamic financial institution called the Islamic Bank of Asia.[27] In fact, one significant motivation behind the promotion of Islamic finance in Southeast Asia has been the objective of attracting capital from Gulf markets.

Chapter 7 explores in greater depth the increasing affinity of Gulf investors for Islamic investments. Gulf investors have historically invested conventionally (meaning through non-Shariah-compliant methods),[28] as they lacked competitive Islamic alternatives that could meet their investment needs. Over the past decade, however, the number and sophistication of Shariah-compliant investment vehicles (both funds and products) has increased manyfold. At the same time, the number of Islamic investment firms and their total assets under management have both risen dramatically. This shift toward Shariah compliance has real implications for asset values in Muslim markets abroad, as Islamic investors flock toward assets that meet their investment criteria. The shift has also reduced the relative appeal of non-Shariah-compliant offerings within the Gulf. In Saudi Arabia, for example, the strong preference for Shariah-compliant investments has motivated asset managers to concentrate their efforts on developing Islamic products more than non-Islamic ones. Similarly, family businesses and corporations increasingly see Shariah-compliant capital structures as highly desirable, both for religious reasons and to attract domestic capital and investors.

Two key forces may act to drive greater interest in Islamic investments by large GCC institutions. First, the Islamic investment industry continues to mature and to develop broader and deeper products and services to meet the needs of sophisticated investors. Second, and perhaps more important, there is increased pressure from the stakeholders of Gulf institutions to consider Islamic investments. As beneficiaries, citizens, government officials, and the management of these investment bodies become more aware of (and comfortable with) Islamic investments in their personal lives, they may naturally be motivated to explore Shariah-compliant alternatives at the institutional level. Considering the size of some Gulf institutional investors, even modest shifts in their allocations toward Islamic investments could have a massive impact on the size of the Islamic investment industry.

In addition to these main forces, other environmental shifts may also support greater interest in Islamic investments by Gulf investors. The global financial crisis has fostered a greater appreciation among Muslims of the prudential aspects of Islamic investment principles and revealed the risks of certain speculative conventional investment modes. Furthermore, as Gulf family businesses expand and rationalize their business portfolios, the "growth capital" that they will require is a natural need that fits well with the spirit of Islamic investment principles. As Gulf investors look to stimulate their local economies, Islamic investment modes are a suitable channel, as many business owners in the region prefer Shariah compliance.

A final trend that we explore—discussed in Chapter 8—is the heightened visibility and transparency of Gulf investments in overseas markers. Despite their significant scale, GCC-based investors have traditionally maintained a low profile because of the traditional and conservative nature of their investments and their relatively small equity stakes in global firms. As GCC investments have become more sophisticated and equity-oriented, demands for disclosure and transparency have grown. The controversy regarding Dubai Ports World was a watershed event in raising the visibility of GCC investors and their potential influence over global companies.

In 2008, the Abu Dhabi Investment Authority issued a published letter declaring its investment objectives. The letter marked a major step toward disclosure, and reflected a drive toward proactive communication so as to allow the discussion to take place on ADIA's terms rather than being imposed by outside bodies. As financial regulations tighten worldwide as a reaction to the global crisis, greater scrutiny of and increased government involvement in regulating investment flows can be expected. In this environment, the trend toward greater transparency by Gulf investors is likely to continue.

Part III: Global Implications

The discussion of key trends in Gulf capital and Islamic finance leads to a consideration of the implications of these trends for international actors and global markets. Part III of the book focuses on what the rise of these global players means for firms, markets, and decision makers worldwide.

Chapter 9 discusses strategies for attracting GCC investors—a topic that has been increasingly important in recent years, and a critical one in these capital-scarce times. We discuss how there is no "one size fits all" approach to tapping into Gulf capital, as the objectives and preferences of Gulf investors vary greatly. Therefore, managers and advisors must make the effort required to understand the strategies and styles of the specific investors they are seeking to attract. As the competition to attract Gulf investors has intensified, some of the old assumptions about doing so no longer hold. A widely held assumption that Gulf investors are "easy sells" who will neither push back nor ask tough questions is now far less accurate, as the region's institutions have become more sophisticated. Also, it has become increasingly important to have at least some level of in-market physical presence in the region. As more and more investment managers seek Gulf capital, having a presence there helps them demonstrate their commitment to the GCC and to its investors, and also allows relationship managers to have deeper ties to their clients. While the actual investment managers may generally be more appropriately based where the assets are, firms that are seeking to build ties with GCC institutions can be well advised to have some investor-facing resources in the region.

Another important change with implications for attracting Gulf capital is an increased focus—at least among some Gulf investors—on strategic partnerships and ongoing co-investment opportunities. For example, certain family investors may seek to invest in sectors in which they have their own businesses or in industries that complement their family portfolios. Such investments can provide not only financial returns but also strategic partnerships and market insights. Likewise, certain investors may be keen to have the right to co-invest alongside private equity funds in specific opportunities that have particular appeal to them as a result of their investment strategies and preferences. Investment managers who recognize these preferences can structure relationships that have added appeal to Gulf-based institutions.

The rise of Gulf capital has implications for firms' investment strategies even if the firms have no direct contact with the region. In Chapter 10, we explore a number of ways in which the activities of Gulf-based actors can have an impact on the investment strategies of international institutions. First, the interest of Gulf investors in a particular market or company can signal a "rising tide" of asset values in that area. As in other investment communities, Gulf investors follow one another's activities and will often be inspired to pursue assets that are similar to those bought by other GCC-based institutions. A vivid example of this phenomenon has been the competition between Borse Dubai and the Qatar Investment Authority for equity in overseas stock exchanges—including vying in 2007 for a stake in the Nordic exchange OMX.[29] Even if a company has no interest in working with Gulf investors, knowing where these investors are going (or from where they are retreating) can provide an important cue regarding future asset values.

The appetite of GCC-based investors for co-investment alongside global firms can also be a key input into the strategies of global firms as they assess new investments. Investing alongside a Gulf institution can make certain capital-intensive transactions more feasible and can also provide a built-in "exit option" for the non-Gulf participants. This may be especially important for funds with a defined timeline for entry into and exit from their investment positions.

Operating companies can also benefit from keeping an eye on the investment preferences of Gulf-based institutions. Gulf capital is funding increasingly global companies, altering some industries' competitive dynamics. In the airline industry, for example, fresh capital has enabled Gulf-based carriers to invest in new fleets of planes and fly from state-of-the art airport hubs, building their appeal relative to competing airlines without access to this capital.[30] Knowing which industries Gulf dollars are likely to fund is thus an important indicator for firms that wish to anticipate changes in their competitive environments.

The regulation of outward investments from the Gulf, a key discussion in public-policy circles, is addressed in Chapter 11. In the public debate, some have called for blanket prohibitions and barriers. Such broad measures, however, drive away valuable capital unnecessarily. A more nuanced approach is required, especially in an environment in which capital is scarce worldwide. Institutions that have the ability to invest will expect accommodation and greater liberty as a result of their "market power" in capital-constrained times. Gulf investors—like their Chinese counterparts—know that they have plenty of choices when it comes to where to invest.

While regulation of investments is often necessary and prudent, the most practical approach going forward may be deal-specific disclosure and regulation. Governments outside the Gulf cannot reasonably expect to impose blanket regulations on investors outside their jurisdiction, but the terms and conditions of particular investments, especially in strategically sensitive areas, can conceivably be reviewed on a case-by-case basis. Regimes that have a sophisticated approach to the regulation of investments, neither blocking capital needlessly nor risking a loss of control of key economic sectors, are likely to win the battle for capital from the Gulf and from other net exporters of wealth.

One key implication of the rise of Islamic finance is the heightened importance of Islamic finance capabilities within global financial institutions. As we discuss in Chapter 12, financial services providers must increasingly understand Islamic finance in order to service a broad base of customers in the Gulf and in other key Muslim markets effectively. Shariah structuring is a complex endeavor, requiring specialized expertise and a distinct governance and compliance model. Shariah authenticity is a key imperative for competing in the Islamic finance sector, and the "window" model by which conventional institutions service Islamic and conventional clients through the same entity is facing additional pressures in the marketplace.

While the cost of entry in terms of the expertise required to provide Islamic financial services can be significant, it is increasingly evident from the examples of HSBC, Citigroup, and others that no financial services institution can be truly global without Islamic finance capabilities. At the same time, regulators in the OECD world—most notably the United Kingdom—are identifying Islamic finance as a growth sector within an otherwise troubled financial services sector. Initiatives are therefore underway to make participation in the Shariah-compliant market more prevalent and easier for Western-based institutions.

Conclusion

We conclude our review of Gulf capital and Islamic finance as new global players with a discussion of their potential roles in a changed international financial order. The rise of the Gulf and of Islamic finance may be seen as part of a broader evolution toward a multipolar financial system. The Gulf's role in this system will be largely dependent on the ongoing scale of GCC surpluses—surpluses that may be significant but that are based on unpredictable energy prices. Islamic finance may expand faster or slower depending on the growth of Muslim markets, but it is evidently a long-term trend that has demonstrated its ongoing importance in the international financial system.

Though it is impossible to fully predict the Gulf's role in the future, indications suggest that the Gulf is likely to remain a key player in global investments for years to come. The involvement of Gulf-based investors in international markets can have an enriching effect, both financially and otherwise, and generate opportunities for firms and professionals who understand the aspirations and needs of such investors. At the same time, the Gulf's engagement in global markets has been—and can continue to be—a driver of reform within the GCC region itself. Robust strategies for both global institutions and entities in the Gulf rely on embracing change and recognizing the opportunities created by an ever-evolving world.

DISTINCT—YET RELATED—PHENOMENA

Gulf capital and Islamic finance, although related, must be understood as distinct phenomena. The vast majority of Gulf investment has been—and remains today—conventional in its structuring rather than Shariah-compliant. At the same time, Islamic finance is a genuinely global phenomenon, with products and services being offered in Asia, Europe, Africa, the United States, and elsewhere. Why, then, do we discuss them together in a single book?

There are three chief reasons for linking these two separate topics in a single volume:

1. GCC countries represent the bulk of the addressable Islamic finance market. The Gulf region's markets—in particular, Saudi Arabia—have been leaders in terms of market size and relative market share of Islamic finance. Although non-Gulf

markets such as Iran have experienced full or partial "Islamization," these markets are generally less accessible to global institutions as a result of regulatory constraints or market risks.

2. The growth of Islamic finance has been—and remains today—deeply linked to growth in GCC wealth. Although Islamic finance also has its origins and key institutions in other parts of the world, the most notable periods of expansion in the Islamic finance market have been correlated with periods of expanded prosperity in the Gulf.

3. Gulf investors are increasingly favoring Shariah-compliant investments when such investments are available. This trend, discussed in Chapter 7, is a central one in both the development of Gulf markets and the evolution of the Islamic investment industry.

Thus, while the phenomena we discuss remain fundamentally distinct, they are intrinsically linked and should be examined with reference to each other.

FROM *DUBAI & CO.* TO *GULF CAPITAL AND ISLAMIC FINANCE*

In 2007, I published a book with McGraw-Hill entitled *Dubai & Co.: Global Strategies for Doing Business in the Gulf States*. That book is a strategic guide for multinational companies and international organizations on how to integrate the Gulf region into their global strategies. The first part of *Dubai & Co.* discusses the GCC in the context of the broader Middle East, addresses common misconceptions about the region, discusses the drivers of market attractiveness in the Gulf, and provides essential background on each GCC member state. Its second part covers corporate strategies for doing business in the region, commenting on each major business function: market entry, marketing, human resources, finance, operations, and organization. The book closes with a discussion of how to raise awareness of the GCC at corporate head offices in order to craft winning global strategies. *Dubai & Co.* has been sold worldwide since 2008, with its first translation—a Chinese-language version—produced that same year.

Gulf Capital and Islamic Finance: The Rise of the New Global Players builds on the analysis in *Dubai & Co.* and extends the thinking in a number of new directions. Whereas *Dubai & Co.* was designed for corporate leaders who are interested in conducting business in the region, *Gulf Capital and Islamic Finance* is principally for financial professionals who are seeking to understand Gulf investments, Islamic finance, and their impact on global markets. In a sense, the two are companion volumes, with one being focused on happenings within the region and the other addressing the worldwide impact of the region's wealth. *Gulf Capital and Islamic Finance* also has the benefit of having been written after the onset of the global financial crisis and economic recession, both of which have had a deep impact on the Gulf region.

Aside from discussing the origins of and outlook for GCC wealth, *Gulf Capital and Islamic Finance* will not provide comprehensive background on the countries of the Gulf and their economies. That information—which is important for observers seeking an in-depth understanding of the region—is available in *Dubai & Co.*

TOO IMPORTANT TO IGNORE

As the world of finance and global markets has become more complex, the set of "essential" knowledge and capabilities grows larger. For today's financial professionals—especially those involved in formulating global investment strategies—deep knowledge of a single market or asset class may no longer be sufficient. In an ever-changing environment, insight regarding new players can help firms and professionals identify and tap into new opportunities or anticipate and outmaneuver potential competitive threats. Gulf capital and Islamic finance are simply too important to ignore.

As a new financial order emerges, Gulf capital and Islamic finance are likely to have an impact far beyond those who deal with them directly today. Private equity and principal investors are likely to run into them as counterparts in transactions or as competitors for attractive assets. Bankers will increasingly service them as clients and as crucial sources of capital. Analysts will observe their impact on international markets. Regulators will be faced with them as important phenomena with implications for public policy.

Consider this book your introduction to two new, important players on the stage of global finance. Hitherto, you have not come across them much. If you work in investments or financial services, however, you're likely to cross paths with Gulf capital and Islamic finance quite often in the years ahead.

PART I

BACKGROUND AND CONTEXT

CHAPTER

Floating on Wealth: The Origins and Sources of Gulf Prosperity

We come from the desert, and we have been living on camel milk and dates . . . and we can easily go back and live in the desert again.
—King Faisal of Saudi Arabia (ruled 1964–1975)[1]

Decades ago, when wealth in the Gulf was far scarcer, one prominent Gulf family subtly began sending a regular stipend to another leading family to help the latter meet its expenses. The recurring payment became standard practice, and continued for decades—even after successive oil booms had multiplied the wealth of each family manyfold. When a financial review by the benefactor family found that this small payment was still being paid regularly, the family stopped the practice for fear that the small gift—negligible compared to both families' current incomes—could be a source of embarrassment for the recipient.

Shortly thereafter, the head of the recipient family placed a call to his former benefactor. While of course he was in no need of the stipend, he noted that the modest payment was something that he had deeply appreciated. He went on to explain the reason why: "because it used to remind me of the time when I was in need."[2]

Judging from their current appearance, it would be easy to forget that the countries of the Gulf have long but modest histories. A look at the business centers of Dubai and Doha, with their sleek skyscrapers, slick roads, and fast cars, reveals hardly anything that looks more than 15 years old. The financial centers of Bahrain, Kuwait City, and Riyadh do feature edifices from the 1970s and 1980s, but these are fast being eclipsed by new icons such as Riyadh's Kingdom Tower. Even the populations are strikingly young, with over 40 percent of the people in the Gulf being below the age of 15.[3] All in all, the Gulf Cooperation Council (GCC) is a region in which one is overwhelmed by "newness" and signs of recent prosperity.

In truth, the countries that now make up the GCC have long histories of commerce and trade. For centuries, trade has been pivotal to sustaining the regional economy—the Gulf's agricultural and livestock base is very modest, and therefore the trade of goods was always crucial to developing the Gulf's wealth. In the area that is now the UAE, for example, the core economic sectors were historically pearl production, fishing, (modest) agriculture, and herding.[4] Artisans produced some goods for local consumption, but the finest goods were imported from the Levant region of the Middle East (*bilad al-Sham* in Arabic, or what is today Syria, Iraq, Jordan, Lebanon, Palestine, and Israel), North Africa, and South Asia. The sparse agricultural endowments of the Arabian Peninsula and the reliance on trade were even mentioned in the Qur'an. Abraham, when leaving his family on the peninsula, prays, "O our Lord! I have made some of my offspring to dwell in an uncultivable valley by Your Sacred House"[5]—with the last phrase being a reference to Makkah. Elsewhere, the Qur'an mentions "the journeys of the winter and the summer"—a reference to the trade routes that sustained the region for centuries.

The Gulf played an important role in the ancient trade route known as the Silk Road. The term refers to a longstanding trade pattern in which goods flowed between China, other parts of East Asia, India, Persia, the Arabian Peninsula, North Africa, and Europe. In this elaborate flow of trade, Gulf ports and the merchants therein were important intermediaries and enablers. Along with the exchange of goods came a mixing of cultures, ideas, and families, such that families with a broad range of ethnicities settled in the Gulf, and merchants from the Gulf settled elsewhere. Significant populations in Indonesia and Malaysia, for example, trace their roots back to Yemeni traders.[6] In contemporary times, observers like *BusinessWeek* have discussed the rise of a "New Silk Road" as historical trade links between Asia and the Middle East have been revived.[7] There is even an investment firm today by the name of New Silk Route (chaired by the former managing partner of McKinsey) that invests in businesses related to these growing economic flows.[8]

Another key driver of the premodern Gulf economy—and one that remains important today—was the economic activity related to the Hajj. This pilgrimage to Mecca, required of all Muslims of means, now brings around 3 million pilgrims to Saudi Arabia each year. In premodern times, the numbers were far smaller, but the journeys were more elaborate. It was not uncommon for pilgrims to travel for several months and then to stay on the peninsula for several more months before returning home.[9] The "Hajj economy"—in addition to pumping funds into the Saudi economy each year—has strategic implications for the development of key sectors. If fostered and applied more deeply, the capabilities and skills linked to the Hajj can be pivotal in developing and expanding world-class initiatives and companies in sectors such as infrastructure and logistics management, public health and safety management, and Shariah-compliant savings and financial services. Besides being an economic boon each year, the Hajj can also be—as it has been for centuries—a strategic component of the region's economic development.[10]

The discovery and export of oil—especially during the successive oil booms of the 1970s and 2000s—have, of course, transformed GCC economies. Nonetheless, modern versions of the premodern sectors that supported the Gulf for ages remain visible today: massive ports like Dubai's Jebel Ali Free Zone facilitate trade between Asia and Europe; luxury goods inspired by the trade in gold and precious stones persist in modern form. Furthermore, the diversity of ethnicities integrated into Gulf society, especially in the western parts of Saudi Arabia, strongly reflects the heritage of the Silk Road and the Hajj economy.

A few decades ago, few would have imagined the massive wealth and rapid development that can now be seen in the Gulf. In a remarkably brief period of time, the countries of the GCC have made the transition from being minor economic actors (and often-overlooked markets for goods and services) to playing a meaningful role in the international economy. As discussed in length in *Dubai & Co.*, this rapid growth has brought both benefits and challenges. One such challenge is a tremendous "backfill imperative to develop the social institutions—universities, cultural institutions, civic institutions, and the like—that are required for long-term economic competitiveness.[11] Senior leaders in the Gulf remember a time when the region was in need. Today, the world recognizes Gulf capital—the fruits of GCC prosperity—as a new global player on the rise.

LARGE—AND GROWING—RESERVES

Over the past decades (but largely in the boom years of the 2000s), the economies of the Gulf have accumulated significant reserves. Consider the following figures:

- As of 2006, Gulf economies had about $1.9 trillion in foreign assets built up over the past decades.[12]
- This pool of foreign wealth corresponds to over $47,000 per person living in the Gulf, and over $70,000 per GCC citizen.[13]
- In contrast, the public debt of the United States in 2009 is over $11 trillion. This corresponds to over $37,000 in national debt per person living in America.[14]

These figures are truly striking and reflect the changing topography of the global economy. For every Gulf citizen born in 2006, the Gulf economies had a pool of foreign assets more than three times the region's annual GDP per capita. In the United States, however, for each baby born today, there is a national debt of about one year's GDP per person. Put roughly, a GCC citizen is born with national assets over three years ahead of the game, whereas an American is born with a national debt about one year in the hole. Large national debts can also be seen in the United Kingdom and other leading economies of the Organisation for Economic Co-operation and Development (OECD) world, making the GCC's accumulated wealth all the more remarkable.

Not only is Gulf wealth significant, but it's also growing. Figure 1.1 envisions the potential growth of GCC foreign assets under three different scenarios.

If the oil price per barrel for the period 2007–2020 averages $70, the McKinsey Global Institute forecasts that the GCC will hold foreign assets of about $8.3 trillion by 2020. If the average price of oil is $100 per barrel—a scenario that appeared likely in early 2008 but now is in question—the foreign asset pool would be $10.3 trillion.[15] Therefore, Gulf foreign assets may grow to three or four times their 2006 size in the decade ahead.

F I G U R E   1.1

Gulf Foreign Assets Are Set to Grow through 2020

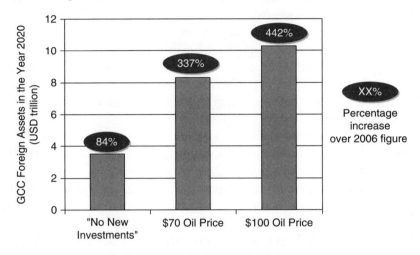

Source: McKinsey Global Institute, author analysis.

A third, intriguing scenario is one of "no new investments." It is projected that, even if the GCC "never invested another penny," the earnings on its existing investments would be about $1.6 trillion in the period through 2020.[16] If all these earnings were reinvested abroad rather than being spent, foreign assets would end up being around $3.5 trillion—84 percent higher than they were in 2006. However, such reinvestment would require fiscal discipline on the part of public and private investors to preserve foreign asset returns rather than use them to fund consumption or local projects.

As is evident in these three scenarios, the pace of growth in Gulf assets is inherently linked to oil prices. The McKinsey forecasts cited here were developed at a time when oil markets were booming, leading McKinsey to assert that "in any plausible oil price scenario, Gulf nations' wealth will continue to grow rapidly."[17] Today, the range of plausible oil prices seems wider. Nonetheless, it is fundamentally important for observers of the region to bear in mind that (1) the Gulf's existing asset base is substantial and is able to generate significant income, and (2) this base is likely to grow through both the reinvestment of returns and infusions of new capital. Just how much new capital will be available for investment depends heavily on the region's ability to generate the kind of budget surpluses it has enjoyed in years past.

HEALTHY SURPLUSES

The large reserves that the Gulf enjoys today have been enabled by healthy budget surpluses over the past decades. Surpluses have varied greatly from year to year based on the market price of oil, and some years have seen deficits. In fact, Saudi Arabia—the core economy of the region—expects a deficit in 2009 as a result of an expansionary budget designed to stimulate the local economy.[18] Nonetheless, sizable surpluses have been the norm in the wealthier Gulf states, especially in recent years.

Table 1.1 shows the budget surpluses of all GCC states and the GCC overall in 2008. It also includes the figures for a number of other countries for comparative perspective.

The key message from this chart is that in 2008 –(a year of remarkable volatility in oil prices), the GCC overall generated an estimated surplus of $161 billion. That's about 14 percent of the total GCC economy and $4,000 per person living in the Gulf today. It's also (at May 2009 valuations) more than the market capitalization of GE, Google, or Apple—and about eight times the market value of troubled Citigroup.[19]

When examined further, this analysis of nations' surpluses reveals a number of other interesting insights. Although China's

T A B L E   1.1

Gulf Surpluses Are in the Double Digits of GDP[1]

Country/Region	2008 Surplus as % of GDP[2]	Surplus in $
Kuwait	32%	$50 billion
UAE	19%	$35 billion
Qatar	15%	$12 billion
GCC overall	14%	$161 billion
Saudi Arabia	10%	$59 billion
Oman	5%	$4 billion
Bahrain	5%	$1.4 billion
China	0%	$18 billion
India	−2%	−$52 billion
United States	−3%	−$455 billion
United Kingdom	−6%	−$135 billion

[1] **Source:** *CIA World Factbook*; accessed February 2009.

[2] GDP in purchasing power parity terms has been used for this calculation.

economy dwarfs that of the GCC (about seven times as large in PPP terms),[20] China's public-sector surplus in 2008 (in absolute terms) was only about half that of the UAE alone and around a third that of Saudi Arabia. China's government-funded investment vehicles therefore had significantly less fresh capital to draw on for foreign investment than their counterparts in the GCC. At the same time, India, while having a large and fast-growing domestic market, experienced a deficit of 2 percent of its GDP.

Comparisons with the United States reveal that the Gulf, despite its growing significance, remains a relatively small economy when compared to that of the United States'. The US economy was about 13 times that of the GCC in total, and around 24 times the size of the Saudi economy. And although the Gulf surplus figures seem large, it would take about three times the GCC's 2008 surplus to pay for the US deficit in that one year alone. The Gulf does have significant public-sector prosperity, but the scale of its economy is a fraction of that of the United States and about half that of the United Kingdom.[21]

"HOT" ECONOMIC GROWTH . . .

In recent years, economic growth in the GCC region has significantly outpaced growth in other parts of the global economy. This fast growth has led to sustained prosperity in the region—a key component of the "opportunity formula" that is driving the Gulf's attractiveness as a place to do business. In addition, the region's favorable demographic trends—young populations, high literacy, increasing global connectivity, and the like—make its consumers a prime market for global firms. Finally, ongoing regulatory reform—with all GCC states now being members of the WTO, for example—has made Gulf markets more accessible than before. This opportunity formula of prosperity, demographics, and reform (discussed at length in *Dubai & Co.*) has made doing business in the region a key strategic initiative for many global firms.

Figure 1.2 shows the annualized growth rates of a range of international economies during the five-year period 2002–2006.

Over the period—boom times for the Gulf—economic growth in the GCC far outpaced growth globally and in the world's developed markets. The cumulative annualized growth rate (CAGR) for the GCC economies (in aggregate) was 6.5 percent—more than 40 percent higher than the world average of 4.5 percent. In the same period, the world's most developed economies grew at about one-third the

FIGURE 1.2

GCC Economies Have Grown Much Faster than World and Core
OECD Averages

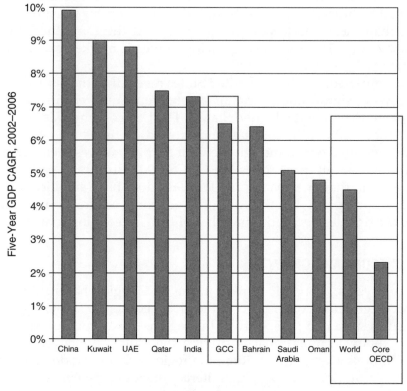

"Core OECD" excludes Czech Republic, Hungary, Mexico, Poland, Slovakia, and Turkey.

Source: Economist Intelligence Unit and *CIA World Factbook*, 2006.

Gulf's pace: 2.3 percent. Kuwait, the UAE, and Qatar grew faster than
India, although China outpaced them all with an astonishing annualized growth rate of 9.9 percent.[22]

   While this economic growth was fueled by natural resource
income, it has enabled economic development across a wide range of
industries. Major expansion in infrastructure, financial services,
tourism and hospitality, retail, heavy industry, and a whole host of
other sectors was achieved as wealth flowed into Gulf economies. GCC
states have actively pursued economic diversification strategies supported by government initiatives such as projects, the establishment of
government-linked companies, and deregulation through free zones
in key sectors like financial services. As discussed in *Dubai & Co.*,

economic growth in the GCC has not been "all about oil"—oil has driven wealth creation, but this wealth has created booms in a wide range of economic sectors.[23]

Were the Gulf to maintain the growth rate it experienced between 2002 and 2006, its economy would double every 11 years. By contrast, the core OECD markets would need more than 30 years to double in size were they to maintain their rate of expansion for the period. In reality, of course, the healthy growth period of the early to mid-2000s has been followed by a deep recession that has affected economies worldwide—including those of the Gulf.

... "COOLING" IN A GLOBAL RECESSION

The cooling effect of the global recession on the Gulf economies has been substantial. Figure 1.3, based on analysis and projections made by the Economist Intelligence Unit in 2009, illustrates expected real growth rates for each GCC economy and a number of other economic clusters for comparison.

While world economic growth generally slowed in 2008 relative to 2007, the major energy exporters of the Gulf—including the UAE,

F I G U R E   1.3

GCC Economic Growth Has Cooled, but Remains Stronger than That of Other Regions

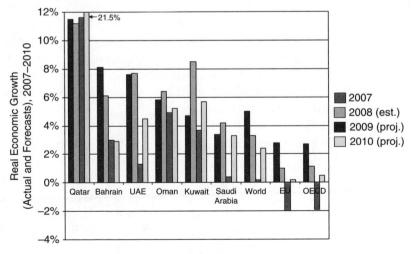

"EU" includes 27 EU economies.

Source: Economist Intelligence Unit, January 2009.

Kuwait, and Saudi Arabia—enjoyed stronger growth in 2008 than they had had the year before. While 2008 was a volatile year for oil prices and for the global economy overall, the average oil price was a strong $97.[24] This enabled the GCC economies to outperform world averages significantly that year.

For 2009, however, far cooler economic growth is expected. Saudi Arabia (the region's largest economy, with over half the Gulf's total GDP) is forecasted to grow at only a 0.4 percent rate. For the UAE, the growth forecast is 1.3 percent—less than one-sixth of the 2008 figure of 7.7 percent. All six GCC economies are expected to see a slowdown in economic growth in 2009, followed by a return to higher growth in 2010. This 2010 rebound coincides with projections for a return to growth in the overall world economy, which is expected to grow 2.4 percent percent in 2010 compared with a mere 0.2 percent in 2009.

When compared to projections for the world's most developed economies, however, the outlook for the GCC region appears relatively strong. The OECD and EU economies are both expected to experience negative growth (−1.9 percent and −2.0 percent, respectively) in the year 2009. In contrast, none of the GCC economies are expected to shrink for the year. When world growth returns in 2010, the countries of the Gulf are expected to again outpace other regions—the OECD is forecasted to expand by 0.5 percent, whereas all Gulf economies are forecasted to grow at about 3 percent or higher.

A closer look at these growth forecasts also highlights the starkly differing scale of projected growth across GCC counties. Expansion in Qatar is expected to continue at an extraordinary rate: 11.6 percent in 2009 (while the global economy shrinks) and above 21 percent in 2010 (literally off the chart displayed in Figure 1.3). This breathtaking 2010 projection assumes ongoing expansion of Qatar's natural gas exports, which continue to increase as additional fields are brought online and export capabilities develop further. Meanwhile, growth in Saudi Arabia is expected to return at a more modest rate of 3.3 percent. The Gulf states with small populations and significant energy wealth—Qatar, the UAE, and Kuwait—can look forward to a different growth trajectory from that of their peers in the GCC. The ongoing prosperity of these small states enables the substantial, high-profile international investments discussed in this book. The Gulf may be a single economic cluster, but the economies of its member states have important differences that lead to different investment approaches.[25]

Growth projections are, of necessity, imprecise and subject to change as conditions evolve. Gulf economies may grow more slowly or faster than current forecasts suggest, and their fates remain deeply linked to global energy markets. It appears, however, that through the world recession and the expected recovery, the Gulf states will enjoy stronger growth than the world and developed-country averages.

THE "BREAKEVEN IMPERATIVE"

Fundamental economic growth, discussed in the previous section, is of course important to the Gulf's role in the global economy. In assessing the region's potential for making investments, however, its ability to sustain budget surpluses is a key factor to consider. When government incomes exceed budgetary requirements, wealth flows into international, regional, and domestic investments. On the other hand, when public-sector income is insufficient to meet the governments' needs, reserves must be tapped, and the rate of investment becomes negative.

The single most important metric in assessing a Gulf government's ability to generate a surplus is its breakeven oil price. This figure reflects the per-barrel oil price at which a state's income covers its public-sector expenses. Above this price, oil income creates a surplus; below it, there is a deficit. The estimated breakeven oil price of each GCC state in 2009 is shown in Figure 1.4.

As is evident from Figure 1.4, the breakeven prices for GCC states vary greatly from country to country. Qatar (for which natural gas prices are also a key determinant of national income) and the UAE can break even with oil prices of $24, and Kuwait breaks even at a modest $34. Even with the high volatility seen in oil prices since 2008, ongoing surpluses in these three countries appear highly probable and can be expected for the foreseeable future.

Saudi Arabia, the world's leading oil exporter, faces an estimated 2009 breakeven price of $54. In the current environment (oil was trading around $60 per barrel at the time of this writing), Saudi Arabia's ability to generate a surplus for 2009 is uncertain. The key question over time will be which grows faster: the steady-state oil price or the Saudi public-sector budget requirements. Oman and Bahrain, both of which require oil prices of around $80 for a surplus, are unlikely to see surpluses in 2009 and 2010, based on current IMF estimates.[26]

FIGURE   1.4

Breakeven Oil Prices in the Gulf Vary Widely

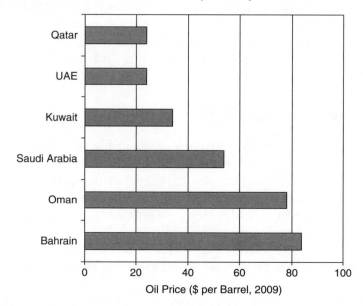

Oil Price ($ per Barrel, 2009)

Source: CMBC, "Which Oil Producers Are Making Money?" October 2008.

The breakeven imperative" of GCC states highlights the heavy reliance of Gulf governments on natural resource income for public-sector revenue. Unlike some other oil exporters, such as Norway, Gulf governments rely primarily on oil and gas income as their main source of funding. Taxation—the key lever that governments typically use to manage their incomes—is nonexistent or minimal in GCC member states. Gulf governments, at present, are missing some of the tools for managing their public-sector incomes that are available elsewhere. Greater diversification of government revenues beyond oil and gas income could, over time, significantly change the Gulf states' reliance on energy markets to meet their breakeven imperative. Today, however, governments' breakeven points are best defined in terms of oil prices.

ILLUSTRATION: DUBAI'S DIVERSE INCOME

Dubai's economic development and deregulation strategies, in addition to diversifying the emirate's overall economy, have greatly diversified its sources of government income. These strategies were, in a way, born out of necessity—Dubai's oil reserves pale in comparison with those of Abu Dhabi, the UAE's capital and dominant contributor to oil exports as a percentage of GDP. By the year 2005, for example, Dubai and its neighboring emirate Sharjah exported a mere 6 percent of the UAE's total oil exports.[27]

Through investment in (and promotion of) nonoil sectors such as shipping and logistics (Dubai Ports World), transportation (Emirates airlines), financial services (the Dubai International Financial Centre), and telecom (Etisalat), the Dubai government has broadened the scope of economic activity in the emirate. The creation of free zones, in which foreign entities can fully own their businesses, has attracted a large pool of multinational firms. If nobody is paying direct taxes, how is the government generating income?

Some sources of public-sector income include

- Real estate income, including rental fees on office space in free zones and other property-related charges
- Income related to companies in which the emirate is a majority or significant shareholder
- Privatization initiatives in which stakes in government-owned companies are either sold or publicly listed
- Fees collected by utility companies
- Fees for visas and other government services
- Municipal surcharges on the hospitality sector
- And so on

Another potential source of public-sector income, returns from international investments by government-linked investment vehicles, has come under significant pressure during the financial crisis and global recession as a result of the use of leverage and the choice of investments. Many people have questioned elements of the emirate's overseas investment strategies and the use of debt to support them. As the dust settles, it is becoming increasingly apparent that not all of Dubai's major investments will be winners. Dubai's public-sector revenue model certainly has both strengths and weaknesses, but its diversification serves as an important case study throughout the region. As noted recently by an executive based there, "Dubai may have no taxes, but its government has plenty of ways to generate income."

LONG-TERM OIL PRICE DYNAMICS

No discussion of the outlook for Gulf prosperity and investment flows would be complete without some consideration of future oil prices. The fact that the Gulf has substantial investable wealth today is undeniable. Whether new wealth will be added or its coffers will be drained to fund local needs will depend largely on what happens in global energy markets. Over the course of 2008 and 2009, oil prices have been extremely volatile, peaking at above $147 per barrel in July 2008, then plummeting to the $42 level in February 2009, and returning to around $60 by late May. Oil's volatility has been greater than that of the Dow Jones Industrial Average, which has traded in a band around 45 percent of its summer 2008 values, as opposed to oil, which has seen dips of around 70 percent.[28]

Though these markets are impossible to predict with certainty, observers of the Gulf are well advised to take note of the forces that are likely to shape them in the years ahead. Figure 1.5 illustrates some of the key forces influencing oil markets in the medium to long term.

FIGURE 1.5

Oil Prices May Face both Downward and Upward Pressures

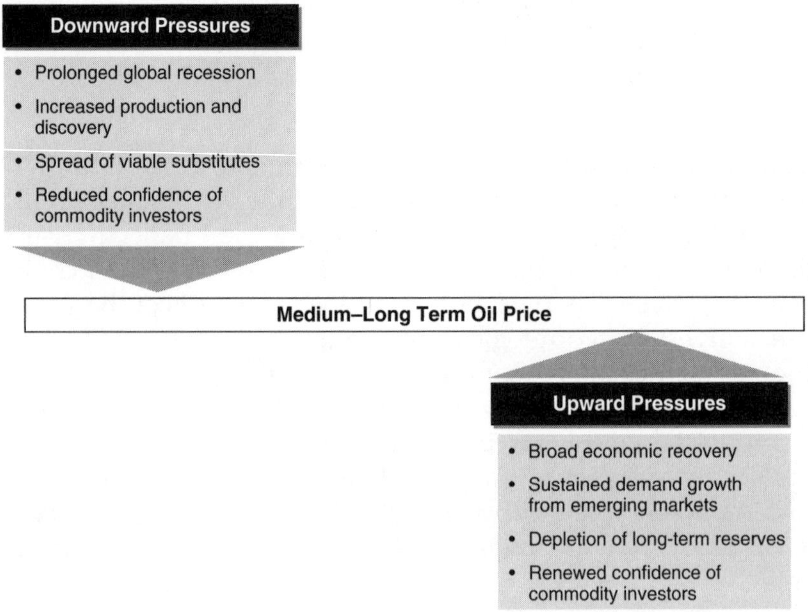

Downward Pressures

- Prolonged global recession
- Increased production and discovery
- Spread of viable substitutes
- Reduced confidence of commodity investors

Medium–Long Term Oil Price

Upward Pressures

- Broad economic recovery
- Sustained demand growth from emerging markets
- Depletion of long-term reserves
- Renewed confidence of commodity investors

Downward Pressures

On the one hand, certain foreseeable pressures could keep oil prices low for the medium to long term, and could (possibly) reduce the currently enormous importance of oil to the global economy. First, a prolonged global recession could keep fundamental demand for oil lower than it was during the boom years of the 2000s. Household consumption of oil for heating and for driving is, relatively speaking, fairly inelastic (although some individuals can, of course, trade in gas-guzzling SUVs for fuel-efficient compacts or switch from oil heat to other alternatives). A greater cause of elasticity in oil demand is changes in consumption by manufacturers that use oil as an input. As demand for all sorts of manufactured goods (appliances, machines, toys, clothes, and so on) has slipped, factories have started operating at lower capacity or even shutting down. Furthermore, fewer ships and trucks with lighter loads are needed to transport the goods to market. The aggregate effect is that less oil is needed, putting downward pressure on the trading price of the commodity. If the recession lasts several more years, depressed demand for oil could become the new norm.

While a recessionary environment naturally lowers the demand for oil, in some ways it also tempts certain oil producers, especially smaller ones, to increase production. Producers know, of course, that higher production pushes market prices down. However, short-term budgetary pressures are sometimes so great that countries will choose to sell more (even at a lower price) in order to meet their immediate needs. The Gulf states tend to be highly compliant with OPEC production quotas—as the most important members of the cartel, they need to be, or else the system would fall apart. Smaller oil producers, however, have been known to break away from quotas in order to generate immediate income. If the global recession deepens and extracts greater human costs, governments will feel added pressure to cash in on their natural resource wealth. In addition, worldwide oil exploration is continuing, and new sources of oil have the potential to meaningfully add to the world supply. Additional discoveries, aided by ever-improving technology, make oil less scarce and therefore less valuable.

A third downward pressure, and perhaps the most profound, is the spread of viable substitutes for fossil fuels. As was the case during previous oil price booms, the boom of the 2000s has led to increased momentum toward developing and marketing alternative energy sources. It is worth noting, for instance, that the US Department of Energy was itself established in 1977, in the wake of the oil booms of the 1970s, which motivated Americans to seek alternatives to Middle Eastern oil.[29] In fact, there has been a longstanding pattern of spikes in oil prices leading to greater efforts in the alternative-energy sector—efforts that have typically lost momentum when oil prices came down and the sense of urgency was lost. It was not surprising, therefore, that both Democrats and Republicans in the United States made "energy independence" a core theme of their 2008 election campaigns—oil was trading well above $100 per barrel during the summer months of the campaign.

More than previous alternative-energy initiatives, however, the initiatives of the Obama administration appear to be central to a long-term US economic strategy. When oil prices plummeted in early 2009, the administration's enthusiasm did not. In May 2009, President Obama requested a budget of over $26 billion for the Department of Energy, with significant emphasis on the department's Office of Energy Efficiency and Renewable Energy. According to the Department of Energy, its revised budget "makes significant investments in hybrids and plug-in hybrids, in smart grid technologies, and in scientific research and innovation." Proposed funding for alternative-energy initiatives is up dramatically: a rise of 83 percent for solar energy, 70 percent for building technologies, 36 percent for wind energy, and 22 percent for vehicle technologies.[30] Promoting renewable energy is seen as an important element of the government's stimulus package and long-term economic vision.

Recent initiatives look more like a genuine strategy than like a reactionary fad. In addition, renewable energy has been positioned as a priority for US national security. As president-elect, Obama combined economics and security in his declaration that "the future of our economy and national security is inextricably linked to one challenge: energy."[31] Throughout the 2008 campaign season, candidates from both the Republican and Democratic parties argued for decreased US dependence on foreign oil, with Republicans often advocating for increased domestic drilling and Democrats emphasizing renewable energy. While the security argument generally overlooks the fact that Gulf oil producers are key US military allies (US Central Command for the war in Iraq is, after all, in Qatar), it does resonate with many Americans, who see oil states as a potential threat. Adding security to the rationale for renewable energy gives the movement increased strength and momentum.

The search for viable substitutes for fossil fuels is by no means an easy one. In addition to addressing the inherent scientific challenges, alternative-energy advocates need to work out the challenging economics of making such energy affordable. The infrastructure required for making the transition to alternative energy (for example, developing fueling stations for electric cars) could be massive. Although developers have been working on renewable energy for decades, oil still remains dominant. It remains very difficult to predict how viable certain alternative-energy sources will prove, and how they will affect the volume of oil consumption. That said, it is undeniable that the spread of viable substitutes for oil could have a profound impact on oil prices in the long run and that the current US administration has made alternative energy a clear priority.

Upward Pressures

At the same time as the factors just discussed put downward pressures on oil prices, there are also contrary trends and economic forces that have the potential to push oil prices upward in the medium and long term. These contrary trends cannot be overlooked, as they are rooted in certain economic realities that have long shaped energy markets.

First, a broad-based economic recovery (whenever it takes place) will naturally bring with it increased demand for oil to be used in manufacturing, transportation, and other areas. Segments of oil demand that soften during a recession rebound when there is a recovery, sending oil prices back up. The "spike" in oil prices during this rebound can be especially sharp if production levels have started to sag during a recession. Often, recessions also lead to underinvestment in exploration and capacity building—a phenomenon that sparks quick booms during a recovery because the growth in production cannot keep pace with the growth in demand. If this pattern holds in the current recession, there could be a quick rise in oil prices before a longer-term stabilization.

In addition, the basic demand for oil has grown steadily over the past years, largely as a result of increased industrialization and development in emerging markets. This trend, which is a long-term phenomenon, marks one of the key contrasts between previous oil booms and the boom of the 2000s. Whereas previous booms were largely event-driven (based on embargos or political events), the boom of the 2000s was rooted in a sustained increase in fundamental demand. Figure 1.6, based on US federal government projections, illustrates the rapid growth in oil demand from emerging markets expected in the years ahead.

F I G U R E   1.6

Oil Consumption by Region, 2003 and 2030

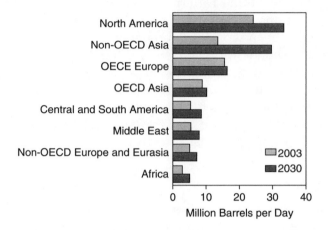

Sources: 2003: Energy Information Administration (EIA), *International Energy Annual, 2003* (May–July 2005), www.eia.doe.gov/iea/. 2030: EIA, System for the Analysis of Global Energy Markets, 2006.

While oil consumption is expected to increase everywhere, its expected growth is most striking in non-OECD Asia—a cluster that includes China, India, and other emerging Asian economies. In 2003, non-OECD Asia consumed roughly half the amount of oil consumed in North America; by 2030, the gap is expected to be much smaller. In the most developed European and Asian countries (the OECD member states within these regions), growth in oil consumption is expected to be quite modest when compared to other parts of the world. Growth in basic demand for oil is a factor that drives prices upward over time.

The steady trend toward increased oil demand is linked to the general development of these emerging markets. As industry and urbanization expand, so does the demand for energy. As standards of living rise, so do the use of automobiles, the transportation of packaged goods, and so on. It's also worth noting that when it comes to consumption of oil, emerging markets are likely to be more price-sensitive than other areas when it comes to the adoption of alternative-energy sources. Policy makers and consumers in the wealthier markets of Western Europe and the United States may, because of environmental or other concerns, choose alternative-energy sources even if they are somewhat more expensive than fossil fuels. Developing countries, in contrast, will tend to be more conscious of cost and will be eager to utilize the least expensive means for fueling their economic development.

A third basic driver of higher long-term oil prices is rooted in the simple fact that fossil fuels are not renewable. Over time, reserves are depleted, making the commodity scarcer. Advances in exploration and production have the potential to increase the base of known reserves, but the rate of growth in known reserves may not exceed the pace of demand growth. In developed markets, where finding new reserves can be especially challenging (such as in the North Sea in Britain), investment in exploration tends to decrease when oil prices are low. When prices rebound, exploration efforts come back—but these efforts can take time to bear fruit. The reality is that fossil fuels become scarcer with each passing day, suggesting that future prices may well be higher than they are at the moment.

Besides the fundamental factors just discussed, the influence of commodity investors (sometimes referred to as "speculators") is critically important in shaping energy prices. Decades ago, oil was bought almost entirely by companies that were end users of the commodity. Today, oil—like other commodities—has become an asset class for investment by funds and other entities that have no interest in actually using the oil. Financial investors buy oil futures because they think their value will increase and sell them when they think their value will decline—making decisions based on an outlook for the market rather than a genuine need for the commodity.

This financial investment or speculation in oil can have the effect of accelerating or amplifying volatility in the marketplace. As oil prices rallied far above $100 per barrel in 2008, much of the buying was being done by speculators who expected the price to rise even further. As other speculators behaved the same way, the upward spiral became a self-fulfilling prophecy. When, on the other hand, financial investors began selling oil futures, the price began to plummet and continued falling based more on investor confidence than on fundamental oil supply and demand.[32] Especially as hedge funds and other investment vehicles unraveled in the financial crisis of 2008–2009, commodity investors were forced to liquidate their positions, and this speeded the decline in oil prices. A thorough assessment of potential oil prices in the future must, therefore, also take into account the key role that financial investors play in commodities markets. Their confidence in the oil market can drive prices upward; a lack of confidence (or a lack of available capital by financial investors) can drive prices downward.

Predicting oil prices in any era is difficult, and in volatile times like the present, it is impossible to make a forecast with much certainty. A few things, however, can be stated with confidence. First, oil prices will continue to be a driving factor in the wealth of the Gulf and the key source of GCC surpluses. Second, there are fundamental forces at work on both sides of the price dynamic—some trends exert downward pricing pressure, and others exert upward pressure. How the two sets of pressures will balance is unknown. Third, the future of commodity prices is likely to have a lot to do with the perspectives of financial investors and commodity traders, in addition to the fundamental questions of oil supply and demand.

LASTING POWER: THE GULF'S "RESERVE ADVANTAGE" AND LOW-COST PRODUCTION

The fact that the Gulf is pivotal to energy markets today is obvious. What is less apparent is the fact that as long as oil and gas remain central to global energy, the importance of the Gulf region to oil markets will probably only increase.

The reason in rooted in two key statistics:

1. The GCC states combined provide 22 percent (between one-fifth and one-quarter) of the world's oil supply.
2. At the same time, these states hold 40 percent (two-fifths) of the world's known oil reserves.[33]

The Gulf states therefore enjoy a huge "reserve advantage" over other oil producers. Their long-term ability to supply is far greater than their actual output amounts. As other producers either exhaust their reserves or scale back production to preserve what they have left, Kuwait, the UAE, and Saudi Arabia will have plenty of oil left and will be even more dominant as global suppliers.

The scale of Gulf energy reserves is astounding. Consider the following estimates of how long Gulf oil and gas will last:

- Kuwait's oil reserves are expected to last for 105 years, and its gas will last 169 years.
- The UAE can continue exporting oil for another 97 years and gas for another 130.

- Saudi Arabia—the world's largest producer—has supplies lasting 66 more years.
- Qatar's oil may run out in 38 years, but its natural gas is abundant enough to last for an eye-popping 594 years.[34] That's a longer period than the period between the invention of the printing press and today.

This reserve advantage means that as oil grows more scarce, the Gulf states will proportionately have more of it. As long as oil is precious, the Gulf can expect sustained prosperity. It's no wonder, therefore, that countries with booming demands for energy— namely, China and India—are building ties with the Gulf like never before.

The reserve advantage also means that Gulf exporters can raise output to meet global demand with minimal risk of draining their long-term reserves. Another advantage that key Gulf producers have stems from their remarkably low cost of production. The geology of the region makes drilling for oil far cheaper in the Gulf than it is in certain other regions. This is critical, because if the market price of oil drops globally, producers with higher cost bases start to cease production. For high-cost producers, it does not make economic sense to produce when the prevailing market price is below their costs. Gulf producers, however, can still generate profits at low oil prices. Well past the point when other countries would drop out of the market, Gulf producers can keep pumping.

Like any other business or organization, national oil companies in the Gulf have a straightforward revenue equation: revenues = price × volume. If the price goes up and volume remains the same, revenues increase. Revenues can also, however, increase even if prices go down—if volume increases enough to make up the difference. By making the region one of the few feasible producers of oil in a low-price environment, the Gulf's cost advantage creates the potential for growth in overall revenues as other producers of oil scale back or exit the market.

HIT BY THE CRISIS

As discussed earlier, the GCC region has no doubt been affected by the global financial crisis and economic recession. Investor confidence plummeted in late 2008, destroying billions of dollars of market capitalization on public exchanges. The collapse in energy prices put surpluses at risk and reduced fresh liquidity dramatically. Economic growth (though expected to remain significantly higher than that in developed markets and world averages) has slowed substantially. While the root causes of the current crisis may not be linked to the Gulf, its effects have certainly reached the GCC region.

Another way in which the financial crisis affected the region was in the form of overseas investment losses. In early 2009, a working paper published by the Council on Foreign Relations offered estimates of investment losses incurred by major GCC wealth funds in the year 2008.[35] The paper estimated losses as deep as 41 percent for the Qatar Investment Authority and 36 percent for the Kuwait Investment Authority, with Saudi sovereign wealth losses estimated at a more modest 12 percent. While the paper may be estimating larger losses than were actually incurred (it seems to assume greater exposure to risky alternative investments than others would expect), it is certainly reasonable to assume that Gulf investors faced the same pressures on their overseas investments as other global investors.

The experiences of the current financial crisis and global recession have, in a number of ways, accelerated key trends that are already underway in the evolution of Gulf capital and its role in global markets. Heavy investment losses have prompted GCC-based investors to increase the sophistication of their investment strategies and structures, and the crisis has also made world-class principal investment talent more readily available for recruitment by Gulf institutions. Slow growth outlooks and struggling capital markets in the OECD world, while creating some bargains in developed markets, have also encouraged Gulf investors to increase their focus on domestic, regional, and emerging-market investments. These markets are seen as pockets of reasonably high growth in the years ahead. Furthermore, the financial crisis highlighted the risks associated with excessive debt, highly leveraged investments, and debt-collateralized instruments. As a result, many observers—both in the GCC region and beyond—have looked more closely at Shariah-compliant (Islamic) investments as a more stable alternative. The GCC's growing affinity for Islamic finance and investments has been a steady long-term trend that has continued through the current crisis.

In formulating policy responses to the crisis and the recession, Gulf decision makers have been working with a unique set of

FIGURE   1.7

Gulf Decision Makers Have Severe Constraints regarding Economic Policy

<table>
<tr><td>Monetary Policy</td><td>Fiscal Policy</td></tr>
<tr>
<td>

• Dollar peg remains firmly in place in all countries but Kuwait

• Maintaining the peg is important for both economic and political reasons

• Effect of peg is that the Gulf's interest rates are effectively set by the United States and driven by US domestic needs

</td>
<td>

• Government investment has a degree of flexibility, particularly with regard to large projects

• State benefits are quite inelastic because of expectations and pressures

• Income tax is largely absent, although fees and other mechanisms are used to generate supplementary income

</td>
</tr>
<tr>
<td>Key Driver Is the US Federal Reserve</td>
<td>Key Driver Is the Global Energy Market</td>
</tr>
</table>

constraints. In the realms of both monetary and fiscal policy, Gulf states today have certain limitations on formulating policy responses to economic crises. Figure 1.7 illustrates some of the key limitations.

Because all GCC currencies, with the exception of the Kuwaiti dinar, remain pegged to the US dollar, the region's scope for autonomous monetary policy is extremely limited. Interest rates are de facto set by the US Federal Reserve, which makes its decisions based on the state of the US economy, not on the needs of the GCC. Over the years, many have cited the dollar peg as a root cause of high inflation in the Gulf. Rapid economic growth in the GCC would otherwise have dictated higher interest rates to curb inflation, yet the dollar peg kept interest rates low. The dollar peg cannot, however, be entirely to blame for Gulf inflation, as inflation is a natural by-product of the dramatic growth in the region's wealth. There has been much discussion about shifting away from the dollar peg, and much of the thrust behind the envisioned GCC monetary union was to enable greater autonomy in Gulf monetary policy. As discussed in *Dubai & Co.*, however, the likelihood of a monetary union forming in the near future appears slim as a result of significant structural differences in the economies of member states. Furthermore, in 2009, the UAE announced that it was pulling out of the potential monetary union— a critical blow to the initiative, since the UAE is the second-largest economy in the GCC.

There are important economic and political reasons for the dollar peg, and those reasons appear likely to persist in the near term. As long as oil markets remain dollar-denominated, the region's exports and government incomes will continue to be in dollars. In addition, the bulk of the Gulf's foreign reserves remains in US Treasury bills, a practice that is both a cause and an effect of the dollar peg. Currency diversification of oil markets and reserve investments is a matter that is often discussed, but a radical shift in either seems unlikely in the near term.

In the realm of fiscal policy, Gulf decision makers have significantly more latitude, but they nonetheless face constraints. As discussed earlier, public-sector income relies on volatile global energy markets, over which the Gulf has little control. The near absence of taxation takes away a major lever that governments typically have in adjusting their incomes and managing through recessions. At the same time, state benefits paid to nationals are fairly inelastic (and growing) as a result of social expectations and the well-established covenant between Gulf leaders and their citizens. Political participation—though growing, especially at the municipal and parliamentary levels—is limited, but the state looks after the core economic needs of its citizens. Changing this covenant could be highly disruptive for ruling families in the region.[36]

The component of fiscal policy in which Gulf governments have the greatest latitude is direct investment in the local economies through projects, state-owned companies, and other initiatives. Since Gulf reserves are so large, even small changes in the percentage of reserves invested in local projects can have a significant stimulus effect on domestic economies. Saudi Arabia's 2009 expansionary budget is a prime example of the use of government investment dollars to promote infrastructure improvement, job creation, and overall economic activity. As we shall discuss in a later chapter of this book, expanding or contracting the flow of public investment in local economies is in some ways the most important tool available to Gulf leaders in managing through crises and recessions.

"DRY POWDER" AND EXPANDING COFFERS

Like institutional investors everywhere, Gulf-based investors have endured significant losses during the financial crisis and global recession. Though impossible to measure precisely, the losses are almost certainly in the hundreds of billions of dollars, assuming that Gulf institutions' asset allocation models matched those of their international counterparts. Such losses were no doubt painful for the region's sovereign and private investors, and the collapse of local stock markets in 2008 was even more painful for the region's retail investors.

It is important, nonetheless, to keep in mind that Gulf institutional investors have a number of advantages over other investors as they seek to recoup their losses and make winning investments in the years ahead.

First, many Gulf institutional investors are not time-bound in their investment outlook. Unlike private equity funds, for example, they are not required to liquidate their positions within a fixed number of years in order to return capital to their investors. The flexibility of not being time-bound allows most Gulf-based investors to avoid having to sell assets in "fire sales" or at low valuations; instead, they can ride out a cycle and benefit when markets recover.

Second, Gulf investors—especially large, government-linked ones—tend to have substantial allocations for Treasury bills and conservative fixed-income investments. These investments are very safe ones, and in effect are like cash. Cashlike marketable securities act as what is called "dry powder" in the realm of principal investments—funds that are available for new investments and are not affected by previous losses. In a world in which assets are far cheaper than they were a short while ago, dry powder is a source of immense advantage in enabling Gulf investors to pick up assets at attractive valuations.

Third—and perhaps most profound—many Gulf institutional investors are continuing to enjoy fresh injections of cash even in the current recession. Budget surpluses continue in key GCC markets, and part of those surpluses is fed into investment vehicles. These fresh injections of capital, adding to the dry powder of Gulf institutions, extend those institutions' advantage over comparable investing institutions elsewhere. Whereas hedge funds see massive redemptions and withdrawals of cash and endowment funds see new donations dry up in times of recession, surplus-generating Gulf states are in the enviable position of being able to add to their cash coffers and make new investments.

KEY LESSONS

- The economies of the Gulf *have humble origins, but achieved rapid prosperity during the oil booms* of the 1970s and 2000s.

- Successive oil booms have enabled the Gulf to *enjoy large budget surpluses, build reserves, and make foreign investments* of close to $2 trillion in value by 2006.

- The Gulf's foreign *wealth is expected to grow significantly* in the coming decade—nearly doubling from its 2006 level even if no new investments are made, and growing by over 300 percent at an average oil price of $70 per barrel.

- Although the global recession has slowed economic growth in the region, *key GCC economies continue to enjoy surpluses*—a stark contrast with growing deficits in the world's largest economies.

- The *GCC's reserve advantage* and low production costs make it more important over time and enable it to generate revenue regardless of whether global oil prices are high or low.

- The Gulf region has been *deeply affected by the global financial crisis and economic recession*, and has a limited set of policy tools available for addressing the situation.

- Gulf investors *enjoy a significant and growing amount of dry powder* that is available for ongoing investment activity.

2

Entrusted Stewards: The Landscape of Gulf-Based Investors

Not all Gulf capital is the same. Although international headlines often lump "Middle Eastern" or Gulf investors into a single broad category, the reality is far more nuanced. Over time, professionals who work with Gulf-based institutions come to appreciate the differences between various types of Gulf investors—differences in scale, objectives, capabilities, and investment styles. The monolith of "Gulf capital" fades away, and a more contoured landscape of institutions becomes visible.

Some organizations, however, learn this lesson the hard way. In the mid-2000s, an international (non-Gulf) company was raising capital and had offers in hand from two Gulf-based investors. One was a relatively newly created institution with a dynamic brand, a flashy Web site, and a strong PR machine. Representatives of this institution wooed the potential portfolio company with slick presentations and a well-crafted pitch. The second offer was from a leading sovereign wealth fund with a far more understated approach. Although this fund was often written about, it had no substantial Web site or Internet presence. While its reputation was strong, the fund said little about the size of its portfolio or its strategy. When its representatives visited the potential portfolio company, they presented themselves with little fanfare and a simple proposition. The company being courted was significantly more impressed by the first suitor, whose public presence and elegant pitch suggested that it was a more sophisticated institution. It therefore chose to take capital from the newly established institution and declined the offer from the sovereign wealth fund.

Then, however, came the global financial crisis and worldwide recession. Although the crisis affected both Gulf institutions, the newer one was highly leveraged and therefore was more deeply hurt by declining asset values. The sovereign wealth fund, in contrast, took a hit, but weathered the storm more smoothly. Seeing the relative health of the suitor it had rejected, the portfolio company came to regret having chosen its investor based more on perception than on stability.[1]

In introducing Gulf capital and describing its origins and outlook, we have hitherto looked at the phenomenon as a whole. This is often done in commentaries on the topic, even those by financial professionals. More often than not, media reports on transactions and the parties behind them emphasize either the region overall ("Gulf-based investors eye XYZ asset") or the buyer's country of origin ("Saudi investor acquires a major stake in ABC company"). The reasons for this are understandable. First, most Gulf-based investors are barely known internationally, and many of them prefer to keep a low profile. Historically, they have had little incentive to engage in active public relations strategies, and thus their names are not easily recognized. Second, the public discourse regarding Gulf investors is often more concerned with the political and regulatory aspects of transactions than with the "business story" behind them. In the case of the Dubai Ports World (DPW) acquisition of P&O, for example, the US public was far more interested in the fact DPW was a UAE-based entity than in the fact that DPW was already operating several ports internationally (including in Latin America). The focus has been more on the countries than on the institutions involved.

However, such generalizations miss out on important insights that can be gained though a more sophisticated view. In this chapter, we offer a categorization of Gulf Cooperation Council (GCC)–based investors that illustrates the important differences (and commonalities) among them. We review how differences in objectives, typical size, sources of wealth, investment strategy, and management approach naturally lead to very different behavior on the part of Gulf institutional investors. Understanding these broad categories and the characteristics of investors in each category is crucial for observers of the Gulf who wish to attract, advise, study, regulate, or otherwise engage with GCC capital. In addition to laying out these categories, the chapter offers perspective on how the landscape we describe is evolving, as each category is developing with its own set of unique dynamics. This chapter will help you go below the surface of the Gulf investor base and feel the contours of the institutional topography.

SETTING THE STAGE: FOUR BROAD CATEGORIES OF INVESTORS

The landscape of Gulf investors is, of course, complex and dynamic, and therefore impossible to neatly classify into precise buckets. An analysis of key institutional attributes, however, reveals four broad categories:

- "Generalist" sovereign wealth funds
- "Specialist" government investment vehicles
- Private institutions
- Private investment houses

Table 2.1 summarizes the key attributes of each category, contrasting them along five key dimensions.

The relative sizes of the four categories cannot be precisely known, since assets under management are rarely disclosed in public. Analyst estimates suggest, nonetheless, that the bulk of Gulf capital is held by the generalist sovereign wealth funds (SWFs), with the next largest category being private institutions. According to 2009 estimates by the Sovereign Wealth Fund Institute, Gulf SWFs hold about $1.6 trillion in assets.[2] McKinsey & Co. estimates that the category of investors that we have classified as "private institutions" controls about $900 billion in wealth.[3] The other two categories—specialist government investment vehicles and private investment houses—are growing rapidly and may have roughly $150 billion[4] and $65 billion[5] in assets under management, respectively. Generalist sovereign wealth funds and private institutions may therefore be seen as the bedrock of Gulf capital, with the other types of institutions adding diversity and dynamism to the landscape.

T A B L E 2.1

Gulf Institutional Investors Fit into Four Broad Categories

Category	Objectives	Typical Size	Source of Wealth	Investment Strategies	Management Approach	Examples
"Generalist" sovereign wealth funds	Preserve and grow national wealth	$50 billion and above	Governments	Generally conservative; increasingly diversified	Largely external fund managers overseen by portfolio executives	Abu Dhabi Investment Authority (ADIA); Kuwait Investment Authority (KIA); Qatar Investment Authority (QIA)
"Specialist" government investment vehicles	Grow national wealth through strategic investment	$10 billion–$80 billion	Governments	Defined by sectors and investment types	Actively managed by internal teams	Mubadala (UAE); Dubai International Capital (UAE); Saudi Industrial Development Fund (KSA)
Private institutions	Preserve and grow private wealth	Vary widely; typically below $10 billion	Private; typically business families	Vary widely	Typically external fund managers with increasing internal capabilities	Kingdom Holdings (KSA); Kharafi Group (Kuwait); Kanoo family (Bahrain)
Private investment houses	Maximize financial returns for third-party investors	Typically below $10 billion; growing rapidly	Private; typically business families	Often alternative investments, but strategies vary	Actively managed by internal teams	Investcorp (Bahrain); Abraaj Capital (UAE); Global Investment House (Kuwait); (UAE)

"GENERALIST" SOVEREIGN WEALTH FUNDS: UNDERSTATED STEWARDS

The generalist sovereign wealth funds (SWFs) of the Gulf are the region's most prominent investors and, in many ways, its most important. In the global SWF sector, Gulf institutions have been pioneers and today are leading players. According to estimates by the Sovereign Wealth Fund Institute, Gulf institutions hold 41 percent of global SWF assets, and three GCC sovereign funds are among the world's top seven SWFs by asset size (see Table 2.2).

Combined, the generalist SWFs listed in Table 2.2 are believed to hold about $1.6 trillion in assets—two-fifths of the estimated global total SWF asset base of $4 trillion. Remarkably, the Kuwait Investment Authority (KIA) was established in 1953—more than 55 years ago and far before the birth of most Kuwaitis alive today. The SWFs of the UAE and Oman were founded in the wake of the oil booms of the 1970s, whereas those of Qatar and Bahrain were formed in the boom of the 2000s. Saudi Arabia's "SWF"—which is, in fact, an amalgamation of preexisting holdings—was formalized in 1990, but its constituent parts can be traced back further.

T A B L E   2.2

Gulf Sovereign Wealth Funds Are Leaders among Global SWFs[1]

Global Rank (by Assets)	Country	SWF Name	Year of Establishment	Estimated Assets[2]
1	UAE	Abu Dhabi Investment Authority (ADIA)	1976	$875 billion
2	Saudi Arabia	Saudi Arabian Monetary Agency (SAMA) Foreign Holdings	1990	$425 billion
7	Kuwait	Kuwait Investment Authority (KIA)	1953	$200 billion
14	Qatar	Qatar Investment Authority (QIA)	2003	$60 billion
27	Bahrain	Mumtalakat Holding Company	2006	$14 billion
33	Oman	State General Reserve Fund (SGRF)	1980	$8 billion

[1] Sovereign Wealth Fund Institute, Global Fund Rankings, January 2009.

[2] Rounded by author. We emphasize that these are merely estimates by the Sovereign Wealth Fund Institute.

Profile: ADIA's Massive Coffers

The Abu Dhabi Investment Authority (ADIA), established in 1976 by the UAE's founder, Sheikh Zayed bin Sultan Al Nahyan, has been a custodian of Abu Dhabi's oil surplus for decades.[6] Although the organization guards its privacy and its inner workings are strictly confidential, experts estimate its assets to be well above half a trillion. Morgan Stanley believes ADIA's assets to be a breathtaking $875 billion and growing.[7]

Like all massive institutional investors, ADIA invests in a range of asset classes across multiple regions. A large amount of such investors' assets tends to be in conservative, fixed-income instruments. To provide a sense of scale for the income that ADIA's coffers could produce, consider the following analysis. Let's assume that ADIA had $750 billion in assets and that two-thirds ($500 billion) of those assets were in bonds yielding 5 percent per year. The income from those investments alone would be $25 billion per year, or $6,000 per person living in the UAE. If, in a severe crisis, ADIA were forced to start liquidating its assets, even half of the $750 billion estimated total would provide more than $350,000 per UAE citizen. ADIA's assets are, therefore, a tremendous cushion of fiscal security for the emirate and for the broader UAE.

It is not surprising that global bankers sit up and take notice whenever (the typically low-profile) ADIA speaks up. In a 2006 *Euromoney* article, HSBC's chairman, Stephen Green, acknowledged that ADIA was one of the few institutions worldwide that the bank's most senior executives would visit on demand, regardless of whatever else they might be doing.[8] HSBC's bankers are certainly not alone in recognizing ADIA's clout.

Better Described as "Trusts"

In addition to their size, the Gulf's SWFs stand out for their distinct set of purpose. The Sovereign Wealth Fund Institute defines SWFs as entities that "hold, manage, or administer assets to achieve [national] financial objectives, and employ a set of investment strategies which include investing in foreign financial assets."[9] In the case of Gulf-based SWFs, we would suggest a simpler characterization: Gulf sovereign wealth funds exist to preserve and grow countries' national wealth.

Gulf SWFs are marked by an ethos of stewardship, or responsibility for ensuring the ongoing prosperity of their countries. This sense of mission is perhaps best captured by the name of a key Kuwaiti sovereign investment vehicle: the KIA's Future Generations Fund. The fund was born from the recognition that the current generations have been fortunate to enjoy windfall wealth and dramatic prosperity. Today's leaders, therefore, bear a responsibility to provide future Kuwaitis with a standard of living similar to that enjoyed by nationals today. Wealth preservation is thus an overarching objective of the fund, as is growing the wealth to serve the growing population.

Although the term *sovereign wealth fund* has gained global recognition and widespread use, in some ways it is a misnomer. We would, therefore, suggest a different term that better captures the ethos of such entities (especially in the Gulf): *national trusts*. The term *fund*, especially in the principal investments industry, often has a specific meaning and implies characteristics that simply don't apply to the GCC's sovereign investors.

Table 2.3 illustrates some of the salient differences between the "national trust" mindset and the typical attributes of investment funds.

The distinctions described in Table 2.3 are fundamental and have a profound impact on the behavior of these national trusts. Because these trusts are open-ended and take a long-term perspective, they are not subject to the same set of pressures as funds that have defined exit horizons. A typical private equity fund, for example, will have a

T A B L E   2.3

Gulf SWFs Are Better Described as National Trusts

Attribute	National Trust Mindset	Typical Investment Fund
Investment horizon	Open-ended and long-term	Defined fund life with short- and medium-term targets
Strategies	Multiple and evolving investment strategies	Defined strategy, stated at inception
Ownership	Single owner—the government	Multiple shareholders/ investors.
Beneficiaries	The nation overall and future generations	Private shareholders and diverse constituencies of institutional investors
Management	Multiple external managers with internal portfolio executives	Actively managed through a single investment team

five- or ten-year "life," within which it must make investments, realize gains, and return capital to shareholders. In the event of a major
downturn (like the current recession), funds with predefined exit
timelines often find themselves in a squeeze. National trusts, in contrast, can often ride out the storm and stay in positions that are likely
to increase in value in the long term, even if they temporarily incur
losses. This flexibility can give national trusts greater resilience in
their portfolios over time.

Whereas investment funds typically must have a defined strategy that is stated to committing investors up front, national trusts
again have greater flexibility. They may pursue multiple strategies
that evolve over time, adapting to market conditions and to the needs
of the nation. An investment fund that is defined as an equity fund
cannot, for example, transform its portfolio to fixed income, even if
fixed income offers stronger returns. National trusts have flexibility to
do so. As Gulf populations grow and age, governments' liquidity
requirements will grow, and national trusts can adjust their investment strategies accordingly. The Qatar Investment Authority (QIA)
may, for example, migrate to more conservative investments 30 years
from now if the state requires steady income from it.

Ownership is another key difference between national trusts and
investment funds. Since national trusts have a single owner (the
state), they are extremely sensitive to public needs and are not
swayed by general market sentiment. Investment funds, in contrast,
need constant communication and interaction with the diverse set of
investors that provide their capital. It is inevitable that the needs and
preferences of shareholders will influence (for better or for worse) the
investment strategy of a fund.

Another stark contrast between national trusts and funds is that
the beneficiaries of a national trust are the general public and (in fact)
future generations not yet born. These stakeholders cannot yet invest
for themselves, so the institutions do so on their behalf. The provider
of capital (the state) and those making decisions regarding allocation
are not investing their own personal wealth; they are acting as
trustees for a nation. Again, this raises the sense of stewardship and
responsibility as well as fostering a long-term perspective. In this
sense, national trusts are therefore more similar to the US Social
Security Administration or a university endowment than they are to a
typical investment fund. In fact, the analogy with endowments is apt
for another key reason: ideally, national trusts wish to meet national
needs through their returns without dipping into the principal

amount with which they are entrusted. The principal is touched only in the event of a budget deficit and an urgent need for liquidity.

A final key contrast relates to the management model. Investment funds generally rely on the capabilities of an internal investment team—in fact, their very selling point to investors is often the specific strengths of a defined set of managers. National trusts, on the other hand, are run by portfolio executives who, in turn, engage a large number of external fund managers. The people who run national trusts have investment expertise, but their stewardship qualities are more important than their hands-on technical expertise.

Linked to National Governance Model

Following from their objectives and mindset, Gulf SWFs must necessarily be linked to the overall governance models of the states they serve. Preserving and growing national wealth is, ultimately, a government objective to be achieved through a number of channels, of which SWFs are an important one.

As illustrated in Figure 2.1, SWFs are an integral part of the institutional framework for allocating and managing surpluses that stem principally from energy wealth.

FIGURE 2.1

Wealth Is Channeled through an Institutional Framework

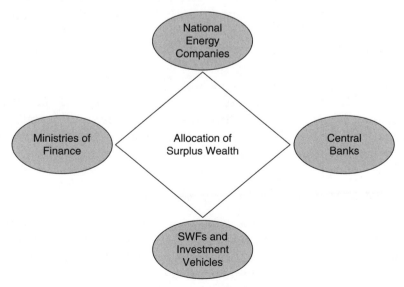

At the start of the flow are national energy companies, which are fully owned by the state and are the governments' core source of income. As discussed earlier, it is the surpluses generated by oil companies that have enabled the remarkable capital formation of the region.

The first demand on energy income is, of course, to fund the national budget. The mechanisms by which this occurs vary from country to country. Each state, as discussed earlier, has a different breakeven point, after which energy income enables new surpluses. When the price of oil is below that level, there are deficits that need funding through reserves or other methods.

At the government level, two types of institutions play particularly pivotal roles as wealth is allocated. Ministries of finance, which are customarily responsible for the public sector's budgeting process, have a part to play in funding ministries, projects, and government initiatives. In years of windfall surpluses, new projects and initiatives may be launched and need to be funded appropriately. Central banks are also important as holders of national reserves. SAMA Foreign Holdings—imperfectly dubbed a sovereign wealth fund for analytical purposes—are assets of the Saudi Arabian Monetary Agency, the Kingdom's central bank.

Sovereign wealth funds (or national trusts, as they may more appropriately be called) absorb the wealth that is available for investment in line with their broad mandates. Sometimes there are specific rules in place for this flow. Under Kuwaiti law, for example, at least 10 percent of Kuwait's oil revenues must be put into the KIA Future Generations Fund.[10] According to Harvard Business School analysis, Saudi Aramco –(the world's largest oil company) retained only about 7 percent of its profits in 2008, with 93 percent flowing into the government for funding the budget and 75 percent being channeled through SAMA (the central bank, discussed earlier).[11] The allocation process may be more or less rules-based depending on the state and the year, but it generally follows a pattern involving multiple elements of our institutional framework.

Traditional Allocation Models

The essentially conservative mandates of generalist SWFs naturally lead to fairly traditional asset allocation models within such institutions. The bulk of SWF assets (like the assets of endowment funds and other large prudential institutions) is understood to be in the traditional asset classes of cash, fixed income, and listed equities in mature markets. These allocation models give priority to the core purpose of preserving wealth, with less emphasis on the pursuit of above-market returns through riskier investments.

McKinsey & Co. researchers and other experts have put forth broad estimates regarding the asset allocation models of Gulf SWFs. Before considering these, it is important to note that the estimates cannot be verified, since the portfolios of these SWFs are not public information. For illustrative purposes, though, it is worthwhile to cite the allocation estimates put into the public domain by other researchers. Figure 2.2, based on the published work of the McKinsey Global Institute, Monitor Group, and the Sovereign Wealth Fund Institute, provides a useful general reference.[12]

The key point that can safely be drawn from these estimates is that the bulk of Gulf SWF assets, especially those held by the largest institutions, are in cash, fixed income, and equities. ADIA and the KIA are estimated to hold, respectively, only 15 percent and 6 percent of their assets in alternative classes like private equity, hedge funds, and real estate. Although the boldest investments by these institutions are often the highest profile (for example, the KIA's 19 percent investment in the Industrial and Commercial Bank of China), "risky"

F I G U R E   2.2

SWF Assets Are Principally Held in Traditional Asset Classes

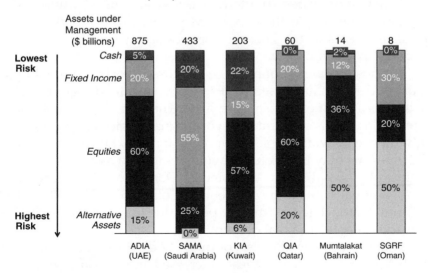

Source: Sovereign Wealth Fund Institute, 2009.

investments seem to represent only a relatively small component of Gulf SWFs' overall portfolios.

Another observation from these estimates is that SWFs' appetites for risk vary substantially from country to country. The QIA, whose allocation for alternative investments is estimated to be a fifth of its total assets, made high-profile investments in the financial sector in the period before the financial crisis. The QIA took an 8 percent stake in Barclay's and a 9 percent stake in Credit Suisse in 2008.[13] Through its UK-based affiliate, the QIA is believed to use financial leverage (debt financing) to support aggressive equity investments such as its bid for a 27 percent stake in the Sainsbury supermarket chain.[14] Such tolerance for risk may be understandable considering the massive scale of Qatar's surpluses and its expected growth in national income. Saudi Arabia's SAMA, by contrast, is believed to have no allocation at all for alternative investments—a reflection of central bank prudence and the Kingdom's slimmer overall surpluses. Gulf SWFs may share a common mandate, but their risk profiles nonetheless vary.

Reactive to the Crisis

As discussed in Chapter 1, Gulf-based SWFs have certainly been affected by the global financial crisis and economic recession. Like other institutional investors, Gulf sovereign wealth funds endured heavy declines in their holdings in listed equity markets and (to the degree they were exposed) alternative investments. Prominent Gulf investors—for example, the QIA, as mentioned earlier—had increased their investments in the financial services sector shortly prior to the meltdown in that industry.

The postcrisis environment, as discussed earlier, offers buying opportunities for Gulf-based SWFs with financial strength and "dry powder" as a result of ongoing surpluses. There are, however, sensitivities regarding the risk of reentering volatile markets too early—prudence might dictate a "wait and see" approach instead. Furthermore, some GCC investors may be careful to avoid being seen as bargain hunting at a time of global distress—as noted by Don De Marino, cochairman of the National U.S.-Arab Chamber of Commerce, the potential PR "firestorm" associated with the perception of "Arabs buying up assets too cheaply" is a real concern.[15]

At the same time, analysis of publicly disclosed investments by Gulf SWFs during 2008 suggests increased interest in high-growth Asia and caution regarding investment in Organisation for Economic

Co-operation and Development (OECD) markets. In fact, 65 percent of disclosed Gulf SWF transaction targets in the third quarter of 2008 were in the Middle East and North Africa (MENA) or Asia region. In the course of 2008, visible transactions in OECD targets fell steadily, from $37 billion in the first quarter to $8 billion in the third.[16] Gulf sovereign wealth funds may not have seen the crisis coming, but once it hit, they exercised heightened caution.

Also of note following the financial crisis has been a visible increase in collaboration between SWFs in the Gulf region and beyond. This trend had begun before the crisis, driven at that time largely by international concerns that SWFs had grown too large and required special regulation. After the crisis hit, the heads of SWFs continued collaborating, but for very different reasons. Bader al-Saad, managing director of the KIA, hosted a meeting of SWF heads in April 2009 and noted that "the crisis places an extra pressure on our group to have increased coordination and greater cooperation."[17]

Understated Stewards

In summary, Gulf sovereign wealth funds—or, as we have called them, national trusts—act as understated stewards of national wealth. Historically, they have eschewed public attention and tried to maintain low profiles. Their equity investments in listed companies, for example, tend to be below the limits required for public exposure (sometimes set at 5 percent), and rarely do they seek representation on public companies' boards of directors. Although today there is a trend toward greater transparency, Gulf sovereign wealth funds have had little need (or, in fact, incentive) to publicize their wealth.

The stewardship mindset of Gulf sovereign investors shapes their investment strategies, asset allocations, public demeanor, and other factors. In terms of assets, these sovereign wealth funds are the biggest single category of Gulf capital. As we turn our attention toward other categories, we shall see a diversity of mindsets and incentives, resulting naturally in very different behavior.

"SPECIALIST" GOVERNMENT INVESTMENT VEHICLES: FOCUSED HYBRIDS

The second category of Gulf institutional investors is the segment that we call specialist government investment vehicles (GIVs). Although the asset base of this category is relatively small compared to that of

T A B L E   2.4

Specialist Government Investment Vehicles Exhibit both Public and
Private Attributes

Public-Sector Attributes	Private-Sector Attributes
Government ownership	Scale akin to private firms
Alignment with overall economic strategy	Pursuit of focused investment strategy
	Often take strategic stakes in portfolio companies
Linkage with institutional framework for wealth allocation	Often use leverage and complex financing
	Active management by internal teams
	Competitors and comparables are generally private firms

generalist SWFs, the category is growing fast and includes some of
the region's most dynamic investors. In fact, many of the high-profile
acquisitions made by Gulf investors in recent years (including, for
example, stakes in Ferrari and Barney's) have been made by these
institutions.

Specialist GIVs are, in many ways, hybrid institutions. These
vehicles exhibit attributes of both public-sector investors and private
investment institutions and are thus largely a cross between the SWFs
we have just discussed and the region's private investor base. Table 2.4
outlines key elements of GIVs' operating model that reflect a blend of
public and private attributes.

Public Ownership

Specialist GIVs may operate much like private investment firms, but
they are ultimately funded by GCC governments. The creation of
such GIVs, from the perspective of governments managing large
portfolios of wealth, serves both strategic and organizational purposes. Strategically, it has become increasingly important for Gulf
governments to diversify their investments beyond the conservative
asset classes favored by SWFs. Like other giant institutional investors
worldwide (for example, university endowments and public pension
funds), Gulf governments have become increasingly inclined to allocate some wealth to alternative investments. These include asset
classes like real estate, private equity, and buyouts—asset classes that
have inherently higher risks but also promise higher absolute returns.

Although large institutional investors allocate only a small minority of their assets to alternative investments, their funding provides the lifeblood for specialist funds that are generally not open to (or suitable for) smaller investors.

Diversification not only brings portfolio benefits (i.e., strengthening the overall return on financial investments) to Gulf states, but also helps meet the broader goal of economic diversification in the region. The chief executive of Mubadala, a UAE-based GIV, has stated that Mubadala "began investigating and investing in business-building activities in strategic sectors at home and abroad through partnerships that ensured diversification and development of the emirate's [Abu Dhabi's] economy."[18] As far back as 1974, Saudi Arabia recognized the need for active government investment in order to support domestic diversification and created the Saudi Industrial Development Fund (SIDF), with the objective of "supporting the development of the private industrial sector, by extending medium to long term loans . . . provision of guidance and advice in administration, finance, marketing and technology to industrial firms in Saudi Arabia."[19] Bahrain's Mumtalakat holds the Kingdom's strategic investments in key companies and sectors, including Gulf Air (transportation), Aluminum Bahrain (manufacturing), and the Gulf International Bank (financial services).[20] GIVs' areas of focus—especially at the time when the GIVs are created—must fit within the broader economic strategies of the states that fund them.

Within the UAE, a number of specialist GIVs have been created over the years to support investment in sectors that have strategic importance. The UAE's federal governance (by which individual emirates have discretion over certain resources, while the federation acts as the sovereign) has fostered the establishment of emirate-level entities. The competition between emirates has generally been healthy, motivating stronger performance and better results, but at times these efforts have appeared unnecessarily duplicative. In the postcrisis environment, it is expected that Abu Dhabi–based entities will exercise more visible influence over investment activities federationwide, in particularly with regard to attractive Dubai-funded assets with growth potential and financing needs.

Table 2.5 (which is not an exhaustive list) provides a snapshot of a few of the UAE's specialist GIVs, their years of inception, and their areas of strategic focus.

The areas on which these GIVs focus reflect key priorities of the emirates that established them. As energy is the cornerstone of the

T A B L E   2.5

UAE-Based Government Investment Vehicles Reflect Areas of
Strategic Focus for the National Economy[1]

Government Investment Vehicle (GIV)	Emirate	Year Established	Strategic Focus
International Petroleum Investment Company (IPIC)	Abu Dhabi	1984	Energy—oil and gas
Mubadala Development Company	Abu Dhabi	2002	Industrials and energy
Istithmar World	Dubai	2002	Real estate and retail
Dubai International Capital (DIC)	Dubai	2004	Diversified private and public equity
RAK Investment Corporation	Ras al Khaimah	2005	Natural resources— energy and minerals
Dubai International Financial Centre (DIFC) Investments	Dubai	2006	Financial services
Investment Corporation of Dubai	Dubai	2006	Real estate and financial services

[1] William Miracky et al., "Assessing the Risks: The Behaviours of Sovereign Wealth Funds in the Global Economy," Monitor Group, June 2008; Zawya, "Wealth Funds in the UAE Lead Way with Transparency," March 3, 2009; miscellaneous details verified from individual GIV Web sites.

Abu Dhabi economy, its vehicle International Petroleum Investment Company (IPIC) focuses on this strategic sector. To support Abu Dhabi's diversification, however, investment in a wider rage of industries is required—hence, the creation of Mubadala in 2002. Dubai's economy has been built through logistics (i.e., ports) and transportation, financial services, hospitality, real estate, retail, and other key sectors. Dubai's GIVs have accordingly been focused on real estate, retail, and financial services, while the government has channeled resources to transportation and hospitality through heavy investment in infrastructure. Ras Al Khaimah, a smaller emirate that has begun pursuing a diversification strategy through its RAK Free Zone, has also established an investment vehicle for key sectors.

Specialist GIVs are linked to Gulf states' broader institutional framework for allocating surplus wealth, as discussed earlier.

Mubadala's CEO illustrated this phenomenon succinctly, noting that "while ADNOC [Abu Dhabi National Oil Company] continued to export oil and gas, and ADIA managed a diverse investment portfolio abroad, Mubadala became responsible for orchestrating change from within the emirate."[21] The allocation framework involving oil companies, central banks, finance ministries, and investment vehicles (both SWFs and GIVs) is guided by governments' overall economic priorities and objectives for longer-term development and competitiveness.

Private Operating Models

One key reason for creating specialist GIVs as distinct entities has been to enable the organizational focus and culture required for alternative investments. States could, of course, have chosen to keep all their investments in the hands of their generalist SWFs. However, creating distinct, focused GIVs brings the important benefits of fostering specialist expertise and giving teams of investment specialists autonomous platforms to mold according to the unique characteristics of the asset classes and industries in which they invest. Generalist SWFs, like endowments and pension funds worldwide, benefit from mature organizations with sophisticated asset allocation models, rigorous macroeconomic and market analysis, and robust governance of external asset managers. Private equity institutions, by contrast, benefit from organizational agility, expertise in specific asset classes and industries, and strong internal teams undertaking fundamental analysis of specific opportunities. Specialist GIVs are better off as separate institutions, since the attributes that drive their success differ significantly from those found in generalist SWFs.

In keeping with their mandates, GIVs often take strategic stakes in their portfolio companies and work actively to add value in the companies they own. For example, IPIC holds a stake of 47 percent (bought in stages) of the oil refiner Cepsa. A large chunk of that equity was bought from Santander in March 2009 for $3.8 billion.[22] Since that acquisition, IPIC has also acquired the firm Nova Chemicals for $2.3 billion in 2009.[23] Both of these investments are related to IPIC's oil and gas expertise and Abu Dhabi's strategic focus on energy. IPIC can thus act as a value-adding investor and a strategic buyer of energy assets rather than simply as a passive investor drawing only financial returns.

DIFC Investments, whose investments support Dubai's aspirations to act as a global financial center, took a 28 percent stake in the London Stock Exchange in 2007 and almost entirely bought out the

Nordic exchange OMX in 2008.[24] Partnership with these exchanges can help the DIFC transfer technology and relationships that support its own development as a financial hub and also, importantly, build credibility concerning its standing among leading international centers. It's not surprising that, based on similar aspirations and rationale, Qatar has also hotly pursued investment in exchanges.

Another way in which specialist GIVs operate much like private institutions is in their use of financial leverage and (at times) complex investment structures. Analysts estimate, for example, that Dubai International Capital (DIC) raises about 30 percent of its capital externally,[25] and that the use of debt financing by Dubai-based investors has enabled them to take larger stakes but also created substantial risks. In the financial crisis, such debt financing has proven especially troublesome. Even Abu Dhabi, with its vast capital reserves, utilizes financial leverage (in the broad sense of the term) to enhance the buying power of its specialist GIVs. In 2006, Mubadala established a $500 million revolving line of credit with a set of leading international and regional banks, including Citibank, Barclays Capital, and others.[26] In November 2008, Mubadala secured a AA credit rating in order to enable future debt financing.[27] IPIC is the majority shareholder of an investment vehicle called Aabar Investments, which is publicly listed and therefore draws on capital from the retail market in Abu Dhabi. In December 2008, Aabar bought a 9.1 percent stake in German automaker Daimler AG for the sum of $254 million. Khadem Al Qubaisi, chairman of Aabar and also managing director of IPIC, has stated that IPIC intends to grow its portfolio to $20 billion in value by 2014 through such acquisitions.[28] Leveraged investments allow GIVs to amplify their returns, but also create repayment requirements that can be brutal when asset values go down.

Unlike SWFs and similarly conservative investors, specialist GIVs in the Gulf sometimes engage in joint ventures (JVs) with leading global players. Beyond providing equity capital (as is done in straightforward acquisitions), entering JVs requires significant involvement in overseeing the commercial aspects of the relationship, and typically participants need to play active roles in the ongoing entity. In the second half of 2008, Mubadala entered into such a JV-like arrangement with GE regarding clean technology. Mubadala and GE agreed to invest $4 billion each (over the course of three years) principally to develop Abu Dhabi's "Green City" called Masdar and also support other renewable energy initiatives.[29] The Qatar Foundation, through its extensive Education City initiative, has essentially entered into JVs with a number of leading US universities. These include the Weill Cornell Medical College, Georgetown's School of Foreign Service, Carnegie Mellon, and others. Each university has been selected for its excellence in the particular area for which it is engaged, and Qatar strictly insists that partner universities maintain the same high standards in Doha as they do at their home campus. This creative form of JV, like regional JVs in the realm of business, allows each partner to bring specialist expertise into the Gulf and transfer world-class knowledge to the local market.

As part of their active management strategy, specialist GIVs need to employ professionals who can directly manage investments in the demanding asset classes of private equity and other alternative investments. Mubadala's professional staff is extensive, with 400 professionals who are split into an "operations" division that is responsible for investments and a financial and corporate affairs group that is responsible for central services and controls.[30] For each dollar invested, specialist GIVs require more people than SWFs do because GIVs are more intensely involved in selecting and managing their portfolio companies. Other GIVs in the UAE are believed to have far smaller teams than Mubadala's, but nonetheless require substantial in-house expertise.

Focused Hybrids

In summary, specialist GIVs may best be understood as focused hybrids. Their strategic approach and core business models reflect predefined strategies akin to those of private institutions. They have a level of specialization and investment focus that are not found in generalist SWFs. At the same time, the visions of GIVs ultimately tie into national objectives, and their focus areas are linked to the overall economic strategies of GCC states. Thus, the category of GIVs is very much a middle ground between massive sovereign wealth funds and the private principal investment firms that have become fixtures of capital markets in the world's most developed markets. In many ways, Gulf GIVs reflect a spirit of public ownership with private operating practices that has become a hallmark of GCC business culture over the past decade.

PRIVATE INSTITUTIONS: BUILDERS OF FORTUNES

The third category in our framework, private institutions, is perhaps the most diverse. This category captures a wide range of entities, including family offices, private investment vehicles, and other entities

used to channel the private wealth of the Gulf. The defining characteristics of institutions in this category are that (1) they are funded by private wealth (not government capital), and (2) their core objectives are to
preserve and grow the wealth of their founders.

Legacy and Stewardship

Private institutional investors in the GCC generally trace their roots to
wealth created during the region's rapid expansion since the 1970s.
While the boom times brought wealth to the state overall through oil
revenues, significant wealth also flowed into the private sector through
the funding of projects, infrastructure, government-backed companies,
and the like. Sizable private fortunes were built by contractors who (literally) helped build the GCC, project management firms that under-
took massive initiatives, financial services enterprises that channeled
wealth through the economy, and captains of business throughout the
broader economy. The phenomenon of private fortunes blossoming as
states experience rapid economic growth is a common theme worldwide, especially in emerging markets; it is visible, for example, in the
large business families of postwar Germany and Japan, in the renowned
business families of South Korea, and in the business networks of South
Asia.

The investment activity undertaken by private institutions is driven by a sense of legacy and stewardship. Private wealth
that was originally held by entrepreneurs and founders of large enterprises has been channeled into institutions in order to preserve the
existing assets and grow them for future generations. In this respect,
much of the ethos of private institutions is similar to that of sovereign
wealth funds. Private institutions differ, of course, from SWFs with
respect to the sources and scale of wealth, as well as their investment
approaches and management styles.

The precise scale of private wealth in the GCC is unknown, as
private wealth is generally not disclosed. Estimates of its size vary
widely; the IMF's estimate was over $1.5 trillion in 2008,[31] whereas
McKinsey's assessment has been closer to $800 billion.[32] Whereas
these estimates seek to capture both wealth held by private institutions and wealth held directly by individuals, our focus in this chapter is on institutional wealth rather than retail investors.

It is believed that about half the private wealth of the GCC is
concentrated in Saudi Arabia.[33] This should not be surprising, since,
after all, the Saudi market represents about half of the GCC's total

FIGURE   2.3

Saudi Arabia Holds about Half the Gulf Cooperation Council's
Private Wealth

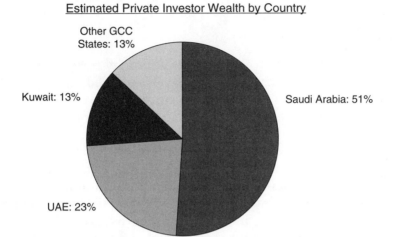

Estimated Private Investor Wealth by Country

Other GCC
States: 13%

Kuwait: 13%

Saudi Arabia: 51%

UAE: 23%

Source: McKinsey Global Institute, 2008.

economy and about two-thirds of its total population.[34] Although
other Gulf states often get more attention, Saudi Arabia is clearly the
core market of the GCC.

Figure 2.3, based on McKinsey research published in 2008, estimates the breakdown of GCC private wealth by country.

It's noteworthy that the UAE, Kuwait, and Qatar—states with
substantial sovereign wealth funds and specialist GIVs—represent a
smaller proportion of the private wealth pool than they do of the SWF
pool. This insight reflects the fact that these three prosperous states
have immense natural resources but very small populations (Qatar's
is roughly that of Manhattan, and the bulk of its residents are expatriates), enabling the dramatic accumulation of state surpluses. Saudi
Arabia, with its population of over 27 million, has a much more substantial base of domestic needs to meet before it can apply government revenues to savings and investments.[35] At the same time, Saudi
Arabia offers a broader pool of private institutions and investors than
any other GCC state. Investment managers and corporations that
seek private funding from the Gulf must therefore look to Saudi
Arabia, as it offers the largest pool of potential partners. Although the
Kingdom lacks free zones and international financial centers like

those of Bahrain, Dubai, and Qatar, it remains the single most important destination for marketing to Gulf investors. Bahrain's appeal as
an offshore banking center, for example, can largely be traced to its
role as a hub for serving Saudi capital and investors.

"Conglomerate Culture"

Most owners of private wealth in the Gulf today trace their fortunes
to family business enterprises that have prospered since the 1970s.
The process of nation building that occurred in the region as a result
of its increased prosperity and resources included a process of "enterprise building" by businessmen who were well placed and able to
deliver on their countries' needs. As each country developed its economic infrastructure across key sectors, business families served as
key partners of the state in bringing about development. This phenomenon, which is by no means unique to the Gulf, has generated
companies and business groups that prosper to this day.

The relatively fragmented nature of the Gulf economies, the
(generally) protectionist economic policies of the time, and the basic
spirit of economic nationalism created an environment in which
business conglomerates could flourish in each country. Families that
built a successful enterprise in one industry were well positioned to
branch out into other industries, using their access to capital, relationships with decision makers, ability to execute, and credibility in
the marketplace. The banking sector is a prime example; each country needed its own set of banks, and merchant families were well
suited to start or invest in such banks. Competition was relatively
limited, since foreign financial institutions had highly limited access
to the local banking market. Similarly, lucrative distributorship and
franchise opportunities helped build merchant families' enterprises.
Leading Gulf business families secured the rights to act as local dis-
tributors for top global firms (selling, for example, consumer goods
from the United States, automobiles from Europe, and electronics
from Japan) and were able to generate revenues based on the
brands, reputations, and business models of international firms. At
the same time, regulations that made it impossible for global businesses to enter GCC markets directly created a substantial opportunity for local businessmen to strike partnerships. Even after the entry
of all GCC member countries into the WTO, key sectors are often
heavily regulated, and partnerships with local companies remain the
norm.[36]

One example of a highly successful family conglomerate in the Gulf is the Al-Futtaim Group of the UAE. Al-Futtaim is, without a doubt, one of the strongest family enterprises in the GCC and one of the most effective local agents any multinational could find. Besides representing an impressive (and comprehensive) list of multinational firms such as IKEA, Toys 'R' Us, Hertz, and Honda, Al-Futtaim has been at the forefront of retail property development through its portfolio of shopping malls (known as "MAF Shopping Malls," for Majid Al-Futtaim). Its City Centre shopping mall in Dubai—a pioneer at the time of its creation and for years considered the city's most popular—has been a convenient venue for locating and promoting Al-Futtaim businesses such as Carrefour and Toyota/Lexus. Al-Futtaim has expanded its shopping mall development capabilities well beyond Dubai, undertaking projects elsewhere in the UAE and the GCC. Muscat City Center in Oman, for example, is an MAF Shopping Malls property. Al-Futtaim's powerful real estate capabilities give multinationals confidence that, if they partner with the group, their outlets will be in prime locations with significant shopper traffic. Carrefour, for example, has chosen Al Futtaim as its franchisee in the UAE, Qatar, and Oman and as a joint franchisee with the Olayan Group for the Saudi Arabian business.

As an illustration of how broad family conglomerates in the region can be, it is worth taking a closer look at the business portfolio of the Al-Futtaim Group. Table 2.6, though far from comprehensive, presents some highlights of the group's activities.

Al-Futtaim has managed to build formidable businesses across a range of industries and has attracted distribution agreements with leading US (e.g., Chrysler), European (e.g., Carrefour), and Asian (e.g., Toyota) firms alike. The breadth and depth of its expertise, along with its capital base, makes Al-Futtaim and other leading local conglomerates key pillars of their local economies and serious investors in regional and overseas businesses.

The journal *Arabian Business* publishes a ranking of the "World's Richest Arabs"—a regional equivalent of the Forbes 400 ranking of America's wealthiest individuals. Estimating private wealth is very difficult to do, since (1) many family businesses are not listed on public exchanges and therefore are not required to provide public disclosure of their financials, (2) the precise shareholding of individual family members in a conglomerate's businesses is rarely known, and (3) individual tax filings (which often provide insight into private wealth) are customarily not required. Nonetheless, the "rich list" is

T A B L E   2.6

The Al-Futtaim Group at a Glance[1]

Attribute	Description
Origins	Founded in the 1930s as a trading enterprise; grew into a conglomerate through the 1940s and 1950s
Number of companies	Over 40 companies bear the Al-Futtaim name, not to mention all the international brands that the group represents through distribution and franchise agreements
Geographic presence	While the UAE is its home market, Al-Futtaim has operations in Bahrain, Kuwait, Qatar, Oman, and Egypt
Operating divisions	• Automotive • Electronics • Retail services • "Overseas" (international) • Insurance • Industries • Real estate
Key retail brands	IKEA, Carrefour, Toys 'R' Us, Marks & Spencer, Seiko, Raymond Weil
Key auto brands	Toyota/Lexus, Honda, Chrysler/Jeep/Dodge, Volvo, Hertz
Key electronics brands	Panasonic, Sanyo, Toshiba, Alcatel

[1] Al-Futtaim profile excerpted from *Dubai & Co.* and based on the corporate Web site and press releases.

useful for broadly illustrating how private wealth in the region is gen-erally rooted in sprawling family conglomerates (see Table 2.7).

Many of the names listed are owners of well-known conglomer-ates in their respective countries. In Saudi Arabia, for example, the Olayan, Al Zamil, and Abdul Latif Jameel families are leading busi-ness groups with high-profile holdings in (respectively) the financial services, petrochemicals, and automotive industries. The Al Rajhi fam-ily is a household name for establishing the Kingdom's first—and still dominant—Islamic bank. Saleh Kamel, founder of the Dallah Al Baraka Group, holds major assets in the financial services sector as well as in the media industry and beyond. The Bin Mahfouz family is a major shareholder in National Commercial Bank, Saudi Arabia's largest bank by market share.[37] The UAE families featured—including the Al Ghurair, Al-Futtaim, and Gargash families—control significant conglomerates, and the Al-Tajir Group is a major retailer. A quick scan of the region's wealthiest people thus highlights the importance of

T A B L E   2.7

Gulf Representation on Top 30 "Rich List" of Wealthiest Arabs[1]

Country	Number on "Rich List" Top 30[2]	Individual/Family Listed
Saudi Arabia	15	Prince Alwaleed bin Talal Al Saud
		Maan Al Sanea
		Sheikh Mohamed Bin Issa Al Jaber
		Mohammad Al Amoudi
		The Bin Laden family
		The Olayan family
		Sulaiman Al Rajhi
		Saleh Kamel
		The Algosaibi family
		The Al Zamil family
		Mohamed Abdul Latif Jameel
		Khalid bin Mahfouz
		Saleh Al Rajhi
		Sheikh Walid Al Ibrahim
		Abdullah Al Rajhi
UAE	5	Abdulaziz Al Ghurair
		The Gargash family
		Mahdi Al Tajir
		Majid Al-Futtaim
		Abdullah Al-Futtaim
Kuwait	3	Nasser Al Kharafi
		The Al Shaya family
		Suad Al Humaidi
Bahrain	1	The Kanoo family

[1] "Special Report: The World's 50 Richest Arabs," *Arabian Business*, December 2008, www.arabianbusiness.com/richlist.

[2] The numbers do not add up to 30 because 6 of the individuals or institutions ranked in the top 30 are not GCC entities.

family conglomerates (and the principals behind them) in building fortunes of investable wealth.

The "conglomerate culture" of local business families, although evolving rapidly, has a profound impact on the way many private institutional investors act. Even when taking minority stakes, many private institutions prefer to focus on sectors in which they have operating expertise and deep familiarity. In addition to searching for financial return, these conglomerates often buy into assets and portfolio companies that have some strategic fit with the conglomerate's existing businesses. In this regard, they differ significantly from returns-focused principal investment vehicles and private equity funds, which look solely for investments that are strong in their own right, as they have no intention of coordinating the activities of their portfolio companies.

Take, for example, the case of the Kharafi Group of Kuwait. Established in 1976 as a mechanical and electrical works, it has expanded into a conglomerate of industrial companies, including construction, development, and infrastructure-related industries. The group also holds a major stake in the National Bank of Kuwait.[38] One strategic sector in which it has invested significantly is telecommunications. Kharafi, through its investment vehicle Al Khair, has taken a 30 percent stake in the Iraqi telecom provider Atheer and is also a significant owner of Zain telecom. Zain has expanded significantly beyond Kuwait, operating in Saudi Arabia and other Middle East markets and potentially evolving into a pan-regional telecom operator.[39] Whereas an investor who was driven solely by absolute return objectives might build a more scattered portfolio of holdings, Kharafi has adopted a focus on key infrastructure sectors in which it has both operational and investment expertise.

Increasing Institutionalization

A major trend among private-sector investors in the region is increased institutionalization. Historically, portfolios and assets were typically held in individual names and financed through personal bank accounts. Family members and friends would invest together in assets, but they generally did so informally and kept their holdings in the personal names of consortium participants. This informal method of investment suited the overall economic environment in which the leaders of merchant families were establishing and growing fortunes. At that stage of development, more attention was paid to building business enterprises than to managing assets and investments.

Over the past decade, however, far greater focus has been placed on developing institutional processes for managing wealth and making investment decisions. One reason for this has been that the scale of fortunes has increased to the point that professional management, customarily made up of nonfamily members, is appropriate considering the sums being invested. Another reason is that decades of interaction with professional asset management firms have led to a natural migration of best practices, expertise, and staff from multinational firms into regional family offices.

Perhaps the most important driver of institutionalization, however, has been the transition of influence and control to a new generation of Gulf leaders. Unlike their fathers and grandfathers, who built fortunes in the post-boom period through entrepreneurship and operating businesses, the generation that has come of age in the 1980s has studied extensively overseas, worked with multinational firms, and interacted heavily with global financial institutions. Formal processes of investment review, portfolio management, and the structuring of asset ownership come naturally to this new generation. Institutional models are also well suited for passing on wealth from one generation to the next, whereas personal inheritance models can be more contentious and complex. This is an important concern as the founders of Gulf business empires advance in age.

The rise of "family offices"—institutions that manage family wealth—is thus a trend that has been embraced and supported by families themselves, the advisors who serve them, and regulators in the region. The Dubai International Financial Centre (DIFC), for example, has developed a distinct set of regulations for "single family offices," or SFOs. SFO regulations facilitate the establishment of family holding companies and utilize family structures for holding and passing on wealth.[40] SFOs, which tap into nonfamily professionals to act as executive asset managers, adopt formal policies for investment review, asset allocation, and portfolio management in ways that informal personal structures historically have not done.

Perhaps the most famous private institutional investor from the region is Prince Alwaleed Bin Talal Alsaud, founder of the firm Kingdom Holding Company and widely considered to be the wealthiest private Gulf citizen.[41] Kingdom Holding Company, established in 1980, has evolved into a significant global investor with assets across a wide range of sectors and countries. Figure 2.4, featured on the Kingdom Holding Company Web site, nicely illustrates the company's global reach and diversified asset base.

As is evident in Figure 2.4, financial services and hotels represent a major share of Kingdom's portfolio. At the same time, the company holds assets in real estate, telecom, automotive, retail, and other sectors as well. Table 2.8 lists some of Kingdom's most prominent portfolio companies and the company's estimated equity stake in those firms.

FIGURE 2.4

Kingdom Holdings Is a Truly Global, Diversified Investment Platform

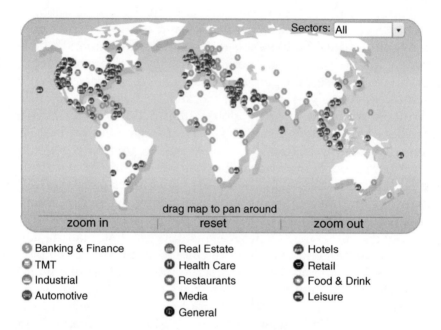

Banking & Finance — Real Estate — Hotels
TMT — Health Care — Retail
Industrial — Restaurants — Food & Drink
Automotive — Media — Leisure
General

Source: Kingdom Holdings Web site; accessed 2009.

TABLE 2.8

Prominent Portfolio Companies of Kingdom Holding Company[1]

Sector	Company	Country	Stake (Estimated)
Financial services	Citigroup	United States	3.6%
	Samba Financial Group	Saudi Arabia	5%
	Cal Merchant Bank	Ghana	14%
	United Bank for Africa	Nigeria	13.7%
	Ecobank Group	Togo	10%
Hospitality	Four Seasons Hotels and Resorts	Canada	45%
	Fairmont Hotel San Francisco	United States	50%
	The Savoy Hotel	United Kingdom	50%
	The Plaza Hotel (New York)	United States	50%
	Monte Carlo Hotel Company	Monaco	25%
	Disneyland Resort and Theme Park	France	17.3%

Retail and consumer	Saks Inc.	United States	1.1%
	Procter & Gamble	United States	1%
	Amazon.com	United States	1%
	eBay.com	United States	1%
	Priceline.com	United States	1.76%
	PepsiCo Beverages International	United States	1%
Media	News Corporation	Australia	1.8%
	Time Warner	United States	0.8%
	The Walt Disney Company	United States	1%
	Saudi Research and Marketing Group	Saudi Arabia	29.9%
Real estate	Kingdom Center (Riyadh)	Saudi Arabia	36%
	Canary Wharf Group	United Kingdom	8%
	Jerusalem Development and Investment Company	Palestinian Territories	5%
	Real Estate Investment Company Limited	Saudi Arabia	38.8%
Technology and telecom	Apple Computer	United States	5%
	Motorola	United States	1%
	Silki La Silki National Telecommunications Company	Saudi Arabia	25.4%

[1] Zawya Company Profile; accessed March 31, 2009.

Kingdom's portfolio companies illustrate the breadth of private holdings by Gulf-based investors. Kingdom holds minority stakes in leading US firms, including Apple, Disney, Citigroup, and Motorola, among others. These investments not only provide financial returns, but also position Kingdom (and Prince Alwaleed) as a serious investor on the world stage. In emerging markets, Kingdom tends to hold larger stakes in portfolio companies—taking, for example, 10 to 15 percent stakes in a number of African banks. This may reflect the fact that overall asset values are lower in emerging markets (hence, the minimum value required to make an investment that is worth Kingdom's time necessarily buys a bigger stake) and Kingdom's appetite for greater control in the context of riskier investments. Kingdom's largest stakes are—not surprisingly—in Saudi investments that are closest to home and perhaps easiest to influence. Even at home, however, Kingdom takes minority stakes (up to 50 percent) rather than majority ownership of portfolio companies.

"Prestige" Investments

Of the four categories of Gulf investors identified in our framework, private institutions are the most inclined toward "prestige" investments. Because private institutions are typically controlled by a family or a small number of individuals, investments can be made based on noncommercial grounds and personal preferences. The same is not true for public-sector vehicles (which are accountable to governments) or for investment houses (which are accountable to their investors).

Sheikh Mansour bin Zayed Al Nahyan, son of the UAE's founding ruler, also makes investments in his personal capacity. As a private investor, he led a consortium buying the UK soccer team Manchester City in 2007.[42] The purchase, though it may prove profitable one day, was generally seen as a "trophy asset" that reflected the preferences and interests of the buyers more than a return-focused financial investment.

Other types of Gulf investor have also bought their fair share of prestigious assets. Bahrain-based Investcorp, for example, has owned Tiffany & Co. and Gucci. Abu Dhabi's Mubadala today owns 5 percent of Ferrari. In the cases of both of these investors, however, business benefits have been procured: Investcorp successfully exited its luxury investments,[43] and Mubadala has used its influence over Ferrari to join the Formula 1 circuit in 2009 and to set up the world's first Ferrari theme park in Abu Dhabi.[44] Private investors, by contrast, are freer to pursue investments that bring nonfinancial benefits, such as soccer teams, ranches, and prestigious buildings.

PRIVATE INVESTMENT HOUSES: MARKET-DRIVEN MANAGERS

The final category of Gulf-based institutional investors is private investment houses—a dynamic and fast-growing category with increasing importance in the region. The fundamental distinction between "investment houses" and the private institutions discussed previously is that investment houses manage wealth on behalf of third-party investors and clients. Whereas private institutions (as defined in our framework) invest their own proprietary wealth, investment houses provide services to Gulf clients and manage funds on behalf of others. This difference creates stark contrasts in investment strategies, operating models, and internal capabilities.

Extensions of Banking and Core Financial Services

As private wealth in the GCC has grown, so has the need to provide financial services to local clients. Expanding prosperity in the region has enabled financial institutions to provide not only basic banking products like savings accounts and personal loans, but also private banking and wealth management solutions for wealthy clients based in the region. Investment services have become a key proposition of GCC financial institutions and can be a key contributor to banks' overall profitability. Although many of the Gulf's wealthiest people keep assets in offshore accounts with global banks in the United Kingdom, Switzerland, Hong Kong, and Singapore, there is also a sizable demand for investment services within the region. In the 1970s and 1980s, for example, Bahrain emerged as a major banking hub for the region, largely because it was a trusted and nearby haven for newly wealthy Saudi investors.

In many ways, the rise of private investment houses is a natural extension of core banking and financial services. There are, however, important differences between the investment services customarily provided by banks and those provided by specialist investment houses, as shown in Table 2.9.

Investment houses specialize in marketing funds to investors and generally do not provide financial services such as daily banking and basic credit services. While many banks offer their clients investment products, they generally do not manage funds directly—they work with external fund managers or feed assets into existing funds

T A B L E   2.9

Investment Houses Differ from Banks along Several Dimensions

Banks	Investment Houses
Provide investment services as part of a broader client relationship	Relationship with clients is focused on investment services
Offer a range of savings and investment "products"	Customarily focus on marketing investment funds
Often act as a distribution channel for external fund managers	Have internal management capabilities and generally manage funds directly
Service retail, commercial, high-net-worth, and institutional clients	Focus on high-net-worth and institutional investors

created by asset managers. Investment houses, in contrast, tend to manage funds directly and develop the internal capabilities for doing so. Unlike banking franchises, which serve a full range of customers, investment houses focus on high-net-worth individuals and institutional clients who are capable of making large investments in sophisticated and risky investment funds.

Not surprisingly, investment houses in the region sprang up in the wake of the oil boom of the 1970s and again in the sustained boom of the 2000s. It's noteworthy that the early pioneers of the investment house category were established using investment banking licenses. Investcorp, for example, has been engaged in transactions since 1982 and is registered as a "wholesale bank" under the supervision of the Central Bank of Bahrain.[45] Investment banking licenses enabled Investcorp and other principal investment firms such as Arcapita (formerly First Islamic Investment Bank) to participate in the arrangement of investments and then sell those investments to third-party investors. While these entities were established as banks, in fact they behave more like private equity shops that elsewhere in the world would be considered nonbanking financial institutions.

It's also important to note that, from the time of the oil booms and associated wealth creation, international asset management firms and fund managers have actively courted Gulf clients. The wealthiest GCC families have long held accounts and assets with leading US and European financial institutions such as Goldman Sachs, Morgan Stanley, Merrill Lynch, UBS, and Barclay's, among others. In the past decade, global firms have increased their commitment to the region, establishing offices in financial centers in Dubai and Qatar, building teams with regional expertise and relationships, and seeing the Gulf as a key growth market for wealth management. The focus of our current analysis, however, is on the rise of investment houses based in the region itself.

Sizable Mutual Fund Industry

As investable wealth in the region has grown, investing in listed equity (stock) markets has been a natural first step for many investors. It is common for Gulf-based banks and asset management firms to offer their customers an array of mutual funds, including funds focused on the home country (e.g., Saudi equity funds), funds focused on the broader region (GCC or MENA funds), and funds that invest globally or in emerging markets.

In the category of GCC equity funds (funds concentrated on stock markets) the firm Markaz Research estimated in February that there were 51 asset managers in the category with a total of nearly $12 billion in assets under management. Of the top ten asset managers in its ranking, five were Saudi entities, four hailed from Kuwait, and one was from the UAE.[46] Several of the top ten institutions, including Riyad Capital, HSBC Saudi Arabia, Samba Financial Group, NCB Capital (Saudi Arabia), and the National Bank of Abu Dhabi,were entities affiliated with full-fledged commercial banks.

The volume of assets under management of mutual fund managers fluctuates as stock markets go up and down. In the highly volatile Gulf markets, swings in market capitalization have been particularly pronounced, with multiple boom-and-bust cycles experienced this decade. Following a strong bull market from 2001 to 2006, equity markets suffered a severe correction in 2006 despite overall economic strength and earnings growth that year. Markets then recovered but declined heavily again in 2008 as a result of the global financial crisis and the expected economic recession. According to the Markaz study, regional equity managers were holding an average of 29 percent of assets in cash by December 2008 (fleeing the sinking stock exchanges), whereas only 6 percent of fund assets were held in cash in April of the same year.[47]

Although regional markets are developing, they remain far less developed than the more established public markets in the United States, Europe, and parts of Asia. Markets remain largely sentiment-driven, with share prices often moving on the basis of retail sentiment more than on the analysis of earnings forecasts and hard numbers. One key measure of this is the percentage of assets held directly by retail investors as opposed to professional asset managers. It is estimated that, in the Arab world overall, total managed assets amount to roughly 6 to 7 percent of total market capitalization, whereas the norm in other emerging markets is 20 to 25 percent. In the more mature markets of Europe, the percentage of managed assets is believed to be around 40 percent, between five and six times the figure for the Arab world.[48] This figure suggests substantial headroom for Gulf mutual funds to grow, and also indicates the challenge they face in seeking to institutionalize what today are largely retail-driven markets.

Private Equity Shops Are Dynamic and Growing

Private equity has been a growing industry in the GCC region, and its rise is one of the hallmarks of the boom of the 2000s. The Gulf Venture Capital Association, a key industry body, estimated that the cumulative funds of private equity and venture capital funds in the MENA region reached nearly $20 billion by 2008.[49] Figure 2.5 illustrates the explosive growth in this sector in recent years:

It is estimated that since 2005, the pool of assets under management by regional private equity and venture capital (PE and VC) firms has increased in volume about five times. At the same time, the average size per fund has also grown (although far more modestly) to over $250 million per fund. Therefore, growth in the industry has come mainly through the introduction of new funds by both established players and new entrants. This is to be expected, since private equity and venture capital funds are

FIGURE 2.5

Middle East and North Africa Private Equity and Venture Capital Assets Reached about $20 Billion by 2008

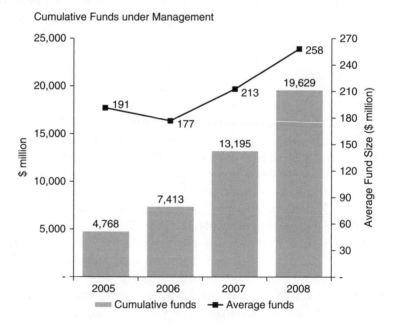

Cumulative Funds under Management

Source: Gulf Venture Capital Association, "Private Equity and Venture Capital in the Middle East," 2008 Annual Report, p, 16.

customarily closed-ended, and therefore new investments are channeled to new funds.

Regional PE and VC firms have shown remarkable success in
some of their investments—even in the turbulent year 2008.
According to the same association report (citing data from the intelligence firm Zawya), a number of leading PE firms exited investments
in 2008 with internal rates of return (IRRs) well above their stated targets.[50] For example:

- Abraaj Capital's Buyout Fund II generated a reported
  annualized IRR of 52 percent on its investment in National
  Air Services (NAS) airlines—a remarkable feat considering
  the large size of the original investment ($177 million).
- Unicorn's Global Private Equity Fund I (a fully Islamic fund)
  achieved a reported annualized IRR of 98 percent on its
  investment in the construction firm Ormix.
- SHUAA Partners Fund I, another pioneer in the region,
  exited its investment in the retailer Damas Jewelry for
  $70 million, having entered at less than half that value
  ($33 million) in 2005. The precise IRR is unknown, since the
  detailed capital structure of the transaction has not been
  made public.

PE and VC shops in the region operate with a unique set of opportunities and constraints. A number of these are outlined in Table 2.10.

T A B L E   2.10

Regional Private Equity and Venture Capital Firms' Opportunities
and Constraints

Opportunity Drivers	Unique Constraints
Fundamental economic growth and earnings potential for portfolio companies	Capital markets are not mature, making exit options less reliable
Restructuring of conglomerates and family enterprises	Available market information is often limited
Active promotion of entrepreneurship	Constraints associated with structuring and operations remain
Ongoing deregulation of markets	Regulatory constraints largely persist

The overall economic outlook for the region—especially when compared to that for other markets worldwide—remains strong, suggesting ongoing potential for profits and earnings growth for portfolio companies. As discussed earlier, there is a major trend underway toward the restructuring of conglomerates and family enterprises, especially as family offices are institutionalized and new generations take positions of leadership. The "rationalization" of business portfolios—focusing on core areas of expertise and shedding businesses that don't fit—can lead to many promising private equity investment opportunities. In addition, governments and public institutions are increasingly stressing the importance of entrepreneurship by young nationals. Small and medium enterprise (SME) funds have been established specifically to support such businesses, and major foundations like the Mohammed Bin Rashid Foundation and the Qatar Foundation actively promote entrepreneurship. In the UAE, for example, the fund Alf Yad (which literally means "1,000 hands") has been established as a for-profit fund with a broader social mission. To quote the fund:

> The premise behind the name is that over the course of ten years, Alf Yad's 1000 investors will have directly contributed towards the Arab Economy and shall constitute the "one thousand hands" that will invest capital and enable privately held businesses to flourish.[51]

In addition to efforts that specifically target entrepreneurship, ongoing investment by GCC governments in establishing universities, research facilities, and other "knowledge infrastructure" helps to foster an environment conducive to creating new businesses. These businesses can become attractive investment opportunities for Gulf-based private equity and venture capital firms in the years ahead.

At the same time, the unique constraints associated with principal investments in the region should not be underestimated. As mentioned earlier, capital markets are not yet mature, and therefore planning exits via IPOs on local stock exchanges is not entirely reliable. According to industry research, only 30 percent of private equity exits in the region between 1998 and 2008 were through IPOs—a strikingly low figure indicating the uncertainty associated with seeking a public exit.[52]

Second, the information available in the market regarding the performance of potential portfolio companies, their competitors, and other actors is often quite limited. This environment of imperfect information can create advantages for actors who have greater access to information than their rivals and counterparties do, but overall it makes the investment process less efficient and more speculative. In addition, there are often significant constraints associated with investment structuring and ongoing operations, especially when portfolio companies are family enterprises. Established stakeholders often retain significant control, and conditions can be placed on matters such as the appointment of key executives, ongoing support for pet projects, and the like. Outside buyers investing in such assets need to be aware of the environment that they are entering.

Finally, although all post-WTO Gulf states are opening up various sectors of their economies, regulations that limit foreign ownership in key industries are still in place today. Thus, PE and VC funds that are domiciled in offshore centers and have international shareholders may be barred from taking majority stakes in otherwise attractive companies. Furthermore, employment laws and other requirements may make it difficult to implement the type of sweeping organizational changes that buyout firms often seek as value-creating strategies in their portfolio companies.

Fund Managers Are Driving Increasing Intraregional Investment

Regional PE and VC funds have played an important role in driving one of the key overall trends related to Gulf capital: an increased focus on intraregional investment. Whereas a number of key pioneers in the region's PE and VC sector, such as Investcorp and Arcapita, have focused almost exclusively on making investments in the West and the broader OECD market, the generation of firms established in the past decade focuses largely on investment opportunities within the Middle East. A number of this decade's most prominent firms—Abraaj Capital (UAE), SHUAA Capital (UAE), Global Investment House (Kuwait), and others—have made their most successful investments in the Middle East region. Within this category of MENA-focused funds, Egypt has been the single largest target market for acquisitions. Figure 2.6, also drawn from the Gulf Venture Capital Association's analysis, shows the breakdown of investments by country.

Egypt's appeal is not surprising, as it is by far the largest Arab market by population and thus is fertile ground for consumer-facing and population-driven businesses. A reported 73 percent of MENA PE exits have been through either IPOs in Egypt or sales to Egyptian

F I G U R E   2.6

Egypt Has Attracted the Most Attention from Regional Private Equity
Investors

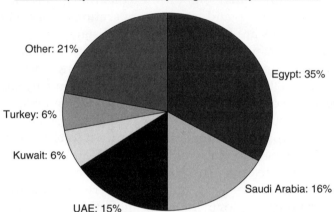

Private Equity Investments by Target Country, 1998–2008

Other: 21%

Egypt: 35%

Turkey: 6%

Kuwait: 6%

Saudi Arabia: 16%

UAE: 15%

Note: Figures rounded and may not add up to 100%.

Source: Gulf Venture Capital Association, "Private Equity and Venture Capital
in the Middle East," 2008 Annual Report, drawing on Zawya data.

firms, illustrating Egypt's viability as an exit market for principal
investors.[53]

It is noteworthy, however, that the three GCC markets featured in
the analysis—Saudi Arabia, the UAE, and Kuwait—combined drew
only 37 percent of investments. This, in our view, is a reflection of the
unique constraints and challenges of investing in the GCC, as well as a
reflection of the high historical valuations in the Gulf that have pushed
asset values up significantly (even for private companies). Principal
investors actively look for "bargain" entry prices, and over the past
years those have simply not been available in Gulf markets.

A CHANGING TOPOGRAPHY

The landscape of Gulf investors has evolved rapidly in recent years,
and the period ahead is likely to see further changes, so that various
categories of investors will face new sets of opportunities and challenges. Generalist sovereign wealth funds are likely to continue to
grow as surpluses are generated in the more prosperous member

states of the GCC. In line with their core mission of preserving and growing national wealth, the conservative, OECD-focused portfolio strategies of these SWFs are likely to continue. Increased international scrutiny is likely to be another reason for these SWFs to concentrate on sovereign debt, fixed income, and diversified equity investments, with minor stakes in listed companies.

Specialist government investment vehicles are likely to become increasingly important as GCC states pursue economic strategies of diversification and skill building. Specialist GIVs are starting to show signs of success in building ties with world-class companies, building assets of strategic importance, and fostering an active investment strategy for a portion of the Gulf states' surplus wealth. In the years ahead, we can expect to see expansion in the specialist GIV category, and also greater coordination among GIVs (especially in the UAE). Partnerships and co-investment relationships between specialist GIVs and private investors may take root, meeting the investment objectives of both groups and (more important) a broader goal of enhancing private-sector involvement in the region's capital formation and deployment.

Private institutions will evolve with the Gulf economies and with the demographic shifts in the region. Increased focus and institutionalization are major trends that are already underway and are expected to continue strongly. Shifts in the operating models of private institutions are likely to create significant opportunities for investment firms seeking portfolio companies, firms seeking to raise Gulf capital, advisors who serve them both, and professionals seeking opportunities in the region.

Investment houses stand poised to benefit from enhanced capital markets, ongoing deregulation, and evolving business structures in the region. As investment houses further prove themselves and their capabilities, deeper relationships can be built with the private investors who fund them and, interestingly, with the specialist GIVs that are taking root in the region. Decision makers are likely to encourage greater collaboration as they seek to ensure that public investors do not "crowd out" the private sector.

While the future topography of the Gulf's investor landscape cannot be precisely predicted, key forces that are at play and are likely to shape the future have been identified. Considering the ongoing importance of the GCC to global markets, financial professionals will be well served by keeping an eye on the moving parts creating the dynamism of the Gulf's institutional landscape.

KEY LESSONS

- Gulf capital is not a monolith—the landscape of GCC-based institutional investors is complex and evolving.

- Generalist sovereign wealth funds (better described as national trusts) are the region's largest and most mature investors. Their mission—to preserve and grow national wealth—leads them to pursue conservative investment strategies.

- Specialist government investment vehicles act as focused hybrids, pursuing specific investment strategies that are relevant to their countries' overall economic development plans while operating like private firms.

- Private institutions, which generally trace their roots to family conglomerates, have long been important investors in the region. They are becoming increasingly institutionalized as new leadership emerges within them.

- Investment houses, although today managing a modest portion of the Gulf's overall wealth, are increasing in importance and play a key role in enabling intraregional investment.

3
CHAPTER

Values and Value: Islamic Finance in the Gulf and Beyond

[The] ethical principles on which Islamic finance is based may bring banks closer to their clients and to the true spirit which should mark every financial service.[1]

—Vatican publication, March 2009

Once, on a flight from Zurich to Riyadh, I was seated next to a businessperson who was visiting Saudi Arabia for the first time. She was a senior executive at a massive global energy conglomerate for which the Gulf region was critical to business success. Although her role was not directly related to the Gulf Cooperation Council (GCC), she was visiting the region as part of a project in her portfolio of responsibilities.

When I mentioned my involvement in Islamic finance, she was noticeably intrigued. She asked me to tell her more about the field. I said I would, but that first I was curious about what the term *Islamic finance* meant to her. "To me," she said, "it sounds like providing financing for mosques or funding for Muslim charities." She then went on to discuss the presence of Muslim charitable institutions in

Europe. Strikingly, her perception of Islamic finance had nothing to do with banking, investments, or commercial financial services.[2]

It's often noted that Islamic finance, which more precisely can be called Shariah-compliant financial services, is a fast-growing sector with increasing importance on the global stage. Major financial institutions, including HSBC, Citibank, Deutsche Bank, UBS, Standard Chartered, and dozens more, have introduced Islamic products and services and see such business lines as key potential engines of growth. Major business publications feature stories on "Islamic finance" with increasing frequency, and financial professionals are coming across the term more often. In fact, a *Harvard Business Review* piece on the rise of Islamic finance as a global player was featured in the journal's "Breakthrough Ideas" issue in 2008.[3] The term is quickly becoming a part of the lexicon of global business.

Despite the heightened profile of Islamic finance, misunderstandings and misconceptions of the term abound. Some people mistakenly think that Islamic finance includes all banking and investments undertaken by Muslims, even though the bulk of such activity is in fact undertaken through conventional (not Shariah-compliant) ways. The Islamic finance sector therefore makes up only a very small portion of Muslims' overall financial activities. Frequently, I have been asked how a financial institution can earn a profit and still be deemed "Islamic." A colleague who leads the Islamic finance program at a leading university is often approached by students who interpret the Islamic finance program as being a scholarship fund. Those with greater exposure to the sector sometimes focus solely on the prohibition of interest (one key principle of Islamic finance) and miss the broader ethical and economic frameworks. Furthermore, observers often note the similarities between Islamic offerings and their conventional counterparts and conclude that there is no "real" difference between Islamic finance and conventional banking.[4] Although this is often a fair criticism, it generally overlooks key procedural and structural differences—differences that have an impact on Shariah compliance even if pricing and economic outcomes are identical.

This chapter provides a brief overview of the Islamic finance sector, introducing it to nonspecialists. The focus is on Islamic finance as a commercial phenomenon that is of increasing importance to the global financial system. We do not seek to provide a comprehensive primer on the principles, structures, and technical aspects of Islamic finance— there are other books available that do so.[5] Instead, we present the commercial and strategic aspects of Islamic finance as a "new global player"—a sector that is of relevance to financial professionals worldwide. The chapter begins with an overview of Islamic financial principles and their grounding in universal ethics. Next, we discuss the evolution of the Islamic finance sector and provide a snapshot of the industry landscape. We then comment on key challenges facing the sector, exploring in depth its "authenticity challenge" and "real economy imperative." Overall, we present the sector as dynamic and growing, but also facing fundamental challenges—challenges that must be addressed if Islamic finance is to continue its growth trajectory in the decade ahead.

PRINCIPLES ROOTED IN COMMON VALUES

Islamic law, referred to as the Shariah in Arabic and in other Muslim languages, is a deep and rich intellectual tradition.[6] Like canon law, rabbinical law, and the secular liberal tradition, Islamic law is replete with well-developed schools of thought. The tradition includes scholarly tomes and detailed analysis rooted in principles, texts, and other proofs. The field of Islamic jurisprudence is referred to in Arabic as *fiqh* (from the root for "understanding"). It signifies the efforts of legal specialists to interpret the Shariah and apply it to particular human circumstances. A trained expert in jurisprudence is referred to as a *faqih* and is often addressed with the honorific title *"shaykh."*[7]

Importantly, there is a distinction between jurisprudence (*fiqh*), which is expressed in guidelines and in opinions referred to as *fatawa'* (the plural form of the word *fatwa*), and legal judgments of the state. A *fatwa* represents the expert opinion of a jurist, but it does not have the status of law and is not backed by the power of the state. Therefore, a variety of expert opinions regarding the same matter can be freely circulating in a society. This is especially true in matters that are contemporary in nature (like modern financial services) and are prone to a diversity of opinions. A legal judgment in a court of law is referred to as *qada'* and is backed by the infrastructure of the state.

Within the field of jurisprudence, one major category of specialization is the jurisprudence of transactions (*fiqh al-mu'amalat*), an area encompassing business transactions, financial arrangements, and so on. Although many people are exposed only to the aspects of *fiqh al-mu'amalat* that pertain to Islamic financial services, it should be noted that the field has deep roots in the classical Islamic tradition and refers to more than just finance. For example, guidelines for paying employees

FIGURE   3.1

Islamic Finance Principles Are Rooted in a Set of Common Values

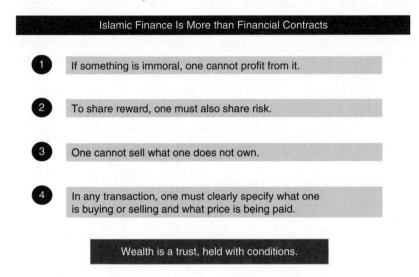

on time and disclosing shortcomings in goods that are being sold are all part of the same body of jurisprudence that governs lending and investments. This should be borne in mind by practitioners and observers of Islamic finance alike, lest the focus be placed solely on the technical aspects of financial structuring, neglecting the broader ethical spirit of the tradition.

The depth of Islamic jurisprudence cannot, of course, be reduced to a handful of pithy maxims. There is, nonetheless, value in stating some core principles that run through the tradition and provide a general ethical framework for understanding the detailed rules that are derived from them. Figure 3.1 features four key principles underpinning Islamic financial ethics that are rooted in common values.[8]

Aligning Financial Activity with Ethics

The first of these core principles—and, in my view, the most fundamental—is that if something is immoral, one must not profit from it. In other words, one's financial activities must be consistent with her overall ethics and values. If an investor believes, for example, that gambling is wrong, it would be inappropriate for her to profit from gambling by owning a casino. This basic principle generally manifests

CHAPTER 3   Values and Value   **93**

itself in social interaction—most people would find it difficult to deeply admire someone whose income is derived from selling illegal narcotics, even if he is an exceptionally pleasant and well-mannered person.

This principle is fairly intuitive and straightforward, yet (strikingly) it is very rarely applied in the world of contemporary investments. Countless teachers' unions, for example, may unknowingly be investing part of their pension funds in tobacco stocks through diversified mutual funds. These teachers might be unpleasantly surprised to know that they are deriving financial benefit from an industry that they consider unethical. Similar issues may exist with regard to defense contractors that manufacture weapons. In the run-up to the war in Iraq, for example, students and faculty at a major university objected when they believed that the university endowment was investing in manufacturers of military hardware and weapons. Such complaints are, however, quite rare—as is evident from the fact that several charities were victimized by Bernard Madoff's extensive investment-scheme fraud discovered in late 2008. Beyond seeking a solid return on their investable assets, it does not appear that the charities probed deeply into whether Madoff's investment practices were consistent with the charities' own ethics and values.

Leading asset management institutions, whether they be third-party managers of funds like State Street and Vanguard or principal investors like university endowments and pension funds, have increasingly accommodated investors who seek "socially responsible investments" (SRI), "green" or environment-friendly funds, and other ethics-based investment criteria. Historically, such constraints have made investment managers uncomfortable—these managers are, after all, trained to optimize returns within a range of possible investment options. It logically follows that the more flexibility they have (all else being equal), the better. In addition, the introduction of ethical screens that rule out certain investments can be complex and time-consuming, possibly detracting from the returns and "distracting" investment committees. Today, there is greater sensitivity toward socially responsible funds, yet the category remains a small fraction of the total universe of invested wealth.

In the case of Islamic investments, the ethical screens are rooted in principles and directives from the Shariah. The bulk of the "prohibited" sectors overlap with the sectors that are customarily screened out of conventional SRI funds, such as (for example) pornography, gambling, and weapons. There are, however, sectors that are screened out by Islamic funds but not by most SRI funds because they relate to practices that are prohibited in Islam but not in other ethical traditions. The largest of these sectors is conventional financial services—since Islamic law views interest-based financial services as impermissible, conventional banking and insurance stocks are screened out of Islamic funds. In addition, Islam's prohibitions on drinking alcohol and consuming pork extend to investing in breweries, bars, and pork-related businesses. Some SRI funds may also screen out alcohol; others may not. A further (also crucial) distinction is that Islamic funds are generally required to "purify" their returns by removing any portion of the return that is deemed to be from impermissible sources. The purification process takes into account the percentage of income of companies in the portfolio that comes from activities that do not conform to the Shariah.

When investing in publicly listed stocks, Islamic funds customarily apply three types of screens during the Shariah filtering process. The first filter looks at the nature of companies' business—companies whose core business is in an impermissible sector (casinos, for example) are excluded from the set of permissible investments. The second filter looks at the percentage of the companies' income that comes from interest or interest-based investments. If a significant proportion of its income comes from interest, a company may be screened out even if its core business is acceptable. Imagine, for example, a technology company that has received private equity funding and holds a great deal of its assets in interest-bearing accounts and Treasury bills. If interest income represents a substantial portion of its total income, this company may not be eligible for investment by an Islamic fund. The third screen looks at a company's overall debt-to-equity ratio. If a company's balance sheet is heavily leveraged (using conventional, interest-based leverage), it can be screened out irrespective of its core business. Conventional real estate development companies are therefore customarily screened out, even though real estate investment itself is allowed in Islam. If the debt on a company's balance sheet is structured in a Shariah-compliant manner (i.e., is not interest-based), the debt-to-equity screen is not applied. This is because the motivation behind the rule is to screen out companies that benefit from the use of interest. Investing in leveraged Islamic banks and Shariah-compliant real estate companies is therefore deemed permissible without analysis of their debt-to-equity ratios.

The principle of not profiting from immoral activities extends beyond the realm of investments. According to the Shariah, Muslims should, for example, avoid working in impermissible businesses such as breweries. Similarly, Muslims storeowners are instructed not to sell alcohol to their customers. Often, especially in the West, practicing Muslims engage in these activities, citing "necessity" or a lack of other options. The intent of the Shariah, however, is that a person's entire economic activity be in conformity with her values.

Bearing a Risk to Enjoy a Return

The most famous injunction of Islamic finance is its prohibition of conventional interest. This prohibition is rooted in the Qur'an, which prohibits a practice that is called *riba* in Arabic and is traditionally interpreted to include modern interest. More precisely, it is understood to include all forms of a guaranteed return on moneylending in excess of the principal amount lent. Demanding repayment of $105 next year for $100 lent today would be considered an impermissible arrangement. There is also a form of interest related to bartering commodities that is called *riba al-fadl* (prohibiting the uneven exchange of the same commodity), which is generally less relevant to modern, currency-intermediated financial activity.[9]

One moral critique of interest-based lending is that it is unfair to the borrower because of the misallocation of risk and reward. The borrower may, for example, be borrowing the money in order to fund a business. In operating the business, he is taking a risk—the business could succeed, or it could fail. The interest-based lender, however, locks in a guaranteed return regardless of how the business performs. In other words, the lender seeks a guaranteed return without undertaking a commensurate risk. Of course, conventional economists would argue that the lender undertakes a real risk in the form of credit risk—the risk that the borrower may not pay back the loan. This highlights an important principle in Islamic law: that agreements should be assessed based on the expectation that they will be fulfilled. One cannot enter into a contract that, if it is fulfilled, is deemed to be "unjust," even if it is possible that the contract will not be fulfilled.

Another rationale cited by economists regarding the prohibition of interest relates to the very role of money in the economy. According to Islamic economists, the Shariah views money as a store of value and a medium of exchange, not as a commodity. Therefore, money should not be exchanged at a price; rather, it should be a means for the exchange of goods and services.[10] This perspective explains why the view that an interest rate merely represents the "price of money" (and should therefore be acceptable) is incompatible with classical Islamic economics.

The prohibition of interest was not a new concept introduced by Islam; in fact, interest was long banned by all three Abrahamic faiths (Judaism, Christianity, and Islam) and by other ethical traditions in the world. As discussed by British economist Ann Pettifor, Christianity's ban on interest persisted until after the Protestant Reformation, when theologians created a distinction between "usury," which was deemed to be excessively high compensation for moneylending, and "interest," which was deemed to be a fair price for extending credit. A rate of 5 percent per annum was considered to be a fair interest rate, and this perspective began to take hold.

Despite the shift in theology, however, public perceptions of moneylending and interest-based activities remained highly negative for a long time. Christians of high standing considered it undesirable to marry into moneylending families, and the business of lending for profit was often looked down on.[11] Over time, however, interest-based financing became the norm, and the social stigma associated with it was dropped. A moral disdain for "usurious" rates of interest has, nonetheless, remained. In the United States, for example, "usury laws" that cap interest rates are quite common. In the postcrisis discussions regarding predatory lending, policy makers have increasingly criticized credit card companies and subprime lenders for practices that trap customers into interest rates of 20 percent or higher. An increased awareness has emerged that high rates of interest can keep individuals and families in cycles of perpetual debt and make the accumulation of wealth extremely difficult.

A key implication of the prohibition of interest is that it also leads to a prohibition of the sale of debt. The discounting of a payment stream of receivables at a price other than the face value of the receivables is not allowed because it is a form of interest. For example, a debt in the amount of $100 to be received one year from today cannot be transferred to another party in exchange for an immediate payment of $95. The prohibition on the sale of debt (a view held by the majority of contemporary Islamic scholars, but not by all)[12] is a crucial difference between Islamic finance and conventional capital markets, in which the packaging and sale of payment streams (for example, collateralized debt obligations, or CDOs) is common and is considered essential to efficient markets. Opaqueness in the transfer of debt, misleading ratings regarding the quality of the debt, and misaligned incentives between the originators of debt and the ultimate holders of the debt have, however, all been cited as key causes of the global financial crisis that came to a head in 2008.[13] The ban on selling debt is the clearest manner in which Islamic finance principles proscribe certain practices that led to the financial crisis.

Although Islamic finance prohibits charging for moneylending and the practice of compounding interest, it is important to note that the Shariah and Islamic economics do acknowledge the time value of money. A merchant can, for example, charge a higher price in the case of a sale with deferred payment (for example, if payment will be made in a year) than she would if the buyer were paying cash today. Similarly, it is acceptable for the price to be lower if a customer pays today for property to be delivered in the future than it would be if the customer paid later on (say, at the time of delivery).[14] There is recognition of the opportunity cost associated with having cash in hand— the merchant could have used these funds for additional trading, and the customer could have invested the money and earned a return elsewhere. Thus, Islamic finance does not neglect the reality of the time value of money.

The key distinction between Islamic finance and conventional lending, therefore, is that Islamic finance is rooted in trade (the exchange of assets) rather than in moneylending (charging interest on money lent). The Qur'an itself emphasizes this distinction and recognizes its subtleties. Addressing the argument that interest-based lending is simply a form of trade, the Qur'an says, "that is because they say 'indeed, trade is like interest;' whereas God has made trade permissible and has prohibited interest."[15] To comply with this ruling, Islamic finance must be asset-intermediated and involve the exchange of goods rather than charging for the use of money.

The financing structure called *murabaha*, or "markup" financing, illustrates this fundamental concept of asset intermediation. The first step in the *murabaha* process—like the first step in a conventional financing process—involves a customer identifying a good that he wishes to purchase (for example, furniture). In a conventional financing, the lender would simply provide the customer with the cash at a particular interest rate. In a *murabaha* structure, however, the financier must itself purchase the furniture, take legal ownership of the furniture, and then sell it to the end customer for profit. Conceptually, the extra step (in which the financier buys the asset) turns the transaction into a trade rather than a moneylending arrangement. In practice, the financier typically appoints the end customer to make the purchase on its behalf (so that the financier technically owns the furniture but does not have to go to the store and collect it). Observers have noted that the *murabaha* structure replicates conventional financing and hardly seems different—in fact, the agency agreement through which the customer buys the asset on behalf of the bank may seem cumbersome. The step by which the financier owns the asset (and thereby takes ownership risk at least temporarily) is nonetheless an important procedural difference, without which the financing arrangement would not be deemed Shariah-compliant.

Table 3.1 provides a brief overview of key structures used in Islamic finance, highlighting the manner in which they incorporate (at least conceptually) aspects of trade and commercial risk.

Table 3.1 is by no means an exhaustive list of all Islamic financial structures, nor does it describe all attributes of these structures. Its purpose is to demonstrate how Islamic financial structures differ from their conventional counterparts in that they are designed (at least conceptually) to take on some aspect of tradelike or commercial risk.

Not Selling What One Does Not Own

A third core principle of Islamic financial ethics is that one cannot sell something that he does not own. This principle is straightforward, but it has significant implications for investment practices in contemporary capital markets. In particular, the principle makes short selling (selling stocks or other financial securities that one does not yet own) impermissible.

Short selling has become so common in today's financial markets that most people find little reason to reflect on it. It's interesting, however, to contrast the ethics of investing in a stock by purchasing it ("going long") with short selling ("going short"). When an investor goes long, it is because he believes that the value of a security will go up, and he wishes to benefit from this rise in value. The person from whom the investor is buying (through a broker) may be selling in order to cash in or to create liquidity to permit the purchase of another asset. When an investor goes short, by contrast, she is seeking to benefit from the decline in a security's value. Her underlying belief is that the asset is overvalued and will come down in price. In addition, in order for the short-selling arrangement to be made, there needs to be an investor (or at least a broker) taking the opposite point of view. A short seller's position, therefore, may be seen more of a bet on the market than something linked to an economic interest in the

TABLE 3.1

Select Islamic Finance Structures and Their Tradelike Features

Structure	Conventional Equivalent	Financing Process	Tradelike and Commercial Attributes
Murabaha (markup financing)	Typical consumer credit	The financier purchases the asset from the original seller and then sells it to the end user	The financier acts as the direct seller and takes ownership risk on the asset (at least temporarily)
Mudaraba (partnership between capital and management)	Agency agreements and asset/fund management arrangements	Investors provide capital, and management takes responsibility for generating profits. Profits are shared between investors and management	Investors take on the commercial risk of the venture; the investment could lose value
Musharaka (equity partnership)	Equity partnership	Investors provide equity capital in return for ownership in an asset or venture	Investors take on the commercial risk of the asset or venture; the investment could lose value
Ijara (leasing)	Leasing arrangement	The financier takes ownership of the asset and leases it to the end user	The financier takes (at least conceptually) ownership risk on the asset for the period of the lease
Sukuk ("Islamic bonds")[1]	Conventional bonds	Investors take ownership in a special-purpose vehicle (SPV) that owns assets. The SPV generates income through leasing the assets to the end user or through other means, and that income flows through to the investors	Investors are in fact equity holders in a vehicle and take the associated ownership risk

[1] There are a variety of structures used for *sukuk*; the description here speaks in general terms that are applicable to a number of *sukuk* structures.

asset. As Islamic finance focuses on actual assets and their appreciation, short selling does not fit its principles.

It's noteworthy that, at the height of the financial crisis in
2008–2009, market regulators introduced temporary bans on short-
selling stocks in the financial sector. Presumably, this was to prevent the
shares of major banks from falling even further after their precipitous
declines. Regulators sought to limit action in this sector to two types of
actors: shareholders who wished to sell down existing positions, and
potential investors who wished to buy the shares and "go long."
Regulators took the view (at least temporarily) that short selling was
unhealthy for the market and excessively destabilizing.

The ban on short selling does introduce a constraint on Islamic
investors that conventional investors may not have. Islamic investors
are required to take a more fundamental view of investments, buying assets that they believe will appreciate, and avoiding those that
they believe will decline in value. An investor who believes that a
security will decline could use this insight to sell down his existing
position or simply avoid buying it in the event that he does not yet
own it. Short selling and benefiting from the security's decline is not
an option.

Knowing (Precisely) What One Is Buying or Selling

A fourth basic principle of Islamic finance is that, in a transaction, one
must specify what she is buying and what price is being paid. The
underlying concept of relevance here is referred to in Arabic as *gharar*,
or excessive uncertainty. A prime example of *gharar* can be drawn
from the famous Monty Hall game show *Let's Make a Deal*. In the
show, a contestant could trade in a prize in hand for the unknown
contents of a box or whatever was behind "Curtain 1," "Curtain 2," or
"Curtain 3" (see Figure 3.2).

The contestant had no idea what was behind each curtain and
had no fact-based way to judge whether the items behind the curtains
were of greater or lesser value than what he already had in hand. At
times, there was an additional layer of *gharar* in that the contestant also
did not know the value of what he had in hand—it could, for example,
be a roll of bills with the value of only the top note revealed. The contestant would therefore need to guess both the value of what he
already had and the value of what was behind the curtains.[16] While
Let's Make a Deal was of course a game and not an actual business,
there are commercial contexts in which assets (for example, foreclosed

F I G U R E   3.2

Let's Make a Deal Is a Prime Example of the Principle of *Gharar*
(Excessive Uncertainty)

Source: *Let's Make a Deal* official Web site; accessed July 2009.

properties that are sold "as is" with no opportunity to inspect them)
are sold with highly imprecise information.

Conventional insurance has traditionally been considered
impermissible by Islamic scholars because of a perception of *gharar*.
The terms associated with the insurance policy and payment scenarios have been deemed to be insufficiently precise—the buyer may
know what premium she is paying, but whether a claim will ever be
made, what the amount of that claim will be, and when it might be
made are all unknown. Irrespective of how much a policyholder contributes, often she will see no return on payments made. The industry
of *takaful* (an Islamic equivalent of insurance) operates differently in
that it employs a mutual assurance model by which policy owners
contribute capital, share any profits from investments, and agree to
pay out "claims" in the event that other contributors suffer a defined
loss. This mutual model is seen as more fair and transparent for all
parties.

In commenting on the financial crisis of 2008–2009, some
observers have viewed the opaqueness of certain debt-based instruments such as collateralized debt obligations (CDOs) as contemporary examples of *gharar*.[17] The misrating (and subsequent mispricing)
of such securities added to the confusion of investors holding debt

traded on capital markets. "Toxic paper" flowed through capital markets while investors remained uncertain as to who, in fact, was left holding the bad debts. As regulators around the world have called for greater transparency and disclosure, the risks of excessive uncertainty have been broadly appreciated.

The principles discussed here are by no means an exhaustive discussion of the rules and procedures of Islamic finance. They do, however, provide a basic grounding in a core set of guidelines that are common and accessible across a range of ethical traditions. Whereas the structures used in Islamic finance sometimes seem complex and technically cumbersome, the guiding principles that direct them can be fairly straightforward. The challenge, as we shall discuss later, has been to design products and services that conform to these principles and also conform to customer expectations.

AN EVOLVING INDUSTRY

Although Muslims have been conducting business and financial affairs in accordance with the Shariah for over 1,400 years, the modern Islamic finance industry is a fairly young sector. Its conceptual roots can be traced back to the 1950s, with modern Islamic financial institutions being established in the 1960s, 1970s, and thereafter. The sector has gained sizable market share, especially in the Gulf region, in the 2000s and is considered to be an integral part of the overall financial system in a number of Muslim countries. In addition, Islamic finance has emerged as a fast-growing niche industry in countries in which there are significant Muslim minority communities, including the United States, the United Kingdom, Germany, Hong Kong, Singapore, and many more. The strategic landscape of the sector is dynamic and rapidly changing, with new entrants appearing in the marketplace, often with substantial capital bases and strong sponsors. As the sector evolves, it faces both promising opportunities and significant challenges.

Diverse Origins

Although a number of today's leading Islamic financial institutions are based in the GCC, many of the pioneers in the sector were from outside the Gulf region. The earliest ideas, institutions, and initiatives in modern Islamic finance and economics appeared largely in

T A B L E   3.2

Pioneering Islamic Finance Efforts from Outside the Gulf

Initiative	Year	Country	Description
Tabung Haji	1962	Malaysia	Savings and investment vehicle for pilgrims performing Hajj
Mit Ghamr Savings Bank	1963	Egypt	Rural bank based on profit-and-loss-sharing financing
Islamic Development Bank	1975	Multilateral; based in Saudi Arabia	Multilateral development bank funded by all member countries of the Organization of the Islamic Conference (OIC)
Faisal Islamic Bank (Sudan)	1977	Sudan	Commercial bank; member of Dar Al-Maal Al-Islami (DMI) Trust
Jordan Islamic Bank for Finance and Investment	1978	Jordan	Institution to mobilize savings for industrial development
Faisal Islamic Bank of Egypt	1979	Egypt	Commercial bank; member of Dar Al-Maal Al-Islami (DMI) Trust
Islamic International Bank for Investment and Development	1980	Egypt	Institution to mobilize savings for industrial development
Mandatory "Islamization" initiatives	1980s	Iran, Pakistan, Sudan	Government initiatives mandating that all financial services comply with the Shariah
Bank Islam Malaysia	1983	Malaysia	Commercial bank

Malaysia, Egypt, South Asia, and other parts of the Muslim world (see Table 3.2).

Tabung Haji, a Malaysian institution, is a key example embodying the spirit of Islamic finance's pioneers. The institution was created in 1963 as a savings and investment platform, specifically to help Malaysians save and build wealth for performing Hajj (the pilgrimage to Mecca). Since its very purpose was linked to the religious practice of pilgrimage, it naturally followed that Tabung Haji's investments must be Shariah-compliant. Tabung Haji continues to thrive today, providing both investment services for millions of Malaysians and logistical support (in Malaysia and in Saudi Arabia) for thousands of Malaysians during the Hajj itself.[18]

As illustrated in Figure 3.3, Tabung Haji's business model reflects a number of themes that motivated the establishment of Islamic financial institutions in the 1960s and 1970s.

F I G U R E   3.3

Tabung Haji Reflects the Spirit of Modern Islamic Finance's Pioneers

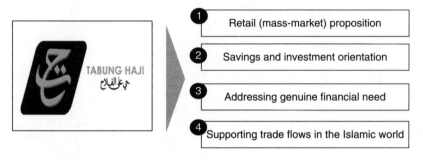

Like other early Islamic financial institutions, Tabung Haji focused on the mass market of retail customers. Although Islamic finance has today evolved to include corporate and institutional client bases, the original customer demand for Shariah-compliant services was rooted principally in the retail market. Customer demand "from the bottom up" has driven the growth of Islamic finance since its inception.

Additionally, Tabung Haji has been focused on savings and investments—helping customers to grow their wealth in a Shariah-compliant way. This orientation is consistent with a broader Islamic ethos that eschews debt for personal consumption and instead favors savings and investment in economically productive activities. This stands in contrast to contemporary lending practices (often copied by Islamic banks as well) that promote personal debt through the aggressive marketing of consumption loans. Tabung Haji focused on a genuine need, savings for pilgrimage, and has maintained its focus on this need. Another pioneer, Mit Ghamr Savings Bank, focused on the needs of rural Egyptians who were underserved by conventional banks. Mit Ghamr's life came to a controversial end (it was shut down by the government amid allegations of impropriety), but the need it sought to address was certainly a real one.

Another aspect of Tabung Haji's business model that was shared by other founders of the Islamic finance industry is the support of trade flows in the Islamic world. The Hajj traffic brings with it significant exchange of goods and services, creating economic links among Muslim countries. One motivation of Islamic finance's pioneers, which is especially clear in the case of the multilateral Islamic Development Bank, was to encourage trade between Muslim countries as a vehicle for economic development.

In the 1980s, three countries (through differing approaches) adopted mandatory "Islamization" programs in their banking sectors: Iran, Pakistan, and Sudan. As a matter of policy, these countries felt that their banking sectors must be entirely Islamic, and edicts to this effect were issued. The mandatory and swift nature of such Islamization initiatives led, however, to unintended consequences—one of which was the superficial "conversion" of banks without sufficiently changing their product structures and operations. Often, customers saw no change in their experience except that names and labels were changed (for example, calling something a "profit rate" rather than an "interest rate"), without sufficiently changing the underlying product. Even though forced Islamization has been revoked in Pakistan and conventional banks have long since dropped the Islamic labels, strongly negative impressions of Islamic banking have persisted among customers who witnessed the "window-dressing" approach. Some assume that all Islamic banks' claims of Shariah compliance are as weak as those of the banks that adopted window dressing out of regulatory necessity. This assumption continues to act as a barrier to the growth of Islamic finance in certain countries.

Gulf Leadership

Although the roots of the modern Islamic finance sector—as is evident from the preceding discussion—are broad and diverse, the largest manifestation of the sector today is in the GCC region. The Gulf today represents the largest addressable cluster of the global Islamic finance sector, and is home to many of its most dynamic institutions. While Islamic finance is by no means limited to the Gulf or simply a "Gulf story," the GCC region is playing a pivotal role in driving the sector forward.

Determining the size of the total Islamic finance market is a difficult endeavor for a number of reasons. One chief reason is that although the assets of fully Islamic banks are generally reported, these assets represent only a part of the total picture. Dozens of conventional banks offer Islamic products, but the assets associated with these businesses are not reported separately. For example, the assets of HSBC Amanah—HSBC's global Islamic finance unit—are not reported separately from the HSBC Group's overall figures. Therefore, the assets of Islamic "windows" of conventional banks generally need to be estimated. In terms of Islamic investment funds, similar challenges exist—and funds often report far less data publicly than banks do.

An additional pool of "Islamic" assets and wealth that usually is not included in estimates but is meaningful for understanding the opportunity is the assets and wealth of Shariah-inclined customers who are holding money in Shariah-neutral products that don't bear an "Islamic" label. For example, a customer who (wishing not to violate the Shariah) holds her wealth in a non-interest-bearing checking account rather than an interest-bearing money market account will generally not be recognized as an Islamic customer. There may, however, be large pools of wealth—especially in countries like the United States, where Shariah-compliant banking services are less readily available—held in Shariah-neutral accounts for ethical reasons.

As illustrated in Figure 3.4, a full picture of Islamic wealth would need to factor in all three layers of analysis. Customarily, however, only the assets of fully Islamic entities (be they banks or funds) are known with any degree of precision, and the assets of windows are then estimated. Shariah-neutral assets of Islamic customers are very difficult to assess and therefore are largely overlooked.

F I G U R E   3.4

Islamic Wealth Includes Three Layers of Assets

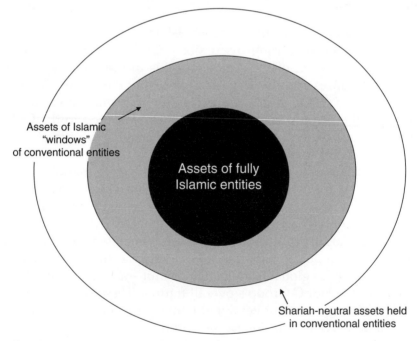

Note: Not to scale.

According to a review of banking assets published in the journal *The Banker*, using 2007 data, the GCC region held more Islamic assets (despite its small population relative to the overall Islamic world) than the rest of the Middle East, Asia, Africa, or any other region. To assess the addressable market, however, one may wish to remove Iran and Sudan (which are included in the published analysis) from the data set. As a result of regulatory constraints in the United States and elsewhere (regulations that affect a large number of multinational firms), access to the Iranian and Sudanese markets is currently limited, if not entirely proscribed. If one looks only at the addressable market, the GCC constitutes about two-thirds of the market (see Figure 3.5).

Although the second-largest Islamic banking market (after Saudi Arabia) is Malaysia, five of the top six Islamic banking markets are in the GCC. Oman, which currently does not have any Islamic banks, is not listed but is likely to have significant Islamic wealth in Shariah-neutral products because of the lack of available Shariah-compliant products. It's striking that the United Kingdom, despite being outside the Muslim-majority world, held about the same amount of Islamic

F I G U R E   3.5

The GCC Holds about Two-Thirds of Islamic Banking Assets in the Addressable Market

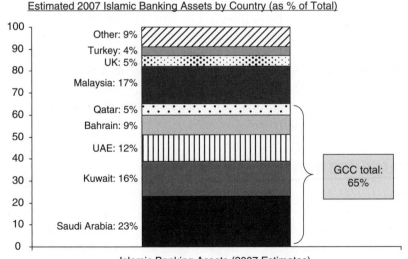

Estimated 2007 Islamic Banking Assets by Country (as % of Total)

Islamic Banking Assets (2007 Estimates)

Source: *The Banker* and International Financial Services, London.

T A B L E   3.3

Islamic Assets and Financial Institutions in the GCC[1]

Country	% of Total GCC Islamic Assets	Number of Institutions Offering Islamic Finance
Saudi Arabia	35%	17
Kuwait	24%	29
UAE	19%	12
Bahrain	14%	27
Qatar	8%	14

[1]**Source:** "International Financial Services," London, Islamic Finance 2009; *The Banker*, November 2008.

banking assets as Qatar and more than Turkey (which is the largest Muslim economy in terms of total GDP)[19] at the time of the study.

Within the GCC, Saudi Arabia is estimated to hold the largest share of Islamic banking assets, and Kuwait has the largest number of financial institutions offering Islamic finance, as shown in Table 3.3.

Saudi Arabia's Islamic assets may, in fact, be significantly higher than 35 percent of the GCC total. It may be that the Islamic assets held in windows of conventional banks have been underestimated. At the retail level, Islamic products and services have been a dominant preference of customers of both full-Islamic banks and windows of conventional banks in Saudi Arabia since the mid-2000s. The number of institutions in each country offering Islamic finance is related more to the level of fragmentation of the banking market in a particular country than it is to the size of the Islamic asset pool in that country. Bahrain, with is plethora of banks because of its role as an offshore banking center, had 10 more banks offering Islamic finance than Saudi Arabia did at the time of the study, despite having less than half the estimated Islamic banking assets.

DYNAMIC INSTITUTIONAL LANDSCAPE

Within the landscape of institutions offering Islamic financial services, there are four main categories of business models, as well as an emerging fifth model that has arisen in recent years and may potentially have a transformative impact on the sector. Each category of institution has played an important role in the development of the sector and is likely to continue to do so as Islamic finance evolves.

F I G U R E   3.6

The Industry Landscape Features Different Models with Relative Strengths and Drawbacks

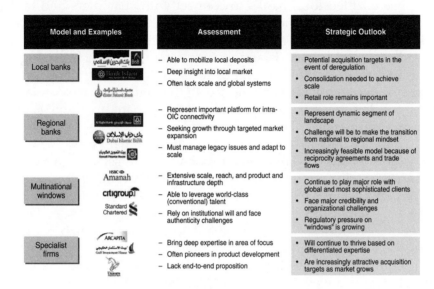

Figure 3.6 outlines the four main categories, providing examples within each category along with an assessment of the category's key strengths and weaknesses. In addition, commentary on the strategic outlook for each segment of the landscape is offered.

Local Banks

The single largest category of institutions offering Islamic financial services is *local banks*—deposit-taking financial institutions that serve a single country or market. As Islamic finance took root in the 1970s and beyond, it became customary for Islamic banks to be created in each country to serve the local market. Dozens of local Islamic banks remain to this day, such as Bahrain Islamic Bank, Bank Islam Malaysia, Qatar Islamic Bank, and many more.

Local banks have played a pivotal role in mobilizing deposits in their home markets, especially from Shariah-inclined customers who were underserved by conventional financial institutions. Local Islamic banks tend to have deep insights into and expertise in their home markets, and they often were the sole providers of Islamic banking services in their respective countries for some time. Being "first movers" allowed them to build solid (and often very loyal) customer bases, and these banks flourished—especially since local competition was historically fairly limited. While their geographic focus has enabled local banks to connect with customers and build successful businesses, they often struggle to achieve adequate scale and procure world-class global systems. Like other small banks around the world, local Islamic banks often find it challenging to build efficient operating models or to undertake investments in the latest systems and platforms. The size of their customer bases relative to the fixed costs associated with operating a bank may make such efficiency impossible.

As the Islamic finance sector evolves, local banks are attractive acquisition targets for larger institutions that are seeking to expand their businesses or for financial investors who are looking for a strong return. Bank Islam Malaysia, for example, is now 40 percent owned by Dubai Islamic Investment Group, a part of the broader Dubai Group of institutions.[20] Within the Gulf, local Islamic banks are prime acquisition targets, pending ongoing deregulation and openness to such acquisitions. Consolidation of smaller-scale banks seems like a natural step in the evolution of the Islamic financial sector, and it is likely to take place if and when regulators allow such consolidation to occur.

Regional Banking Conglomerates

A second category is *regional banking conglomerates*—financial institutions with a presence in more than one country. Much of the dynamism in the sector in recent years has been driven by this category, as banks have expanded from their home countries into new markets and thereby become regional players rather than local ones.

Multimarket banking conglomerates have existed in Islamic finance for decades. Two major Gulf-based conglomerates, the Dar Al-Maal Al-Islami (DMI) Trust and the Al Baraka Banking Group, trace their roots back to the 1970s and have established substantial presences in a wide range of markets. Al Baraka's subsidiaries and affiliates are in no fewer than 12 countries, spanning five geographical areas, as shown in Table 3.4.

More recently, a number of Gulf-based Islamic banks that are leaders in their home markets have begun expanding abroad. Al Rajhi Bank of Saudi Arabia, the Kingdom's dominant Islamic bank, has expanded into Malaysia. Kuwait Finance House (also the dominant

T A B L E   3.4

The Al Baraka Group's Regional Footprint[1]

Area	Countries with Al Baraka Presence
Gulf	Bahrain
Levant	Jordan, Lebanon, Syria
Africa	Algeria, Egypt, South Africa, Sudan, Tunisia
Asia	Indonesia, Pakistan
Europe	Turkey

[1] Al Baraka Group corporate Web site, http://www.albaraka.com/, and author analysis; accessed July 2009.

Islamic bank in its home market of Kuwait) has similarly expanded strongly into Malaysia. Dubai Islamic Bank has established a presence in Pakistan, tapping into the employment and trade flows between the UAE and Pakistan.

As multimarket conglomerates expand, they are likely to drive change in the sector though acquisitions, partnerships, and pan-regional strategies. They also have the potential to achieve the scale required to enable efficiency and profitability levels that are less attainable by small players. To thrive, however, these institutions will need to overcome the legacy issues associated with being originally established as local banks. For example, as Kuwait Finance House (KFH) grows in Malaysia and potentially beyond, one key challenge will be to position KFH as being more than a "Kuwaiti bank" and ensure that it is seen as being committed to the local markets that it serves. Beyond the issues of perception, it is critical that management, operating models, systems, and governance structures all evolve appropriately as multimarket conglomerates expand. As these institutions outgrow their home markets, their entire enterprises need to adapt in order to capitalize on their multimarket presence. If they fail to do so, their ability to win regional market share will be limited.

Windows of Global Institutions

Since the 1990s, leading global banks have entered the Islamic finance market with teams dedicated to Shariah-compliant products and services. Citi Islamic Investment Bank was established by Citigroup in the 1990s as a dedicated business unit, and HSBC Amanah was founded by the HSBC Group in 1998. The entry of Citigroup and HSBC into the Islamic finance field marked a major milestone in the sector's evolution, and it was seen as an important endorsement by the world's financial services establishment. Whereas doubts as to the long-term viability of Islamic finance had abounded prior to this development, the commitment of major banks (such as HSBC, Citigroup, Standard Chartered, Deutsche Bank, UBS, and many more) has affirmed to many the ongoing importance of Islamic finance.

Conventional banks customarily serve Islamic clients through *Islamic windows*—Shariah-compliant business units within the overall bank. Under the window model, the Islamic business unit is not a separate legal entity and does not have a separate balance sheet. This has several business advantages, such as allowing the Islamic business to build off the strength of the conventional business, reducing the costs and complexity associated with entering the Islamic business, facilitating the sharing of resources across Islamic and conventional operations, and so on. It does, however, also have the disadvantage of being perceived as less authentic by some customers and by Shariah scholars, who prefer distinct Islamic entities when possible. Many customers are skeptical of an institution's Shariah compliance if they know that their Islamic deposits will be placed in a general treasury that may be used for conventional loans, or that their Islamic loan may be funded through conventional deposits on which the bank is paying fixed interest.

Windows of global banks are likely to continue to play a key role in the advancement of the Islamic finance sector in the years ahead. Their access to talent and to their institutions' overall expertise allow for product innovation and operational excellence at levels that often exceed those of the other categories of institutions we have discussed. For example, HSBC Amanah's introduction of the international *sukuk* ("Islamic bond") was a major innovation that has since been adopted by both conventional and fully Islamic institutions worldwide. Leading global institutions often have access to the most sophisticated institutional and retail clients in a market, as a result of their international reach and their well-established reputations. They can, therefore, introduce Islamic products and services to segments of the market that are less accessible to fully Islamic banks. As sophisticated clients increasingly see Islamic finance as a viable and attractive alternative, windows of global financial institutions stand to gain considerably.

Specialist Entities

The fourth category in our landscape is that of *specialist entities*—investment firms, advisory firms, and other institutions that focus on specific areas within financial services. Bahrain-based Arcapita, which is registered as an investment bank and focuses on principal investments, is an example of this category, as is the Kuwaiti firm Gulf Investment House and Bahrain-based Unicorn Investment Bank. Specialist institutions and fund managers are growing rapidly in number as demand for Islamic products and services grows in the Gulf and beyond.

Specialist entities often bring deep expertise in their areas of focus and are pioneers in product development. The US-based and London-listed firm Shariah Capital, for example, has positioned itself as a leader in introducing Shariah-compliant alternatives to conventional hedge funds.[21] Since specialist entities are not deposit-taking banks and therefore cannot offer end-to-end propositions to their clients, they often partner with full-service banks to distribute products or provide related services. Specialist institutions' business models allow for significant profit margins and efficient operations, but they can also be constrained in terms of absolute size and scalability.

As the sector evolves, specialist entities can continue to be critical to the ongoing development of Islamic finance. One can expect this category to be a source of innovative ideas, sophisticated product development, and new concepts for the industry. Products initiated by specialist bodies may find their way to the broader marketplace through banks and other large institutions, multiplying the impact of these innovators many times over. Specialized talent is likely to continue to migrate to focused entities that match an individual's skill sets and provide an organizational culture in which innovation and creativity thrive.

Highly Capitalized New Entrants

In addition to the four categories of institutions featured in our landscape, another type of institution has appeared on the scene in recent years: *highly capitalized new entrants*. This category, which is a form of the local bank category, has unique attributes related to having a strong capital base and the potential for significant investment. Highly capitalized new entrants have the potential to shape the industry landscape though investments and acquisitions.

T A B L E   3.5

Well-Capitalized New Entrants in Islamic Finance

Institution	Year Established	Country	Ownership	Paid-in Capital
Alinma Bank	2006	Saudi Arabia	Listed	$2.8 billion
Al-Rayan Bank	2006	Qatar	Listed	$1 billion
Noor Islamic Bank	2007	UAE (Dubai)	Private	$1.09 billion
Al Hilal Bank	2007	UAE (Abu Dhabi)	Private	$272 million

Table 3.5 lists a number of new entrants with substantial capital to support their development.

The appearance of these new entrants reflects a number of key themes in Gulf financial services and Islamic finance. First, all four of the institutions in Table 3.5 have enjoyed the support of government-linked bodies or rulers as founding sponsors and stakeholders. They reflect an increased emphasis on Islamic finance by the leaders of their respective countries. Second, their establishment reflects the recognition that there is a large local demand for Shariah-compliant financial services and that any new large-scale banking institution in the region needs to provide Islamic services. If these entities were set up as conventional banks, their appeal would have been less, and a large segment of the local population would not have been addressed.

In the coming years, these highly capitalized banks can be expected to actively seek growth through heavy investment in their businesses. One form of investment will be investment in organic growth through initiatives like new branches, expansion into new product lines, and targeting new customers. In addition, however, significant investment in inorganic growth initiatives can be expected, including domestic and international acquisitions. In an Islamic finance landscape that is fragmented and includes a large number of small (arguably subscale) institutions, highly capitalized new entrants can be a driving force for mergers, acquisitions, and consolidation. They may, therefore, reshape the industry structure in the years ahead.

As is evident from our discussion, there is no single type of Islamic financial institution—the organizations offering Islamic financial services vary significantly and can be classified into several categories. Each category has played a unique role in the advancement of the sector and will continue to influence the ongoing evolution of Islamic finance.

FUNDAMENTAL CHALLENGES

While the growth and adoption of Islamic finance have no doubt been impressive, the sector also faces fundamental challenges in the years ahead. Challenges exist along a number of dimensions, including customer adoption, product development, organization and business design, human capital development, regulatory enablement, and economic impact. Although each of these areas could be discussed at length, the focus of our current analysis will be on three core challenges: the *authenticity challenge*, the *real economy imperative*, and the need for *regulatory enablement*.

Authenticity Challenge

Islamic finance is rooted in a set of economic principles, including risk sharing, partnership between capital providers and businesses, limitations on debt, and a focus on productive economic activity. Early Islamic financial institutions—many of which, notably, were not formal "banks," but rather were nonbanking financial institutions—sought to embody these principles through equity-based lending, seed funding of "Islamic" companies, expansion into poorer countries in an effort to make access to capital more equitable, and other such measures. These early efforts met with mixed results, and were not always financially successful.

As Islamic finance evolved, adaptive measures were undertaken to enable the sector to conform more closely to the prevailing, conventional financial system. Structuring strategies (referred to as *hiyal* in Shariah terminology) were devised in order to replicate the outcomes of conventional products through Shariah-compliant means. These strategies were often approved by Shariah scholars as "exceptions," with a view that the strategies would be used for a temporary period until alternatives that were more consistent with the spirit of Islamic finance could be introduced.

Table 3.6 lists a few of the key structuring strategies that have been employed by the Islamic finance sector in order to conform to conventional banking norms.

As discussed in Table 3.6, each of these structures has real commercial benefits for financiers and customers. The prevalence of "arranged" *murabaha* structures came about early in the development of Islamic banking as a safe way for lenders to extend credit. Without being arranged, *murabaha* structures would have exposed financiers

T A B L E 3.6

Islamic Structuring Strategies That Conform to Conventional Norms

Structuring Strategy	Description	Commercial Benefit	Shariah Drawback(s)
"Arranged" *murabaha*	Markup financing in which the customer undertakes to buy the asset from the financier (thereby giving assurance of resale) prior to the financier's making the initial purchase from the supplier	Replicates the risk profile of conventional credit more closely and limits the financier's ownership risk	Originally criticized as synthesizing conventional interest too closely by securing the resale prior to the initial purchase
Commodity *murabaha*	A structure in which financial institutions enter into commodity trades benchmarked to prevailing interest rates in order to mimic the returns of short-term Treasury bills or commercial paper	Provides customers with a Shariah-compliant alternative to conventional savings products	The exchange of commodities is generally notional, with no parties taking a genuine economic interest in the commodities
Tawarruq (reverse *murabaha*)	Reverse *murabaha* structure (featuring the exchange of an asset) in which customers receive cash immediately and pay back more cash later	Provides customers with a Shariah-compliant alternative to cash financing	Widely criticized for delinking consumer credit from identifiable needs and thereby departing from the spirit of the Shariah
W'ad undertakings	A broad term used for undertakings (like that in arranged *murabaha*) by which parties undertake to do things that could not be included in the main contract without making the main contract noncompliant	Provide assurances (for example, with some *sukuk* structures) that give comfort to participants and make the structures more conventional equivalent to their counterparts	Criticized as mechanisms to conform with the letter of the Shariah more than its spirit

to greater ownership and commercial risks—risks that pioneers such as Kuwait Finance House took on early in their history, before the industry evolved. On the savings side of the house, the commodity *murabaha* (despite its Shariah drawbacks) gives savers a great deal more comfort and safety than riskier structures would offer. *Tawarruq* (although highly controversial, since it allows for credit with no link to identifiable customer needs) has been hugely popular in some markets because of its convenience for customers.[22]

A number of industry observers, especially economists and academics, have commented that the growth of Islamic finance has come with the introduction of structuring strategies that arguably depart from the spirit of the Shariah. The instruments just discussed, among others, have no doubt contributed to the rapid expansion and increased acceptance of Islamic finance. At the same time, concerns about their Shariah authenticity are well founded and must be appreciated.

Islamic finance's authenticity challenge is rooted in real forces in the operating environment. Figure 3.7 illustrates some of the key pressures that contribute to Islamic finance's challenge in maintaining Shariah authenticity.

Foremost among these pressures is the matter of customer expectations. Islamic financial institutions have generally found that only a small segment of their potential customer base is willing to pay

FIGURE   3.7

Islamic Finance Faces a Multifaceted "Authenticity Challenge"

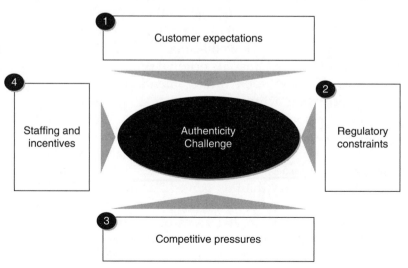

a significant premium (in terms of higher costs or lower returns) for Islamic financial services compared to conventional ones. To capture a sizable market share, therefore, institutions have needed to offer Islamic products that replicate the features, benefits, and pricing of conventional alternatives. This need to replicate conventional products has had real implications for the ability of financial institutions to comply with the spirit of Shariah guidelines.

Consider, for example, an auto financing product. The safest Islamic way for a financier to offer this product may be through an arranged *murabaha* structure—otherwise, the financier may end up owning a car that it cannot sell. In addition, if the financier needs to maintain pricing parity with conventional structures, he will not be able to take ownership risk (for example, being responsible in the event that the car is defective or that major repairs are needed). Doing so would raise the financier's risk and thus result in either a higher price for the customer or lower returns to the financier's shareholders. The principles of the Shariah may have preferred that the financier take greater ownership risk, but doing so could make the product too expensive for the customer.

A second major challenge to greater Shariah authenticity is the regulatory framework governing banks. Islamic financial institutions have found it imperative to incorporate as licensed banks so as to be authorized to collect customer deposits and provide retail financing. Banking laws, however, place constraints on the investment risk that banks can take using customer deposits. Thus, the principles of Shariah might encourage lenders to be genuine partners with homeowners and actively take equity risk in the homes that they finance. This could, theoretically, entail ownership risk related to matters like repairs and maintenance, as well as market risk in the event that the home is later sold for less than its original purchase price. Regulators, however, would view such arrangements as investment activity rather than financing activity. To be a bank, an institution can place only a limited amount of its customer deposits into investments—placing more would make it an investment company.

Some people, therefore, have suggested that Islamic financial institutions should ideally be set up as asset management/investment companies rather than as banks.[23] Doing so would allow for more risk sharing and greater Shariah authenticity. The difficulty with this approach, however, is that asset management and investment companies are unable to take customer deposits (instead, they take investment accounts) and do not enjoy the protection of government deposit insurance and the backing of central banks as the "lender of last resort." Such companies therefore have difficulty becoming customers' primary financial institution.

A third crucial challenge to greater Shariah authenticity is competitive pressures within the Islamic finance sector. When one institution introduces a product or service, it becomes difficult for competitors to refuse to match it—even if the second institution's Shariah preference would be to not introduce the product. Institutions have found that customers generally take comfort in the fact that Islamic banks profess to be Shariah-compliant overall and therefore do not need to assess the Shariah authenticity of each product or service. Therefore, if one Islamic bank has launched a product, then customers expect their own institution to be able to launch a similar one; if it does not, the customer may switch banks. For example, one bank long resisted the commodity *murabaha* structuring strategy on the grounds that its management did not feel that the structure was adequately authentic. Over time, however, the structure became a norm as a result of competitors' activities, and the bank began using it in order to protect its market share.

A fourth, more subtle, force that often contributes to Islamic finance's authenticity challenge is staffing and incentives. As the sector has grown, Islamic finance has needed to staff an increasing number of fast-growing institutions. The most readily available talent pool for staffing Islamic financial institutions has been the conventional banking market, from which professionals are able to bring skill sets and experience bases that are highly relevant for Islamic financial services. Often, senior executives in Islamic banks come directly from conventional banking and take on roles equivalent to those that they have previously held. For example, the head of retail banking in a conventional bank could often be hired as the head of retail for an Islamic institution. Often, little time is given to training this new executive on the principles of the Shariah, Islamic perspectives on financial services, and other Shariah-related matters.

As a result, executives in Islamic financial institutions may often feel inclined to replicate the products, services, and systems with which they are familiar. Not only is this easier and in some ways safer (these are, after all, time-tested and proven products), but also the banks' incentive systems may contribute to the pressures to replicate. Someone who is brought in to grow an Islamic bank's home financing portfolio and charged with generating 25 percent growth in one year will have every incentive to use strategies and tactics that have worked in conventional settings. Considerations regarding the goals of the Shariah and the relative authenticity of different structures are commendable, but they may not be rewarded by the bank's incentive systems.[24]

One could argue that the rapid growth of Islamic finance has come with a trade-off: structuring strategies that have been used to gain market share have at times been seen as less authentic from a Shariah perspective. As reflected in the (highly stylized) curve in Figure 3.8, the evolution of Islamic finance to date may suggest that market share gains have come at the price of introducing less authentic structures such as *tawarruq* and commodity *murabaha*.

As the sector evolves and competition intensifies, a key area to watch will be whether customers (or at least one segment of the customer base) will differentiate among Islamic financial institutions based on Shariah authenticity. One sign that this may happen is that large pockets of Muslim customers, particularly outside the Gulf, often criticize Islamic finance for not being "different enough" from conventional banking and therefore not being worth patronizing. Propositions and entities that are sufficiently differentiated (in terms of business model, financial structuring, or otherwise) may be required if Islamic finance is to tap into this next pool of customers, who hitherto have not been persuaded by Islamic financial offerings. Another development that may break this perceived trade-off would

F I G U R E   3.8

Is There a Trade-off between Shariah Authenticity and Market Share?

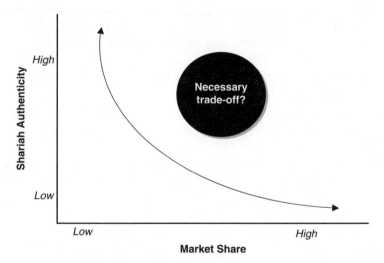

be if Islamic financial institutions are able to identify "Shariah-based" propositions that are simultaneously more authentic and more beneficial to customers. Genuine profit-sharing savings accounts, for example, may be both closer to the spirit of the *mudaraba* fund management model and better for the customer who uses them. Assuming a trade-off between authenticity and market share may be both too easy a mindset and a barrier to innovation—the challenge facing Islamic financiers is to be both more authentic and more appealing to customers and shareholders.

Real Economy Imperative

Another fundamental challenge facing the Islamic finance sector could be characterized as the *real economy imperative*. Although Islamic finance has captured significant market share in the GCC and select markets beyond it, the direct impact of Islamic finance on fostering new businesses, generating jobs, and stimulating the local economies is not as evident as some observers would wish it to be. Given the youthful demographics of the Arab world, the need to create jobs, and the need to enhance the competitiveness of the region's economies, decision makers and observers are looking to the Islamic finance sector as a means for fostering real economic growth.

The real economy imperative arguably applies to financial services overall, conventional and Islamic alike, not just to Islamic finance. For a number of reasons, however, it is more salient in the Islamic finance sector than it is in conventional finance. First, the principles of Islamic finance call for the mobilization of savings into real economic activity and therefore set a high standard for the sector. Second, Shariah guidelines proscribing investments in certain types of derivatives, complex securities, and "notional" assets naturally guide the sector to focus on real businesses and commercial activity. Third, Shariah guidelines related to the nature of portfolio companies' business activities, balance sheets, and capital structures would make it easier for Islamic financial institutions to fund enterprises in the Muslim world, where these guidelines are a smooth fit.

To date, a significant portion of Islamic assets has been deployed either in commodity markets or overseas in the broader international economy. As discussed earlier, the commodity *murabaha* instrument deploys billions of dollars of Islamic savings in metal exchanges and other commodity-intermediated transactions that are designed to replicate the returns on conventional instruments. At the same time, many Islamic equity funds invest (understandably) in Shariah-screened stocks listed on the world's major exchanges—in the United States, the United Kingdom, and other select markets. These exchanges offer the deepest pools of liquidity, the most established track records, and the world's most respected companies. Channeling savings from Muslim markets to the Organisation for Economic Co-operation and Development (OECD) world does not, however, meet the development objectives of policy makers and commentators who wish to see greater real economy development within Muslim markets. As Islamic finance evolves further, pressures and incentives to deploy more savings within domestic markets can be expected to increase. Demonstrating a deep impact on the real economy can be an important way for Islamic finance to show its relevance to economic development and its ability to be a driver of regional growth.

Regulatory Enablement

If Islamic finance is to thrive, an environment of regulatory enablement is generally crucial. Banking laws worldwide, including those in Muslim countries, have been created with the conventional banking system in mind. These laws can often put Islamic finance at a disadvantage, producing a negative impact on the sector's ability to gain market share and flourish.

Table 3.7 lists a few examples of typical banking laws that must be reformed in order to fully enable Islamic financial services.

The prudential limitations on banks' ability to share risks with their customers lead (as discussed earlier) to structuring strategies that arguably reduce Shariah authenticity. Tax laws can pose another obstacle—tax codes customarily treat interest as tax-deductible, creating an incentive for customers to choose conventional finance. To level the playing field, it is important that regulators treat Islamic finance charges as also tax-deductible and thereby not disadvantage Islamic lenders.[25] A third example relates to stamp duties and transaction charges—regimes that charge duties on the transfer of property need to waive potential double taxation in the context of Islamic financing arrangements that involve multiple transfers. Notably, regulators in the United Kingdom have recognized the need for the second and third reforms just listed (tax treatment and stamp duty) and have made changes to enable Islamic finance to better compete with its conventional counterparts.

To date, regulators in the Muslim world have taken adopted different basic stances in addressing Islamic finance. The most common

TABLE   3.7

Examples of Typical Banking Laws That Require Reform to Enable Islamic Finance

Law	Constraint on Islamic Finance	Reform Required
Prudential requirements limiting investment activity by banks	Islamic finance calls for genuine risk sharing between financiers and borrowers; conforming to banking laws requires structuring strategies that reduce risk sharing	Accommodation for investmentlike financing modes intended in Islamic finance while still enabling retail deposits
Tax treatment of interest payments	Interest payments are generally treated as tax-deductible in many jurisdictions, whereas Islamic finance charges often are not tax-deductible	Treatment of Islamic finance charges (e.g., *murabaha* markups) as tax-deductible
Stamp duties/ transaction charges	Regimes often apply a tax when property is transferred from one owner to another. In the case of Islamic transactions, there can sometimes be additional steps that lead to double taxation	Treatment of Islamic finance transactions as a single transfer or waiving the second stamp duty/ transaction charge

approach, adopted in the majority of Muslim countries, could be characterized as an "un-enabling single regime." This approach applies the same set of laws to all financial institutions—conventional and Islamic—without provisions that specifically enable Islamic finance. While such an approach has the benefit of standardization, it has the major drawback of often putting Islamic institutions at a disadvantage as a result of to constraints like those cited earlier.

A second approach can be categorized as an "enabling single regime." Without creating a separate regulatory category for Islamic institutions, this approach seeks to remove the barriers that hinder Islamic financial institutions. The United Kingdom provides a prime example of an enabling single regime—its Financial Services Authority (FSA) does not treat Islamic banks separately from conventional ones, but taxation and stamp duty laws accommodate Islamic transactions by eliminating the hurdles discussed earlier. Importantly, the UK laws make no reference to "Shariah" or to "Islamic finance"—they merely describe the types of structures for which the exemptions from relevant laws exist. This way, there is no favoritism for Islamic finance or limitation of the exemption for a single religious group; the regulator remains neutral.[26]

A third approach, generally viewed by leaders in the sector as most supportive of Islamic finance, can be characterized as a "dual regime." Malaysia and Bahrain, for example, have adopted a separate set of laws for financial institutions that are licensed as Islamic. These laws recognize the distinctive attributes of Islamic finance and apply regulations that are sensitive to these attributes. At the same time, conventional banks are governed by laws that suit the needs and practices of conventional finance.

The "right" regulatory approach for Islamic finance will naturally differ from country to country, and will depend on a number of factors. The country's overall legal framework and tradition, the relative size and importance of Islamic finance, and the stage of Islamic finance's development will all be natural considerations. The core point to bear in mind, however, is that without regulations that are appropriately enabling, the Islamic finance sector will struggle to reach its full potential.

KEY LESSONS

- Islamic finance is rooted in a set of common ethical principles that resonate with the world's great faiths and ethical traditions.

- The origins of modern Islamic finance can be traced largely to pioneering efforts outside the Gulf region, including initiatives in the broader Middle East and in Asia.

- Today, the Gulf region represents the bulk of the world's Islamic assets and around two-thirds of the addressable Islamic finance market.

- The landscape of institutions offering Islamic finance is diverse and dynamic, with four categories of established players and a fifth involving well-capitalized new entrants.

- As Islamic finance evolves, it faces a number of fundamental challenges regarding Shariah authenticity, impact on the underlying real economies that it serves, and sufficient regulatory enablement.

PART II

DEVELOPMENTS AND TRENDS

4

CHAPTER

Smarter Money: The Increased Sophistication of Gulf Investors

Not long ago, an investment banker from a leading global firm was pitching a private equity offering to a Gulf family investor. The investor put forth a query that indicated his interest in negotiating one of the terms of the investment. The banker, seeing his potential customer dressed in traditional Gulf clothing and operating from a family office, launched into an explanation of basic private equity terms. He assumed, based on the investor's appearance and his own perceptions of Gulf investors in general, that the man across the table had little or no familiarity with this asset class. The investor excused himself from the meeting room for a moment and returned shortly with a stack of papers.

The papers were a pile of offering memorandums from the world's most sophisticated private equity firms. Without uttering a word, the investor made it known that he was no novice in private equity and in fact had negotiated with some of the savviest principal investment institutions in the world. The banker quickly got the message. From that point onward, the meeting took a new tone.[1]

Gulf institutions have been prominent as global investors for decades. However, although broadly recognized for their size, Gulf investors have historically not been considered to be among the world's most sophisticated. In fact, a longstanding stereotype in the investment world has been that Gulf investors lack savvy and are therefore prime targets for being "stuffed" with suboptimal investments. Transactions that could not easily be sold to the sharpest buyers in New York, London, and Tokyo might be passed on to Gulf Cooperation Council (GCC) investors in the hopes that they would take the bait. Today, however, many Gulf institutions are far more sophisticated than the stereotype suggests, and have exercised increased savvy in their investment activities.

Historically, Gulf investors have focused on conservative, "plain-vanilla" investments in US and Organisation for Economic Co-operation and Development (OECD) securities. This approach, while generating relatively low returns, suited the objectives and priorities of GCC institutions at the time. Over the past decade, however, Gulf investors have increasingly branched out into more sophisticated investment practices and asset classes—a development that reflects their evolving status and outlook. This migration toward greater sophistication has been accompanied—and largely enabled—by enhanced internal capabilities and human capital within Gulf institutions. At the same time, third parties are taking notice. Reflecting the Gulf's increased savvy and importance, the region today is capturing the attention of many of the world's leading investment firms. In fact, a number of Gulf-based institutions have been positioning themselves (through high-profile transactions, co-investment with other firms, and public appearances) as world-class investment houses. This is a marked change from the time when Gulf investors were largely content to be serviced by marquee firms without building reputations of their own.

This chapter, the first in our section on key trends in Gulf capital and Islamic finance, explores how Gulf investors have grown increasingly sophisticated over time. Appreciating this trend is critical for observers of the region and for those (like the investment banker in our opening anecdote) who wish to do business there. GCC-based investors, long having been taken for granted, are becoming "smarter money." The discussion that follows will give you a sense of why and how this phenomenon is shaping the region's investment activities and affecting global markets overall.

HISTORICAL CONSERVATISM

Gulf-based investors, especially the region's largest institutional investors, have long been recognized as some of the largest buyers of US Treasury bills and other conservative instruments. It is estimated that SAMA, Saudi Arabia's central bank and reserve manager, holds a striking 55 percent of its assets in US Treasury bills,[2] and that the Abu Dhabi Investment Authority (ADIA) has a similar penchant for conservative US fixed-income investments. These two institutions alone may hold several hundred billion dollars of US Treasuries (based on published estimates of their asset size and allocation), not to mention the billions more held by other sovereign and private investors.

Investing in conservative, plain-vanilla securities like US Treasury bills and AAA-rated commercial paper certainly has its drawbacks. The absolute return provided by these investments has been, over time, significantly lower than that from more aggressive asset classes available to institutional investors. The Gulf's longstanding affinity for conservative US dollar investments is, however, rooted in a number of considerations that shape regional investment decisions. As summarized in Figure 4.1, five key decision drivers supporting the rationale for GCC institutions' historically conservative posture can be identified.

The first consideration that has led to a focus on conservative US investments is the dollar denomination of Gulf public-sector incomes. As international oil and gas markets have long been dollar-denominated, GCC governments garner the bulk of their incomes in the form of greenbacks. Sovereign and public-sector investors are, therefore, charged with the task of deploying dollar wealth into an

F I G U R E   4.1

The Gulf's Historical Conservatism Has Been Rooted in Key Investment Considerations

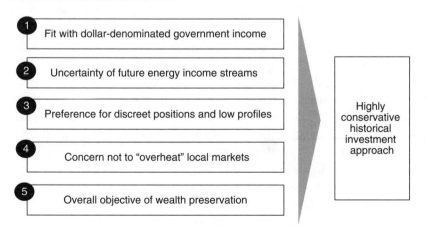

array of investments. Choosing dollar-denominated securities has been a natural choice, one that involves no foreign-exchange risk or bets on the relative strengths of global currencies. Investing in US Treasury bills provides certainty (in dollar terms) of returns. Investing in nondollar securities, by contrast, introduces a built-in currency risk, even if these securities are government bonds or other highly safe investments. The practice of pegging local currencies to the dollar—still the case in all GCC states except for Kuwait—is rooted in a similar line of thinking: economies that are reliant on dollar income have had every incentive to link their currencies to the dollar.

A second reason for conservative investing has been the inherent volatility of energy prices. Along with the famous booms of the 1970s and 2000s, there have also been tremendous busts in oil prices in the late 1970s and much of the 1990s. Crude oil was, in fact, trading as low as $13.11 in the mid-1990s (corresponding to $16.91 in 2008 dollars)[3]—one-tenth its price near the peaks seen a decade later. Treasury bills and other conservative fixed-income securities have played an important role in smoothing out the income available to Gulf investors. If they had allocated the bulk of their savings to more aggressive asset classes like emerging-market equities, their portfolios would have experienced far more volatility. Since the Gulf states—particularly Saudi Arabia—have needed to dip into their reserves and reserve income to fund government budgets during downturns in energy markets, the stable and reliable cash flows of fixed-income securities have been a source of comfort. In addition, conservative investments like US Treasury bills often have the benefit of being exceptionally liquid—positions can be sold almost instantly to provide cash for government projects or other needs. This flexibility has been important in an environment of highly volatile energy prices and Gulf incomes.

It's also noteworthy that conservative investments in US Treasury bills, commercial paper, and large-cap equities have the added advantage of being highly discreet. This has been a consideration for large institutional investors who are sensitive to political perceptions, both at home and in the markets where they invest. As we shall discuss later in this book, Gulf investors have historically preferred to maintain low profiles for a number of internal and external reasons. This is changing rapidly today, with Gulf institutions making more prominent investments and entering asset classes in which disclosure and publicity are essential. Nonetheless, the ability to enter and exit massive positions discreetly has been a key benefit of conservative asset classes—markets that are so deep that the actions of even the largest Gulf investors are mainly unnoticed.

A fourth—and more subtle—consideration of Gulf investors is their concern that they not "overheat" their local markets. The scale of assets managed by Gulf institutional investors, particularly by the leading sovereign bodies, simply dwarfs the local investment market and the domestic investment opportunities that are available. In Abu Dhabi, for example, the top 10 listed equities (which dominate the public market) had an aggregate market capitalization of about $50 billion in early August 2009.[4] While this is an impressive figure, it represents far less than 10 percent of the estimated assets held by ADIA alone, and about 5 percent if we use 2007 estimates of ADIA's asset base. Therefore, if ADIA were to allocate 10 percent of its assets to the local stock market, it could more than double the market capitalization of the leading listed equities. Such an action could severely distort the market, leading to a valuation bubble that would be very difficult to manage. In the event, for example, that ADIA then wished to liquidate its local holdings, it could not do so without causing a massive crash in the market.

Local investment markets have, therefore, been too shallow to allow massive Gulf institutions to allocate a meaningful amount of capital to them. Other emerging markets with more substantial investment activity have greater ability to absorb Gulf capital, but have also been fraught with risks and volatility. Today, Gulf investors are showing an increasing appetite for local and emerging-market investments. Historically, however, managers of the largest institutions have preferred to focus on the deep markets of the United States and other OECD countries, in which their investments will not fundamentally alter the course of the markets. In these deep markets, the risk of causing valuations to overheat or to collapse is not a significant concern.

Finally, the conservative investment outlook that has historically been a hallmark of Gulf investors is consistent with the core missions of these institutions. As discussed in Chapter 2, sovereign wealth funds, perhaps more accurately called national trusts, have focused first on preserving national wealth and next on expanding it. Their purpose has not been to pursue the maximum return possible; rather, it has been to safeguard wealth and generate reliable returns. As captured in the mission statement of the Qatar Investment Authority (QIA), its aim is "to secure the future prosperity of its people . . . the QIA's investment strategy is based on the responsibility to generate a strong and sustainable return."[5] The key words of the statement—*secure, strong*, and *sustainable*—all point toward conservative and safe investments like the ones that Gulf investors have been making for decades.

INCREASINGLY SOPHISTICATED INVESTMENTS

Over the past decade, Gulf investors have been expanding on their legacy of conservatism and venturing into increasingly sophisticated investments. This transition is not a radical shift in core objectives, but rather reflects a natural evolution. As Gulf institutions have achieved greater scale, stability, experience, and capabilities, they have expanded the scope of their investment activities into new asset classes and markets.

To understand this evolution toward greater sophistication, it's worthwhile to assess some of the core attributes of sophisticated investors and the applicability of these attributes to the Gulf context. Of course (as discussed in Chapter 2), there is no single profile for all Gulf investors. Nonetheless, the basic framework given in Table 4.1

T A B L E   4.1

Core Attributes of Sophisticated Investors and Their Applicability to the Gulf

Attribute	Applicability to Gulf	Comments
Scale: Large pool of wealth available for investment	High	The accumulation of savings has propelled Gulf investors to a new level of scale
Investment horizon: Freedom from need to generate period income from investments	Moderate	Some Gulf institutions have assets that dwarf their current needs; others require steady income
Stakeholders: Limited number of stakeholders and decision makers	High	The bulk of GCC institutional investors have centralized decision-making processes
Experience: Substantial experience in a wide range of investments	Moderate	The experience base varies significantly from institution to institution
Capabilities: Ability to independently assess complex investments	Moderate	Internal capabilities have been increasing dramatically in recent years

can help guide the discussion and highlight the causes of Gulf investors' increasing sophistication.

Scale

Over the past decades, accumulated reserves and savings have helped Gulf-based institutions grow tremendously. As discussed in Chapter 1, Gulf investors are believed to hold roughly $2 trillion in foreign assets today, and this figure is expected to grow significantly by 2020. Even if there are no additional budget surpluses, the reinvestment of returns on this asset base will lead to substantial growth in the scale of Gulf wealth. Private investors, who have also benefited from the region's economic expansion and excess liquidity, have amassed fortunes that are often sizable enough to compare with those of prominent principal investors worldwide. As families have professionalized their approach to managing wealth, the savvy with which they do so has increased.

The link between scale and sophistication follows a pattern that is seen worldwide. When an institution has less wealth to invest, caution dictates that its investments must be conservative, protecting the existing principal while seeking a gain at the same time. Riskier investments, even through they promise a higher potential return, are eschewed because the possibility of loss is not acceptable. As the asset pool grows, however, more wealth is available for higher-risk, higher-reward opportunities. Allocations for the "alternative investments" sector are created—a category of investments to which managers allocate only funds that they could tolerate losing. Within the alternative investments space, common categories include real estate, private equity, direct investments, and "absolute return"/hedge fund investments.

US university endowments provide a prime example of how an investor's appetite for alternative investments increases with scale. Yale University, globally admired for its savvy investment strategies, transformed its asset allocation model over the 20-year period 1986–2006, as shown in Figure 4.2.[6]

In 1986, the endowment allocated over 70 percent of its resources to the traditional asset classes of US stocks, bonds, and cash. By 2006, however, the single largest asset class (by value) had become "real assets" (e.g., properties), and there was a roughly equal allocation between foreign and domestic (US) equities. Both private equity and absolute return instruments enjoyed allocations of around 15 percent

F I G U R E   4.2

Yale's Asset Class Allocation Has Been Fundamentally Transformed
as the Endowment Has Grown in Scale

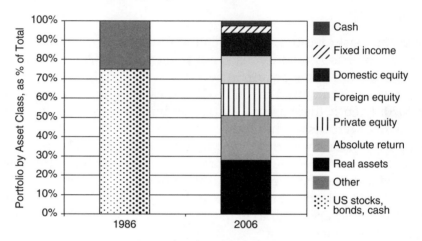

Source: Yale Endowment annual report, 2006.

each—sizable chunks that smaller investors would have much less
appetite for. Endowments smaller than the one at Yale tend to follow
more traditional asset allocation models, just as Yale itself did in the
1980s. Although the recent financial crisis and global recession have
exposed the risks associated with alternative investments by large
endowments, the migration toward sophisticated asset classes over
the past decades has had a positive impact on absolute returns.

While Gulf institutions have increased their allocations for alternative investments, their core assets generally remain in traditional
asset classes such as Treasury bills, fixed income, US equities, and
OECD equities. The "Yale model" reflects an appetite for risk and a
desire for active management that generally does not match with the
priorities of Gulf investors today. Nonetheless, Yale's example provides a useful illustration of how allocation models can evolve over
time and how attention to sophisticated investments increases along
with the scale of an institution's wealth.

Investment Horizon

One drawback of sophisticated investments is that they often require
a longer investment horizon than conservative securities do. Private

equity investments, for example, will generally not provide returns to investors until a fund is liquidated—a window that could be five to ten years in length. Similarly, real estate investments lock up investors' cash for extended periods of time and are often quite illiquid. Plain-vanilla investments like Treasury bills and listed equities, in contrast, are highly liquid and can be sold right away if cash is needed. They can also provide steady streams of coupon payments (in the case of fixed income) or dividends (in the case of shares) that give investors reliable returns on a regular basis.

Earlier in their evolution, Gulf institutional investors customarily had a higher need for liquidity than they have today. Oil income, as discussed earlier, has been volatile and unpredictable. Reserves needed to be fairly accessible and liquid so that they could be applied to current funding needs if required. This is still the case for a number of leading investors—SAMA, for example, needs to be ready to plug a shortfall in the Saudi budget if necessary. Similarly, family investors for whom an annual dividend is an important source of income will be constrained in their ability to undertake sophisticated alternative investments. At the same time, sovereign entities with lighter requirements to support domestic spending (for example, the Kuwait Investment Authority) can take a longer-term approach and invest in less liquid opportunities.

Stakeholders

Another attribute that can be a key enabler of sophisticated investments is having a manageable number of stakeholders involved in decision making and policy setting. Sophisticated investments are often complex in their structures or subtle in their investment cases and rationale. In addition, they are often time-sensitive: in a private equity transaction, for example, decisions may need to be made in a matter of days. Furthermore, concerns related to confidentiality often make it easier for sophisticated transactions to be marketed to institutions with a small number of stakeholders and decision makers.

In both the public and private sectors, Gulf investors generally use decision-making processes that are streamlined enough to allow them to manage sophisticated investments. Although sovereign wealth and public-sector funds are run for the good of the general public, management decisions are customarily made by a small group of professional managers. These managers are overseen by boards of officials, who themselves are generally closely networked and interact with one another in multiple forums. In private institutions and families, there is a wide range of decision-making models, but customarily decisions are centralized. As families have grown and a new generation of leadership has come of age, leading families have instituted formal mechanisms for decision making through family boards and constellations of legal entities. Besides enabling better decision making overall, these structures provide the nimbleness required to make sophisticated investment choices.

Experience

The Gulf's leading investors have benefited from decades of experience in allocating assets and making investment decisions. These institutions have often enjoyed privileged access to the top advisory and professional services firms in the world, leveraging external experience and expertise to help them manage sizable portfolios. For at least the largest Gulf investors, significant track records and experience sets have been built up over the years.

That said, the operating models of Gulf institutions have not always been conducive to retaining "institutional memory." The external advisors supporting investment decisions often have high turnover themselves, with the staff members managing client accounts changing from time to time. Internally, Gulf institutions have often drawn heavily on expatriate talent that may or may not stay long in the region. Compared to institutions elsewhere, Gulf-based principal investors may experience less consistency in staffing and higher turnover in the professional ranks because of the norms of expatriate hiring in the region. Expatriates, being fully aware that settling in the Gulf for the long term is unlikely because of a lack of naturalization options and other legal barriers, all too often look at roles in the region from a mercenary perspective. They may, therefore, collect valuable experience and expertise while working at a Gulf institution, but stay for only a few years and therefore not transfer their experience to the broader organization. As discussed extensively in *Dubai & Co.*, the model of expatriate hiring has significant drawbacks and benefits, and institutions operating in the region must strike a delicate balance between local and expatriate hiring.[7]

A final key attribute that is essential to sophisticated investing is the presence of internal capabilities. Although this aspect is related to experience, it is not identical: institutions can have experience (as a whole) while relying on external expertise, and expertise can be brought into organizations that do not have a long history of collective experience. As is increasingly understood in the wake of the global financial crisis, the ability to independently assess investments using an organization's internal capabilities is crucial for safeguarding the long-term interests of the portfolio. Gulf-based institutions have been rapidly developing their internal capabilities—a trend that both reflects and supports their evolution toward greater sophistication.

ENHANCED INTERNAL CAPABILITIES

Considering the size and importance of Gulf investors, it's no surprise that the world's leading financial firms go out of their way to serve them. HSBC's chairman, Stephen Green, has publicly acknowledged that ADIA is "one of the few clients I would drop everything and see."[8] The CEOs of Goldman Sachs and investment giant BlackRock have both paid personal visits to ADIA,[9] signaling its importance to their firms. A slew of international firms that are eager to tap into Qatar's capital outflows, including Credit Suisse, Barclays, Morgan Stanley, Deutsche Bank, Goldman Sachs, State Street, and HSBC, have flocked to open offices in the Qatar Financial Centre rather than service Qatari clients from a distance.[10] Reflecting both the priority that investment firms place on Gulf capital and the increased appetite of Gulf investors for private equity investments, the private equity firms KKR and the Carlyle Group have both opened offices in Dubai.[11] Carlyle even announced, in 2009, a $500 million fund focused on investing in the Middle East and North Africa region.[12] Gulf institutions have, at least recently, been lavished with attention from the world's leading investment houses.

At the same time, the development of internal capabilities has been a key priority for the region's leading investors. One reason for this push is the recognition of the inherent challenges associated with engaging third-party advisors—challenges that are often referred to as the "principal-agent problem" or the "agency dilemma." However much an external advisor may strive to put the interests of his clients first, advisors are ultimately employed and compensated by firms whose interests are not identical to those of their clients. A relationship manager may, for example, be rewarded more on the basis of how much he sells to the client than on the basis of how the investments that he sells actually perform. In addition, agents may have an incentive to maximize the volume of transactions undertaken by a client—even if the client would be better off sticking to its current portfolio. This misalignment of incentives can lead to questionable behavior on the part of advisors, or at least cause principals to wonder whether, in fact, the agent is always putting the client's interests before his own.

In the case of investment managers, terms are typically structured to align incentives more closely. The prevailing model for private equity managers, for example, is to receive an annual management fee of 2 percent of the total fund and a 20 percent share of the profits ("carried interest") when the fund returns gains to investors. Overall, this aligns incentives between the investors and the managers quite well—the managers have the drive to maximize returns for investors in order to receive a greater amount of carried interest. There are, however, still some areas of misalignment between management and investor interests. One such area is the pressure to exit investments—since managers are rewarded only when they liquidate a position (and funds have a defined life of five to ten years in any case), they will seek to exit an investment even if the investors could profit more in the long term were they to continue to hold the position. Furthermore, commentators have noted that fund managers have an incentive to take greater risk than investors might themselves, since managers share proportionally in rewards in the case of gains but receive the same management fee whether they generate small losses or big ones. In other words, managers share 20 percent of the upside gain but none of the downside risk and therefore may have a bias toward more risky investments.[13]

In addition to principal-agent issues, the sheer costs of using third-party managers can be substantial. Although the 2 percent management fee and 20 percent carried interest model has been the prevailing norm, some of the top-performing funds demand even higher fees. Renaissance Technologies' Medallion Fund, for example, has a whopping 5 percent management fee and 36 percent carried interest.[14] Mammoth institutional investors, including those in the Gulf, have increasingly felt that such fees were an unnecessary drag on returns, since their own asset pools are large enough to justify hiring a world-class investment team and rewarding it handsomely. Although smaller investors cannot efficiently access top talent, larger ones often have the luxury of building their own teams.

Over the past decade, leading Gulf investors have successfully attracted investment professionals with world-class backgrounds to join their internal teams. As shown in Table 4.2, which focuses on a handful of UAE entities, senior executives at Gulf institutions increasingly are boasting strong global pedigrees.

T A B L E   4.2

Senior Executives of Gulf Institutional Investors Have Global Credentials[1]

Executive	Role	Selected Credentials
Jean Paul Villain	Head of strategy, ADIA	Former head of Paribas Asset Management
David Jackson	CEO, Istithmar	Yale MBA, Princeton BA, and Wall Street background
David Smoot	CEO, DIC Private Equity	Former managing director and cofounder of Morgan Stanley's Private Equity Group
Eric Kump	Head of European private equity, DIC	Former managing director of Merrill Lynch Global Private Equity; Harvard MBA
Kenneth Shen	Head of private equity, QIA	Co-head of Asia-Pacific Corporate Finance Group at Salomon Brothers; Harvard MBA
Martin Harrison	Chief investment officer, Emirates Investment Authority	Global partner, Invesco; head of Asset Management, QIA
John Knight	COO, Mumtalakat (Bahrain)	Managing director and chief operation officer for Southeast Asia, JPMorgan Chase
Chris Koski	Global head of infrastructure, ADIA	Infrastructure team, Canadian Pension Investment Board
Maurizio La Noce	Executive director, energy & industry, Mubadala	Chairman of Dolphin PRC; board member of Masdar
Derek Rozycki	Executive director, project and corporate finance, Mubadala	Head of Abu Dhabi operations, Barclays Capital

[1] **Source:** "Expat 50," *Arabian Business,* 2009 list; Dubai International Capital Web site; LinkedIn; Mubadala Web site—senior management team; *BusinessWeek* company profiles.

The enhancement of Gulf investors' internal capabilities has been a sustained trend. In the wake of the global financial crisis, in which hundreds of senior investment professionals have entered the job market, Gulf employers have even greater access to top talent. Executives at leading global firms, sensitive to regulatory and social shifts that will curtail compensation packages in the OECD world, are looking more favorably at the Gulf than ever before. In addition to compensation, Gulf firms can offer the opportunity to build an investment portfolio with an entity that has abundant (and growing) capital—an opportunity that has become very scarce since the financial crisis. Once viewed as a backwater or second-rate market, the Gulf is increasingly being seen as a place where professionals can engage in world-class investment activity.

An oft-repeated phrase in financial circles since the recent crisis has been that if one wants to work in finance, the choices are "Shanghai, Dubai, Mumbai, or good-bye." Pithy as it is, the phrase is an exaggeration and not entirely accurate regarding the Gulf—in fact, many of the most engaging investment roles in the region are in Abu Dhabi, Doha, Riyadh, and Kuwait. This mantra does, nonetheless, underscore an important reality: that the financial crisis has helped Gulf institutions further enhance the internal capabilities required for sophisticated investments.

LANDMARK INVESTMENTS

As Gulf portfolios have expanded into more sophisticated investments, the number of prominent assets owned (in part or fully) by GCC investors has multiplied manyfold. It's important to note that a large number of Gulf institutions' more sophisticated investments are in asset classes and structures that are not reported in the public domain. Investments in private equity funds and hedge funds, for example, are rarely disclosed to the public. Similarly, the purchase of structured products and custom-made instruments provided by global banks is strictly confidential. And, as discussed earlier, the plain-vanilla securities that make up the bulk of Gulf portfolios need not be reported. The details of most Gulf investments, therefore, are not in the public domain.

Direct investments in global firms by Gulf buyers, however, are often reported in the press. Sometimes they need to be reported because of regulatory requirements, sometimes the publicity is in fact welcomed, and sometimes the number of stakeholders involved is so great that the transactions inevitably become public knowledge.

Table 4.3 provides a sampling of prominent investments made by Gulf investors over the years, highlighting key sectors and marquee assets.

As is evident from Table 4.3, leading companies and brands—from GE to Gucci and from Daimler to Disney—have taken on Gulf investors as major shareholders. The list of major Gulf investments

T A B L E   4.3

Gulf Investors Hold Stakes in a Wide Variety of Prominent Global Companies[1]

Sector	Asset	Investor	Stake
	Citigroup	ADIA	4.9%[2]
	Citigroup	Prince Alwaleed Bin Talal	4.3%
	Citigroup	Kuwait Investment Authority	$3 billion; stake undisclosed
Financial services	Merrill Lynch (subsequently acquired by Bank of America	Kuwait Investment Authority	$2 billion; stake undisclosed[3]
	Barclays	Qatar Investment Authority	6.2%[4]
	Credit Suisse	Qatar Investment Authority	8.9%[5]
	HSBC	Maan al-Sanea (Saudi Arabia)	3.1%
	Bank Islam Malaysia	Dubai Investment Group	40%
	Industrial and Commercial Bank of China	Kuwait Investment Authority	19%
	Daimler Benz	Aabar Investments (Abu Dhabi)	9.1%[6]
	Daimler Benz	Kuwait Investment Authority	7.1% (subsequently diluted)
Automotive	Aston Martin	Investment Dar and Adeem Investment (Kuwait)	78%
	Ferrari	Mubadala (Abu Dhabi)	5%
	Porsche/ Volkswagen	Qatar Investment Authority	Pending[7]
	P&O	Dubai Ports World	100%
Industrial	GE Plastics	SABIC (Saudi Arabia)	100%
	Doncasters Group (UK)	Dubai International Capital	100%
	Tiffany (floated 1987)	Investcorp (Bahrain)	100%
Retail	Gucci (floated 1996)	Investcorp (Bahrain)	100%
	Saks Fifth Avenue (floated 1996)	Investcorp (Bahrain)	100%
	Walt Disney	Kingdom/Prince Alwaleed Bin Talal	Substantial
Hospitality	Four Seasons Hotels	Kingdom/Prince Alwaleed Bin Talal	22%

(*continued*)

T A B L E   4.3

(Continued)

Sector	Asset	Investor	Stake
	Fairmont Hotels	Kingdom/Prince Alwaleed Bin Talal	16%
	Essex House (New York)	Jumeirah International (Dubai)	100%
	Travelodge (UK)	Dubai International Capital	100%

[1] **Source:** *Dubai & Co*. and company sources, unless otherwise noted.
[2] "Abu Dhabi Reviewing Citigroup Investment: Sources," Reuters.com, March 1, 2009.
[3] "KIA Acquires a Minority Stake in Merrill Lynch," Reuters.com, January 31, 2008.
[4] "Slim Demand for Barclays Offer Gives Qatar 8% stake," Reuters.com, July 18, 2009.
[5] "QIA Raises Its Stake in Credit Suisse Group," Reuters.com, October 26, 2009.
[6] "Daimler Capital Hike to Make Abu Dhabi Biggest Investor," Reuters.com, March 22, 2008.
[7] "Qatar May Buy VW or Porsche Stake," BBC.com, June 9, 2009.

goes on, and is likely to only increase in the years ahead. At a time when crisis-related losses have left most principal investors reeling, Gulf institutions stand poised to find bargains and build portfolios from a position of strength.

BEYOND PLAIN VANILLA: ADIA'S INVESTMENT IN CITI

ADIA's 2008 investment in Citigroup, viewed broadly as a virtual bailout of the global bank prior to the US government's subsequent intervention, is a prime example of a recent high-profile Gulf investment. The transaction represents the increased importance of the GCC as a primary source of capital for large corporations. A close look at the transaction highlights, given in Table 4.4, reveals that the deal was far from a plain-vanilla injection of equity.

ADIA's investment was structured as debt convertible to equity, providing returns in the form of quarterly interest payments for up to four years (depending on when the conversion to equity takes place). The debt was priced at the very high interest rate of 11 percent, locking in a return several times higher than the corporate bond rates prevailing at the time and reflecting ADIA's strong negotiating position when the transaction occurred. When the conversion from debt to equity takes place, the number of shares will depend on how Citigroup's stock

T A B L E   4.4

ADIA's Investment in Citigroup Involved Complex Structuring[1]

Transaction value	$7.5 billion
Nature of investment	Mandatory convertible (debt to equity)
Duration of investment	Four years
Interest rate on debt	11% annual interest guaranteed; payable quarterly
Settlement in shares	Number of shares will vary between 201 million and 235 million, depending on the share price at the time of conversion
Share price on date of transaction	$30.70

[1] "Abu Dhabi Reviewing Citigroup Investment: Sources," Reuters.com, March 1, 2009.

is performing at the time—the worse the stock is doing, the more shares ADIA will receive.

Despite the sophisticated structuring, however, ADIA remains heavily exposed to Citigroup's ailing share price. Were Citi's share price to remain at $30.70 (the price at which it was trading when the transaction took place), ADIA's annualized return would be 11 percent. Any gains in the stock price will add to the base return, and declines will take away from it. With Citigroup trading below $4 per share at the time of this writing, however, ADIA's position remains heavily "under water" (below its initial value), even with the interest payments factored in.

Another Abu Dhabi investment into a global bank, that by Sheikh Mansour bin Zayed Al Nahyan into Barclays, has fared far better. Investing through the entity International Petroleum Investment Co. (IPIC), Sheikh Mansour injected £2 billion into Barclays in 2008 though a mandatory convertible structure that valued Barclays shares at 153p. Barclays entered the deal in order to receive much-needed capital and avoid a government bailout. Eight months later, in mid-2009, Sheikh Mansour exited the investment and realized a gain of £1.45 billion.[15] That corresponds to a return of 9 percent *per month* and more than 100 percent on an annualized basis. Sheikh Mansour's deal was less complex in its structure, yet extraordinarily successful in its outcome. The UK publication the *Telegraph* noted that Sheikh Mansour had spotted an opportunity missed by Barclay's sophisticated investor base, which "barely dipped a toe" when offered the same terms as the Abu Dhabi investor.

WORLD-CLASS POSITIONING

As well as investing in marquee assets, Gulf investors are increasingly taking measures to position themselves as world-class institutions. This is especially true of private investors and investment houses that either rely on third-party investors for funding (and therefore have an interest in maintaining a strong public perception) or compete internationally for attractive deals (and therefore wish to be seen as value-adding shareholders). One way in which this is done is through media, publications, and conference appearances—Arif Naqvi of Abraaj Capital (UAE), for example, appears frequently in the press in outlets such as *BusinessWeek*.[16] The investment houses SHUAA Capital (UAE) and Global Investment House (Kuwait) publish extensive research that is read by financial professionals and cited elsewhere. ADIA and the Olayan Group (Saudi Arabia) have appeared at global summits including the World Economic Forum in Davos,[17] and the Abu Dhabi Investment Council and National Industries Group (Kuwait) have been represented at the prestigious Milken Institute forum in Los Angeles.[18] These events position Gulf institutions as part of a network of global financial leaders.

More concretely, Gulf investors have been co-investing alongside prestigious global partners, signaling their ability to act as peers with leading international firms. For example, ADIA has co-invested alongside the Texas Pacific Group (TPG) in TPG's $44.4 billion buyout of the TXU Corporation, and has also invested alongside KKR in its $19.4 billion buyout of Alliance Boots. It has also invested directly in the investment management firms Apollo Management and Ares Management.[19] Prince Alwaleed Bin Talal invested alongside Bill Gates in the Four Seasons Hotels, again signaling global stature. Actively recruiting at leading business schools like Harvard, Gulf institutions are positioning themselves as significant, world-class organizations that warrant the attention of the best and the brightest. These activities not only help Gulf institutions grow in sophistication, but also send a message that they are serious actors on the global financial stage.

Over the past decades, Gulf investors have gone through a continuous process of institutional development. Today, institutions in the GCC, like those in other markets, span a wide rage of maturity and sophistication. In the years ahead, the increased sophistication of Gulf investors can be expected to remain an ongoing trend, enabling these institutions to act with increasing savvy, confidence, and stature.

KEY LESSONS

- Gulf investors have *historically focused on conservative US dollar investments* because of their investment considerations and circumstances.

- Over the past decade, however, the attributes of *Gulf institutions have increasingly come to match the characteristics of sophisticated institutional investors.*

- Gulf investors have *expanded their portfolios* into sophisticated asset classes and complex structures.

- *Enhanced internal capabilities* have been a key driver in enabling Gulf institutions to make more sophisticated investments.

- Gulf investors are using co-investment, thought leadership, and other platforms to *position themselves as world-class investors.*

- Gulf investors can be expected to *continue increasing their sophistication* in the years ahead.

5

CHAPTER

The Home Front: The Rise of Domestic and Regional Investments

Gulf Cooperation Council (GCC) support of leading American universities is nothing new. For decades, GCC donors have funded programs and academic chairs at top universities, including Princeton and UC-Berkeley. Georgetown's Center for Muslim-Christian Understanding bears the name of a major Saudi donor, Prince Alwaleed Bin Talal.[1] The head of Harvard Law School's Islamic Legal Studies program holds a title named after the Saudi king: "The Custodian of the Two Holy Mosques Adjunct Professor of Islamic Legal Studies."[2] It is therefore not surprising that the Gulf has continued to provide patronage for leading universities during successive economic booms.

Since the early 2000s, however, support provided by the Qatar Foundation for Education, Science and Community Development (QF) has introduced a very different model. The foundation, a major strategic initiative for Qatar, has entered into partnerships with Cornell, Georgetown, Carnegie Mellon, and a number of other universities. The partnerships include extensive funding and elaborate operational support, and insist on academic rigor. What makes QF's patronage different is that, rather than

*funding activities in the United States, the foundation brings these universi-
ties to Qatar's Education City.*[3] *International partnerships have become part
of a domestic education strategy—a strategy to develop the region's own
human resources and intellectual capital.*

*Gulf investments, especially those of the region's largest institutional
investors, continue to be principally allocated to the world's most developed
markets. The United States and other member countries of the Organisation
for Economic Co-operation and Development (OECD) continue to offer the
deepest, broadest, and best-established capital markets. In recent years, however, an increased focus on domestic and regional investments has been a key
trend in the activities of GCC investors. Understanding this trend and its
impact on local economies is critical for observers of the region. At the same
time, assessing the growth of (and gaps in) local capital markets is crucial to
understanding the prospects for directly investing in the GCC's growth and
for understanding the overall allocation choices of Gulf investors. As the
"home front" has become more important, its impact on major institutions
has grown.*

*We begin by contrasting the Gulf's focus on "hard" infrastructure in
previous booms with its increased focus on "soft" infrastructure in the 2000s.
This shift in emphasis, which is rooted in the long-term economic strategies of
countries in the region, has resulted in more creative forms of domestic and
regional investment seeking to develop knowledge-based economic activity.
The shift also reflects increased appreciation of the importance of the private
sector and of privately led initiatives—a sense that governments should act
more as enablers and less as principal economic actors.*

*Next, we discuss the booms and busts experienced in local equity
markets and real estate over the past decade. Listed equity markets in the
region have experienced a number of booms and busts, including two cycles
over the past eight years. From 2001 to 2006, a swell in liquidity and an
increased regional and domestic focus led to a tremendous boom in stock
prices. The market capitalization of key Gulf companies reached meteoric
heights—UAE-based property developer Emaar, for example, became the
highest-valued developer in the world.*[4] *Then a sharp correction in 2006
wiped out more than half the total market capitalization in the UAE, Saudi
Arabia, and Qatar, and more than a third of the value in other GCC markets.*[5]
*This decline, though painful, brought valuations more closely in line with
emerging-market standards. Stock prices rose again in 2007 and much of
2008 before the global financial crisis led to another severe downturn. Gulf
equity markets remain largely sentiment-driven, with retail investors
contributing the bulk of invested capital and typically trading more on confidence than on the fundamental analysis of companies. This was particularly*

evident in the bust of 2006, in which many companies lost more than half of their market capitalization despite achieving earnings growth and solid fundamental results.

We close with a discussion of how the Gulf's capital markets, despite their rapid growth, remain underdeveloped along a number of dimensions. As a result, the most attractive investment opportunities are generally found in direct corporate investments outside of public equity markets. Therefore, both Gulf-based and international investors may be best served by exploring high-growth direct investment opportunities rather than passively investing in local stock markets.

FROM "HARD" TO "SOFT" INFRASTRUCTURE

In each successive oil boom, the Gulf states have used part of their surpluses to invest in domestic infrastructure. The types of infrastructure investments made, however, have evolved along with the region's economic needs and its long-term development strategies. Table 5.1 contrasts the investments in "hard" infrastructure made during the 1970s and 1980s with the investments in "soft" infrastructure made in the 2000s.

In previous booms, the Gulf countries needed to establish their basic transportation infrastructure: roads, airports, and shipping capabilities. This task was especially daunting in Saudi Arabia, because of its vast size and the need for regional airports and highways to connect its various cities. Smaller countries also needed to

T A B L E 5.1

Contrasting Hard and Soft Infrastructure Investments by Gulf States

Hard Infrastructure of the 1970s and 1980s	Soft Infrastructure of the 2000s
Basic transportation (roads and airports)	Upgraded transportation and logistics
Core utilities	Upgraded and "green" utilities
Basic education	Aspirations for world-class higher learning
Government facilities and plants	Business parks, free zones, and commercial enablement
Public projects	Partnerships with private sector

build their capabilities for domestic and international travel, and transportation projects were a key priority in the region.

In the 2000s, investments in transportation took on a different tone. As the projects of the 1970s and 1980s have aged and Gulf populations have skyrocketed, there has been a push for an upgraded transportation and logistics infrastructure. The UAE offers a number of prime examples of such upgrades in infrastructure: Dubai's Jebel Ali Port was a forerunner of substantial investment in Dubai Ports World and other logistical capabilities. The UAE launched two new airlines, Emirates and Etihad, in the 1990s and 2000s, both seeking to be carriers of choice for the region and key hubs for long-haul flights between Europe and Asia.[6] Qatar Airways, launched in 1993, has positioned itself as the world's only "five-star airline" in an attempt to differentiate itself and capture market share. Dubai, Abu Dhabi, and Doha are undertaking or have recently completed massive airport improvement projects.[7] These initiatives are a far cry from the modest investments in roads and simple airports of the 1970s.

In previous decades, the GCC states needed to establish their core utilities infrastructure—power, water, and other basic services required for modern living. Prior to this time, those segments of the population that lived away from urban centers were often underserved and did not always have access to basic utilities.[8] The prosperity of the 1970s was instrumental in enabling governments to extend the reach of utilities to their entire population. In the 2000s, utilities investments have also been crucial, largely to keep up with the region's growing populations. There has, however, also been a focus on research and development related to "green" technologies and utilities of the future. The global conglomerate GE and Abu Dhabi's Mubadala have agreed to invest $4 billon each over a three-year period in order to develop the Abu Dhabi "cleantech" sector. Their main focus has been on an initiative called Masdar, envisioned as being Abu Dhabi's Green City.[9] The demographics of the Gulf indicate that significant ongoing investment in utilities will be needed in the decade ahead. While the bulk of it is likely to involve traditional forms of energy (in which the GCC has inherent cost advantages), interest in renewable and green energy is also present and may shape the region's energy future.

Gulf governments used part of the surpluses of the 1970s to establish basic educational systems in their countries. Naturally, the emphasis was on primary and secondary education, since these areas were generally underdeveloped in the region. As a senior GCC executive who worked for the same global bank for decades once told me, he was deeply loyal to the bank because "it was my school"—it was through his job at the bank that he had developed his reading, writing, and mathematical skills. Before the booms of the 1970s and 1980s, Gulf nationals of modest means had limited access to education.

By the 2000s, the challenge of access to basic education had been addressed, and GCC countries turned their attention to major initiatives aimed at enhancing advanced learning and university-level educational institutions. In 2007, Saudi Arabia launched the King Abdullah University of Science and Technology (KAUST), which was established with the third-largest endowment of any university in the world.[10] In the UAE, Mohammed bin Rashid pledged a $10 billion investment in 2007 to support the development of a "knowledge based society" through a foundation that bears his name.[11] In Qatar, the Qatar Foundation for Education, Science and Community Development has spent more than $2.6 billion since 2001 to create the knowledge hub of "Education City" in Doha and to bring leading US universities to Qatar. Passport Capital estimates that Saudi Arabia has $600 billion of domestic investment (overall) in the pipeline over the next 20 years, and that envisioned in this investment is the funding of no fewer than 20 universities.[12] In addition to Qatar's partnerships with Cornell, Georgetown, Carnegie Mellon, and other universities, Abu Dhabi has entered into a relationship with New York University (NYU) to establish a campus in the UAE.[13] Investment in the region's educational infrastructure now aspires to world-class standards, and substantial resources have been allocated to support these ambitions.

Vast government facilities and plants—power plants, utilities companies, telecommunications companies, government-owned airlines, and the like—have been created in the GCC over the course of successive oil booms. Public-sector companies tended to dominate capital-intensive sectors (telecommunications is a prime example), as governments were best positioned to make the investments required to set up the core infrastructure required. The majority of these public-sector companies survive to this day, even if, like the UAE's telecom provider Etisalat, a portion of their equity is publicly listed.[14]

With new initiatives, however, partnerships between the public sector and private institutions have become increasingly common. As mentioned earlier, Abu Dhabi's Green City initiative is being undertaken in partnership with GE. In Qatar, Qatar Science & Technology Park (QSTP) applied a model similar to a venture capital incubator, with the Qatar Foundation investing $600 million and its 21 partners agreeing to invest $225 million in research and development.[15] There is also a drive toward creating business parks and commercial districts in hopes of sparking private-sector business activity. The UAE has been a trailblazer in establishing free zones, including Dubai's Jebel Ali Free Zone (Jafza), the Dubai International Financial Centre (DIFC), Dubai Internet City, Dubai Media City, and Dubai Knowledge Village, among others. Other emirates, including Sharjah and Ras Al Khaimah, have launched free zones of their own, largely to attract spillover demand that is not being served in Dubai or is seeking a lower-cost environment.[16] Bahrain, with its long legacy as an offshore banking hub, has the Bahrain Financial Harbour free zone as well as industrial initiatives to attract manufacturers. The Qatar Financial Centre (QFC) has attracted a large number of global financial institutions and has thrived as Qatar's prosperity and investment capabilities have grown. Saudi Arabia has envisioned the creation of six Economic Cities throughout the Kingdom, designed to stimulate growth and development and to diversify the Saudi economy.[17] A key open question has been whether the new Economic Cities will (in whole or in part) be free zones, or whether ownership restriction will be enforced in these new developments.

Business parks and free zone initiatives throughout the GCC reflect governments' drive to stimulate the private sector and jump-start local entrepreneurial ventures. Governments are increasingly recognizing that the public sector alone cannot create the volume and quality of job opportunities and economic growth needed to maintain and improve the region's standard of living. To build economic competitiveness, the private sector needs to drive growth and innovation. Government efforts are increasingly focusing on giving the private sector all the tools it needs to drive economic diversification and growth. This is an important departure from the previous model of using state-owned companies as the key drivers of the local economy, and a step toward more vibrancy and diversity in the economies of the Gulf.

LOCAL EQUITY MARKETS: BOOMS AND BUSTS

In addition to enabling the investments in infrastructure discussed previously, the prosperity of the GCC has made wealth available for investment in local stock markets. Although the informal trading of shares in the Gulf dates back to 1935,[18] it was only in the late 1980s that organized exchanges were formed in the region, and it was not until the 2000s that serious growth in Gulf equities markets took place. By the end of June 2009, the seven GCC bourses had a combined market capitalization of $655 billion.[19]

The story of Gulf equities markets since 2000 has been one of both remarkable growth and severe crashes, and extreme volatility and significant swings in value have been witnessed. In the first half of the decade, total market capitalization increased more than tenfold, from $120 billion in 2000 to a peak of over $1.5 trillion by 2006.[20] Local markets went nowhere but up during this period: between 2001 and 2004, total market capitalization in the UAE grew sevenfold, while the Saudi market more than tripled.[21] One Saudi firm even had a market capitalization close to Google's at the time. Through 2005 and the early months of 2006, the frenzy continued, and "irrational exuberance" akin to the 1990s dot-com bubble on the Nasdaq market set in. Remarkably, at their 2006 peaks, Gulf markets accounted for about 20 percent of the value of all emerging-market exchanges.[22]

The majority of the investors in the market—an estimated 70 percent—were individual investors, of which as many as 90 percent may have been short-term speculators.[23] These were the Gulf equivalent of day traders during the dot-com bubble—investors who had little understanding of or interest in the fundamental performance of the businesses they were investing in, but who were eager to capture returns that could be as high as 5 percent per day. Even local companies found the frenzy too tempting to resist. In 2004 and 2005, for example, it was not uncommon for companies to have more "extraordinary income" from gains on the stock market than operating profits from their core business.

Stock market euphoria in the Gulf got out of hand quickly and reached extreme heights. Some investors sold their cars to finance shares, and banks would lend investors cash to buy stock and participate in IPOs. Some lending behavior became downright irresponsible. According to the local Saudi press, some lenders could garner 20 to 30 percent returns in a single week by financing shares; the Saudi Arabian Monetary Agency had to intervene.[24] In Kuwait, lending to purchase shares grew 337 percent between 2000 and 2005.[25] As a sign of the times, some ATMs were enabled with brokerage capabilities so that customers could day-trade as they withdrew cash from their accounts. When a hot IPO was open to investors from around the GCC, it was not uncommon for nationals to drive across borders, sleep in their cars if need be, and stand in long lines to register for shares. Many people quit their jobs entirely when day trading became too lucrative. I recall a striking scene from a visit to the Abu Dhabi stock exchange in 2005. The floor had a frenzy and a buzz, as all exchanges with human traders do. Unlike the New York and Chicago exchanges, however, the bulk of the people on the floor were individual investors, not professional brokers and dealers. When the petrochemical company Yansab was listed in Saudi Arabia, almost two-fifths of the Saudi national population—more than 8 million people—participated in the IPO.[26] In the United States, in contrast, only about half of all households own any individual stocks at all, and no single stock would be universally owned by all of them.[27]

Figure 5.1 illustrates the performance of the Saudi stock market, by far the GCC's largest and representative of the phenomenon witnessed in the UAE and Qatar as well.

Stocks continued to climb until March 2006, when they plummeted. Ironically, the crash began at a time when oil prices (and therefore liquidity in the region) were at all-time highs. This is yet another sign that the high valuations were simply a bubble and were not

F I G U R E   5.1

Saudi Stock Market Boom and Crash, 2001–2007

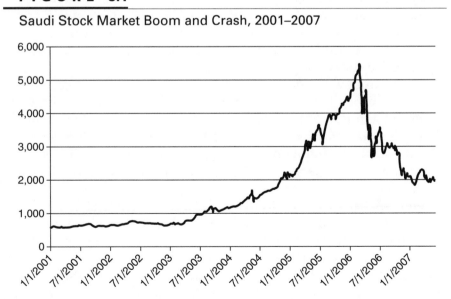

Source: Bloomberg.

based on fundamental economic realities. The correction, which continued throughout the rest of 2006, wiped out most of the gains since early 2005. As of June 2007, however, the market was up around 250 percent from its 2001 level. The investors who were most hurt by the correction were those who came in at the peak of the frenzy in 2005 and 2006—and these, unfortunately, tended to be the least sophisticated and most vulnerable retail investors.

It is noteworthy that the market corrections in Kuwait and Bahrain were far less pronounced than those in Saudi Arabia, the UAE, and Qatar. One reason for this is that Kuwait and Bahrain had more sophisticated stock markets: Kuwait's had been the first in the region, and Bahrain's was heavily weighted toward more stable financial institution shares. Both exchanges also enjoyed a high proportion of institutional investors, who are less likely to succumb to the temptations of valuation bubbles. Oman's stock market, quite interestingly, grew at a healthy pace in 2006—a sign that it was insulated from the frenzy elsewhere in the GCC.

While the sharp market correction was certainly jarring for many investors, observers saw it as a necessary step and a maturing experience for the region. As of February 2007, average price-to-earnings (P/E) ratios for shares traded on regional exchanges were far more in line with emerging-market averages worldwide than they had been a year before. In February 2006, Saudi and UAE shares had been trading at unsustainable P/E ratios above 50. The precorrection P/E ratios were, in some cases, four times the average for emerging markets worldwide. Figure 5.2 illustrates market-average P/E ratios before and after the correction.

Since mid-2007, the story of Gulf stock markets has continued to be one of significant volatility driven by consumer sentiment rather than underlying fundamentals, and by sharp declines following the US credit crisis. The first half of 2007 was characterized by relative stability, following the precipitous declines of 2006, in which the region's largest exchange, the Saudi Tadawul All Share Index, lost 60 percent of its value between February and December.[28] However, by March 2007, the markets had entered the beginning of another 18-month boom period, with the Dubai Financial Market (DFM) index gaining 68 percent between April 1, 2007, and September 1, 2008.[29] While mid-2007 is typically thought of as the height of a bubble in the United States, to put the gains in perspective, all of the Gulf stock markets grew significantly faster than US markets during this period, with the Dow Jones Industrial

FIGURE   5.2

Gulf P/E Ratios Before and After the 2006 Crash

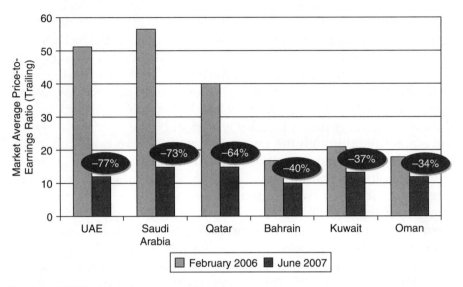

Source: MSCI, research team analysis.

Average increasing only 16 percent compared to the 68 percent increase in the Dubai Financial Market.[30]

Local Markets Hit by the Global Crisis

This second, post-2006 rally was followed by another bust in 2008. This time around, the correction was linked to the global recession and financial crisis, which spared none of the world's major markets in 2008–2009. When US investment banks began announcing large writedowns as a result of losses on subprime mortgages, stock markets in the United States and United Kingdom began to fall immediately. In the Gulf, however, the reaction was not so immediate. The delay between the beginning of subprime losses and the effects on the Gulf and other emerging markets led to hopes among investment banks that a "decoupling" of emerging markets had made them "well positioned to weather a US slowdown, thanks in part to high commodity prices and strong demand for exports."[31] There were even (temporarily) hopes that the continued buoyancy of emerging markets could help prevent a global recession.

The Saudi Tadawul index and the Dubai Financial Market peaked three months after the Dow Jones, in January 2008. However, despite only slightly weakened fundamentals and with positive real GDP growth across the GCC in 2008, Gulf stock markets suffered catastrophic losses as the global financial crisis played out. The DFM lost 77 percent of its value in the 13 months from its peak in January 2008 to its trough in February 2009, and the Saudi exchange lost 64 percent of its value over the same period.[32] Interestingly, someone who had invested $1,000 in the Saudi stock market in July 2004 and held it there for five years until July 2009 would still have almost exactly the same amount, although the investment would have risen and fallen by over 300 percent during those same five years.

Assessing the performance of Gulf stock markets over the past three years leads to two fundamental observations. First, the stock markets of the Gulf, like those of other emerging-market countries, are not immune to global crises and economic shocks. The decoupling of emerging and developed stock markets that was widely predicted in 2006 and 2007 has not materialized. Gulf stock markets proved not to be resilient against the global economic downturn for a number of reasons. Most directly, the economic downturn led to a collapse in oil prices—from $150 per barrel in July 2008 to $50 per barrel in January 2009—which severely hurt Gulf incomes.[33] Also, the global downturn in investor sentiment certainly affected Gulf investors, the largest of whom keep the bulk of their portfolios outside the region and therefore felt the decline in global asset values immediately. In addition, the freezing up of global credit markets definitely had an impact on Gulf institutions, many of which rely on debt-based financing for projects and other investments. In the case of Dubai, public debt reached a staggering 103 percent of GDP,[34] making the financing of new projects and initiatives extremely difficult. Adjusted growth outlooks for oil-dependent Gulf economies affected the prospects for listed companies, and investors fled stock markets en masse as the global downturn worsened.

A second fundamental observation is that the Gulf exchanges appear to be prone to far greater volatility than their mature-market counterparts, enabling both speedy gains and rapid losses for investors. In just one month at the end of 2007, the Saudi stock exchange increased in value by 20 percent, only to lose 20 percent of its value in just seven days a month later.[35] When the Gulf stock markets eventually crashed, their falls were deeper and swifter than those of US markets. Consider, for example, the following figures:

- From its peak valuation to the low point of the 2008–2009 crisis, the Dow Jones Industrial Average lost 53 percent of its value over a 17-month period.
- The Dubai Financial Market, the worst hit of the Gulf exchanges, lost 77 percent of its value in just 13 months.[36]

This significant volatility in Gulf stock markets has often left investors and observers "bewildered," and it reduces the appeal of these markets to sophisticated investors.[37] The fact that the Gulf's losses were more severe than those of the Dow is especially remarkable considering the fact that subprime lending and the "toxic paper" in the financial system did not originate in the Gulf and were largely tangential to Gulf investors' portfolios. Observers in the Gulf noted that they did not cause the global crisis, but—at least from a stock market perspective—they suffered more severely from it than their OECD counterparts.

SHIFTING ENVIRONMENT: FOREIGN OWNERSHIP LAWS AND PRIVATIZATIONS

The scale of domestic and regional investment in GCC public equities markets is inevitably linked to the institutional frameworks that govern those markets. Changes in the limitations on foreign investment, sale of state-owned enterprises (SOEs) and licenses, changes in the IPO processes, market concentration, partial listing, and a large number of other factors will all continue to affect investment levels within the GCC over the coming years and must be understood by anyone who is looking to invest in the region.

Regulations governing foreign share ownership have historically limited the stakes that outside investors could take in GCC companies. These regulations, though rapidly changing, remain in place, keeping Gulf companies in GCC hands and also limiting the amount of foreign investment flowing into the region. Ownership regulations customarily differentiate among three categories of investors: nationals of the country itself (on whom there are no restrictions), nationals of other GCC countries (for whom the restrictions are sometimes less onerous), and international investors. Table 5.2, based on a 2008 study, summarizes foreign ownership limits for certain Gulf states.

Bahrain and Saudi Arabia differentiate significantly between nationals of other GCC states and other (non-GCC) foreigners.

T A B L E   5.2

Foreign Ownership Limits on GCC Public Equity Markets[1]

	GCC-Based Investors	International Investors
Saudi Arabia	49%	0%
UAE	0–49%	0–49%
Kuwait	49%	49%
Qatar	25%	25%
Bahrain	100%	49%
Oman	25–70%	25–70%

[1] Florence Eid, "The Other Face of Arab Wealth: Domestic Investment Opportunities," Passport Capital, Syrian Banking Conference, November 2008.

Bahrain, in a posture reflective of its legacy as an offshore hub for Saudi Arabia and other Gulf states, allows full ownership by nationals of any GCC state. Nationals of other countries, by contrast, are not allowed stakes in Bahraini companies greater than 49 percent. Saudi Arabia allows nationals of other GCC states to own up to 49 percent of Saudi companies, whereas other foreigners are not allowed to have any direct ownership in listed companies. That said, recent regulation has allowed foreigners to hold economic interests in the shares of listed Saudi companies as long as the legal ownership of the shares remains with Saudi brokers.[38] This reform makes it possible for foreigners to benefit from gains in the Saudi market, but keeps them from having ownership rights in their own names.

More favorable ownership laws for GCC nationals have been a force enabling increased intraregional investments. In 2007, 41 percent of shares on the Bahraini exchange were owned by Bahraini nationals, 49 percent were owned by other GCC nationals, and 10 percent were held by foreign investors.[39] In July 2008, 9 percent of the total value of shares on the Abu Dhabi Securities Exchange was held by non-GCC investors,[40] with the remainder being held by UAE citizens and other GCC nationals. The provisions of the GCC Common Market (which came into place in January 2008) will ultimately mean that there are no limits on share ownership by other GCC nationals,[41] and this is a key step in increasing intraregional investment by GCC nationals and companies.

In the UAE, the pace of this change will be set at both the national and the individual company level: the equalization of the status of nationals and other GCC nationals must still be approved by a company's board of directors through a change in the company's charter, by the national ministry of economy, and by the capital market regulatory body, the Emirates Securities and Commodities Authority.[42] The investment firm SHUAA Capital has noted that "treating GCC nationals at par with UAE nationals, when it comes to foreign ownership limits, could act as a catalyst for stock prices of a number of firms in the UAE that have seen their foreign ownership limits reached and, hence, waning investor activity. In general, when foreign ownership limits are relaxed for companies with sound fundamentals, they witness an increased buying flow into their stocks, driving the share prices upwards."[43]

For more than a decade, the UAE's free zones have thrived, largely as a result of provisions allowing 100 percent foreign ownership of free zone businesses. Onshore companies, by contrast, are required to have 51 percent Emirati ownership. In 2009, various media reports suggesting that the UAE may allow majority foreign ownership outside of the free zones in certain sectors, including health care, education, and financial services, appeared.[44] One possible outcome, according to commentators on international law, may be the division of foreign ownership restrictions in the UAE into three groups:

- Sectors and activities in which the UAE Council of Ministers (Cabinet) may from time to time decide to allow greater foreign participation, up to and including 100% foreign ownership;
- Sectors and activities in which the current restrictions on foreign participation would remain (eg, real estate, telecommunications and defense); and
- Sectors and activities which would allow increased foreign participation, but less than 100% (eg, trading in consumer goods).[45]

A second key trend that is leading to an increase in domestic and regional investments is the deregulation and sale of formerly state-owned industries and licenses. Liberalization of telecom markets in the GCC through the auctioning of new licenses has been a source of revenue for Gulf governments and a method of introducing competition into the marketplace, but one of its key impacts has been an increase in intraregional investment. In 2004, the UAE telecom provider Etisalat paid $3.4 billion for Saudi Arabia's second mobile license,[46] starting a wave of license auctions across the Gulf. Saudi Telecom Company (STC) is reported to have set aside a fund of $10 billion for the acquisition of telecom licenses in the Middle East and North Africa (MENA) region, and in January 2009 it acquired Bahrain's third mobile license for $230 million.[47] This wave of acquisitions has now progressed from licenses to the exploration of mergers and acquisitions between publicly listed telecom operators in different GCC countries: in July 2009, Etisalat announced an interest in acquiring a majority stake in Kuwaiti mobile operator Zain.[48]

Over time, it is likely that greater liberalization of ownership laws and additional privatizations will make Gulf equity markets more accessible and deeper. Such changes would make them more attractive both for local investors and for international investors seeking to profit from the GCC region's strong growth prospects and long-term potential. That said, it is crucial for international observers to note that Gulf capital markets today remain less developed than many of their counterparts elsewhere, and that these markets' development gaps have a real impact on their relative attractiveness.

LIMITATION OF PUBLIC MARKETS

As illustrated in Figure 5.3, public capital markets in the Gulf, although developing rapidly, have a number of important limitations that affect their overall attractiveness today.

Unlike the situation in the US market, many offerings on Gulf stock exchanges are partial floats in which the bulk of the company's ownership remains in the hands of the founders or (in the case of privatizations) in the hands of the government. In 2002, for example, Saudi Telecom was listed on the Saudi TASI, but only 30 percent of the shares in the company were sold. Even within this float, a third of the shares were allocated to two Saudi public-sector investors, General Organization for Social Insurance (GOSI) and the Pension Fund.[49] Similarly, in its 2007 IPO, Dubai Ports World sold only a 20 percent stake and targeted individual UAE investors, with a minimum threshold of $6,000 and the opportunity to subscribe being offered at branches of leading UAE banks.[50]

Although shares certainly can perform well even in the case of partial listings, such floats introduce governance issues that can be of concern to sophisticated investors. When only a minority interest in a company is floated, it is difficult to ensure that the company will be run to maximize shareholder value rather than to meet the objectives of the majority owners (either the founding family or the government). For example, if the company's majority owners seek to make

FIGURE   5.3

The Region's Capital Markets Today Have Key Limitations

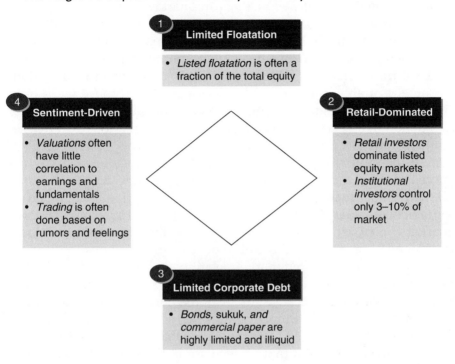

an acquisition that meets their institutional objectives but does not maximize shareholder value, the owners of listed shares cannot prevent the acquisition, since they control only a minority of the company. In more subtle cases, not being principally responsible to public shareholders (but rather being responsible to the majority-owning institution) naturally fosters a culture in which management is more sensitive to the needs of its major shareholders than it is to the needs of its public investors. If the majority owners want a dividend and the retail investors prefer to reinvest earnings, chances are that a dividend will be issued. In recent privatizations, however, there are increasing instances of majority-stake listings on public equities markets. In April 2008, Saudi Arabia's Shariah-compliant Alinma Bank sold 70 percent of its equity to Saudi nationals in an IPO,[51] and Zain subsidiary Zain Saudi Arabia floated 50 percent of its equity in February 2008.[52] This shift toward the listing of majority equity stakes is a promising sign of increasing maturity in the Gulf IPO market.

Second, Gulf stock markets continue to be dominated by retail investors, who tend to be driven by sentiment rather than by economic or market fundamentals. Unlike mature-market exchanges, which are dominated by institutional investors such as mutual funds, Gulf stock markets are dominated by individual investors. According to Jadwa Investment, Saudi individual investors accounted for nearly 95 percent of TASI trades in 2008, with mutual funds accounting for less than 2 percent of shares traded.[53] In December 2008, there were only 51 domestic and regional mutual funds in the Gulf,[54] with a total of $12 billion in assets under management,[55] compared to a total market capitalization on the Gulf bourses of more than $700 billion. Even within the mutual fund sector, holdings are fragmented—only 7 had more than $500 million in assets under management (AUM), and only 23 had more than $100 million in AUM.[56] This phenomenon is extremely unusual for an exchange that has reached such high levels of market capitalization, and in part explains the apparently irrational boom and bust cycles of the Gulf indexes, where "unhealthy trading practices have exacerbated market volatility and hurt investors."[57] The result is that the behavior of these indexes bucks fundamentals in favor of investor sentiment because "many of these investors are day traders who tend to invest according to sentiment, rather than analysis."[58]

Tom Healy, the CEO of the Abu Dhabi Securities Exchange, among others, has noted that an increase in the share of institutional investment in the GCC stock markets will bring greater stability, which will benefit both institutional and individual investors. "Established, long-term, large investors would bring more stability to the UAE stock markets, which have always been heavily dominated by individual investors. Where large, stable institutions invest, more transparency by listed companies and more widespread and in-depth research will follow. With more transparency comes better corporate governance standards, more analysis, more appropriate stock valuations and potentially higher share values and more protection—which will also benefit the smaller, individual investors."[59]

Third, limited corporate debt markets in the GCC have meant that companies have historically raised equity rather than debt. In 2003, only $2 billion in new corporate debt was issued in the GCC, and even by 2007, when $26 billion in corporate debt was issued,[60] the total amount of corporate bonds issued was just 3.2 percent of GDP in the GCC, compared to 112 percent of GDP in the United States.[61] As a result, the capital structure in MENA and the GCC is heavily skewed toward bank assets and equity—the capital structure of world capital markets included 36 percent debt securities, compared to just 6 percent in MENA.[62]

The primary reason for issuing equity rather than debt has been the fact that the GCC region currently lacks a formal bond market. Recently, however, there have been significant developments in the GCC debt markets to encourage more intraregional investment. The Saudi Capital Market Authority announced the creation, in principle, of a regional bond market in June 2009.[63] In the first half of 2009, debt issuance in the GCC reached $12 billion, a 50 percent increase over 2008, and Qatar's QTel announced the issuance of $1 billion in corporate bonds to international investors.[64] Somewhat ironically, it is actually the pressures generated by the significant financial leverage of governments in the region that have been the impetus for creating deeper sovereign and corporate debt markets. In February 2009, the government of Dubai issued $20 billion in five-year bonds in order to meet its financing needs and roll over its debt, and Bahrain announced an $800 million debt sale to finance housing projects.[65] If debt markets continue to mature, they will provide a valuable source of intraregional investment by GCC institutions and will also provide corporate treasurers with a wider range of options in raising capital.

Finally—and as a result of the factors discussed earlier—Gulf capital markets have shown themselves to be extremely turbulent. The business journal *Middle East Economic Digest* has commented on the "insane volatility" in Gulf stock markets, saying that "share price levels not remotely related to sensible valuations have turned them into cockpits for speculators."[66] The Saudi TASI and Dubai Financial Market began to fall from their peak in January 2008, six months before oil prices peaked at $150 per barrel in July 2008, and while both underlying GDP and earnings growth remained strong. As markets correct, small investors may tend to panic, resulting in a "snowball effect . . . [with] frightened investors getting out while they can."[67] It is therefore no surprise that sophisticated Gulf investors are doubly wary of investing in national public equities markets, given their volatility and apparent irrationality with respect to fundamentals, opting instead to invest in private equity and pre-IPO acquisitions.

PROCEED . . . BUT WITH CAUTION

As discussed in Chapter 1, the overall economic outlook for the Gulf region remains fairly positive—particularly when compared to other regions of the world. While the area has certainly been affected by the global financial crisis and recession, the core "opportunity formula" that has driven the attractiveness of the Gulf over the past years remains largely in place. Economic growth and prosperity—though tempered by the recession—remains a long-term trend for the region. Attractive demographics (a youthful population, increased literacy and connectivity, and other positive trends) bring commercial benefits, but also major challenges to create employment and opportunities. Regulatory reform continues, making the region more accessible to global firms and more flexible for companies that are already operating there. These three broad trends suggest a generally attractive market for long-term investment.

At this juncture, it's worth noting that the sharp effects of the crisis felt in Dubai have not been pervasive throughout the Gulf. By the end of 2008, Dubai had $46.7 billion in public debt, amounting to 103 percent of GDP,[68] and was facing a falling real estate sector. There have been highly visible job losses in the construction and financial services sectors, as well as widespread commentary regarding the emirate's economic challenges. However, what has happened in Dubai does not give an accurate picture of the impact of the crisis on the rest of the GCC. In the more prosperous parts of the region, accumulated oil surpluses provide a budgetary cushion, and leverage ratios are far lower than those in Dubai. Across the GCC, growth in 2009 is expected to be much lower than during the boom from 2001 to 2008, but nonetheless is forecasted to remain positive. The IMF estimates that in 2009, GCC real GDP will grow at 3.5 percent, with Global Investment House research pointing to a slightly lower estimate of 2.4 percent, with national growth ranging from a low of 1.4 percent in Saudi Arabia to a high of 9.4 percent in Qatar.[69]

As discussed in Chapter 1, the currency peg to the US dollar found in all Gulf states but Kuwait significantly limits Gulf governments' monetary policy options in addressing economic downturns. That said, Gulf governments have attempted to stimulate their economies through direct investment and expansionary budgets. Fiscal stimulus packages have been implemented in all GCC countries in 2009 and range from 3 percent of 2008 nonoil GDP in Bahrain to 9 percent in Saudi Arabia.[70] In March 2009, Saudi Arabia set up a National Investment Fund to funnel capital to the small and medium-sized enterprises (SMEs) that employ the majority of the Saudi labor force, and the government has announced that $2.3 billion in loans will be available to low-income borrowers to ease their credit constraints.[71]

Gulf central banks have also followed the lead of the United States in innovative monetary policy, taking more "creative" steps to secure the financial and real estate sectors. In Kuwait, where the banking sector was destabilized by defaults by counterparties on eurodollar derivatives contracts, leading to significant provisions for currency trade losses, the central bank provided a guaranteed loan facility of $5 billion as an initial step to shore up the country's banking sector.[72] In the UAE, the Emirates Central Bank bought the entire $10 billion initial tranche of Dubai's $20 billion bond issue in February 2009, at what many have seen as an artificially low "bailout" interest rate of 4 percent.[73]

Overall, a combination of the cushion from the oil surpluses accrued up to the end of 2008 and sufficient freedom driven by creativity in fiscal and monetary policy means that the Gulf states look set to weather the global financial crisis intact. Global Investment House estimates that the cushion of fiscal surpluses, which stood at $300 billion for the GCC in 2008, will fall to around $100 billion (10.3 percent of GDP) in 2009,[74] having been reduced by lower oil prices and increased spending to stimulate the economies. This reduced level of surpluses should still be sufficient to prevent the Gulf states from running OECD-style deficits if economic recovery takes longer than expected.

Even if the overall outlook remains cautiously positive, the financial crisis has certainly changed the short-term nature of domestic and regional investment opportunities in the Gulf. Capital projects have been delayed in favor of short-term spending, with an estimated 150 major projects being on hold in 2009.[75] Private-sector regional M&A activity has slowed almost to a halt as the financial crisis has dragged on, and government has been the primary driver of M&A activity, particularly in the UAE. The financial crisis may have wiped out gains made on the Gulf stock markets, but it has not significantly reduced domestic and regional investment opportunities in the region beyond the short-term.

A balanced assessment of the Gulf would, therefore, suggest that it is an attractive environment for investment. As discussed earlier, however, public stock markets have severe limitations and—at least today—may not be the ideal channel for sophisticated investors to increase their exposure to the region. Instead, investment in private companies through private equity arrangements or through direct partnerships appears to be a far more stable and reliable way to benefit from the GCC's ongoing growth. John C. Bogle, founder of the investment giant Vanguard, has noted that "the stock market is a giant distraction from the business of investing."[76] Perhaps nowhere has that been truer than in the bourses of the GCC.

KEY LESSONS

- Over successive oil booms, the *focus of infrastructure projects in the Gulf region has shifted* from hard infrastructure like roads and core utilities to soft infrastructure such as business parks, free zones, and upgraded utilities that enable private-sector business activity.

- In the 2000s, Gulf equity markets experienced *a series of booms and busts* and proved highly volatile despite consistent economic growth in the region.

- Changes in *foreign ownership rights and privatizations* of government-owned companies are shifting the environment of local capital markets, adding to their accessibility and depth.

- Gulf capital markets face *significant limitations* today, including limited floats, retail-driven markets, limited debt markets, and sentiment-driven volatility.

- While the fundamental outlook for regional investments appears strong, the optimal channel for accessing the region may be *private equity investments and direct partnerships* with companies.

6
CHAPTER

On the Frontier: The Gulf's Growing Focus on Emerging Markets

When Abdullah bin Abdulaziz formally ascended to the Saudi throne in 2005, the new monarch set about defining and implementing his priorities. Since he had long been the Kingdom's crown prince, one key decision was where to make his first overseas visit as ruler. One natural choice could have been the United States—Saudi Arabia's single most important military and economically and the world's leading power. Alternatively, King Abdullah could have visited the United Kingdom or some other European power, staying in Buckingham Palace (something he did later in his reign).[1] Or, the king might have chosen a humanitarian mission to some of the world's most underprivileged nations as a signal of generosity and compassion.

Instead, King Abdullah's first official overseas trip was to China. In early 2006, he was the first Saudi monarch to make a state visit to China, calling on Chinese president Hu Jintao and forging economic ties with the People's Republic.[2] Later the same month, King Abdullah paid a visit to India, where he was chief guest at India's Republic Day celebrations. In his comments, the Saudi king went so far as to refer to India as his "second home."[3] Soon thereafter, the king's counterparties began reciprocating— President Hu came to Saudi Arabia a few months later.

These state visits between dignitaries were quickly converted to business results. Leading from the top, the rulers mobilized state-controlled enterprises to increase their collaboration, particularly in the strategic oil and gas sector. In March 2007, two joint ventures in China's Fujian province were announced—Fujian Refining & Petrochemical Company Limited and Sinopec SenMei (Fujian) Petroleum Company Limited—involving Saudi Aramco (the national oil company), Sinopec, and ExxonMobil, with total investment of about $5 billion. These were the first fully integrated refining, petrochemicals, and fuels marketing projects with foreign participation in China.[4] In some respects, the partnership should not be surprising: Saudi Arabia is the world's biggest oil exporter, and China is the second-largest and fastest-growing oil consumer. Similar results were achieved from the increased focus on Saudi–India relations. According to the Indo-Arab Chamber of Commerce & Industries, more than 270 major deals involving Indian and Saudi businesses were signed in the year and a half since the king's visit in 2006. The value of the two-way trade, including oil, in 2006–2007 was $16 billion—a 360 percent increase over the previous year.[5]

The depth of this focus and relationship has gone further than trade alone. In 2008, when a major earthquake hit Wenchuan, China, Saudi Arabia immediately provided 60 million US dollars in cash and goods.[6] Also, on the cultural side, programs such as the King Abdullah Scholarship, created in 2006, have sponsored more than 150 Saudi students studying in China. This may be a small number compared to the number of Saudi students in the United States and the United Kingdom, but it nonetheless reflects an important measure in terms of diversification and strategic skill development.

While the bulk of Gulf investments remain directed toward the world's most developed economies, a key trend in recent years has been an increased interest in emerging markets. In addition to allocating more of their resources to China and India, Gulf investors have invested more in the broader Middle East and North Africa (MENA) region, Southeast Asia, South Asia, Turkey, and Africa, expanding their global exposure and geographic coverage. This trend, which has been a sustained pattern over the past decade, represents an important shift in the investment behavior of Gulf institutions, and a change that those wishing to partner with Gulf investors should monitor in the years ahead. This chapter serves as an overview of this increasing focus, its drivers, and its manifestations.

We begin with a review of the traditional geographic allocation models of Gulf investors, through which the bulk of the Gulf Cooperation Council (GCC) overseas assets have been channeled to the United States and other developed markets. Next, we explore the factors that have driven the trend toward a greater emerging-market focus by Gulf investors. These can be divided into two categories: external factors, such as the growth of emerging markets and shifts in their overall attractiveness, and internal factors related to leadership changes in the Gulf and evolving affinities. In closing, we discuss the reasons why, despite this trend toward emerging-market investment, the world's most developed countries are likely to remain the top destination for Gulf capital, albeit as part of a more balanced geographical allocation model.

LONGSTANDING DEVELOPED-MARKET ORIENTATION

Throughout the successive oil booms of the 1970s and beyond, the GCC has invested heavily in the United States and developed countries. Despite the political differences that inspired the Gulf states' 1973–1974 oil embargo of the United States and other key Western countries—an embargo that was both shocking and painful—Gulf investments in developed economies continued to flow. There were, after all, good reasons for Gulf investors to focus on developed markets. One key reason why GCC investments were focused on the Organisation for Economic Co-operation and Development (OECD) was a lack of local or even regional capital markets that were sufficiently developed to absorb the massive liquidity created by oil wealth. The most prudent investment strategy at the time was to invest in developed markets, where returns would be liquid and safe. Investing large amounts of capital in small markets would also have driven prices up and yields down, as well as limited large investors' liquidity and ability to exit with good returns. This would have been especially true of the Gulf, where large-scale domestic investment would have distorted asset values upward because of the amount of investable wealth compared to the available asset base, exposing Gulf investors to undue risk.[7]

In addition, the dollar denomination of oil revenue has made US Treasury bills and other dollar-denominated investments natural choices for Gulf investors. A 1975 US Treasury estimate of OPEC's investment direction offers a good gauge of the extent of the Gulf's developed market focus. Of OPEC's $26 billion total foreign investment of oil earnings in 1974, nearly half (according to the Treasury estimate) was channeled to the United States, as shown in Figure 6.1.

Together, the United States and the United Kingdom were believed to have received roughly three-quarters of all overseas investment of OPEC surpluses. Other developed markets received about a fifth, with only 8 percent of capital being allocated to developing markets.[8] Although these data pertain to all oil exporters, not just the Gulf states, they nonetheless provide a useful reference for estimating GCC allocations. Over time, the allocation to the United Kingdom relative to other developed markets has been reduced, as other OECD states have

FIGURE 6.1

Oil Exporters' 1970s Allocations Were Weighted Heavily toward the United States and the United Kingdom

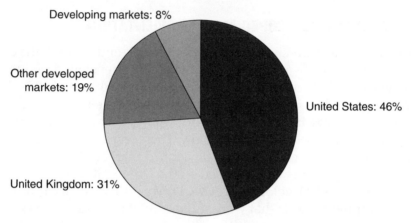

Estimated Foreign Investment Destinations of OPEC Member Oil Surpluses, 1974

Developing markets: 8%

Other developed markets: 19%

United States: 46%

United Kingdom: 31%

Note: Total exceeds 100% due to rounding.

Source: US Treasury Department, 1975.

increased in relative attractiveness. Nonetheless, the general theme of concentrating mainly in the most developed markets has continued.

One of the earliest landmark transactions by Gulf-based investors took place in 1975, when the government-controlled Kuwait Investment Company bought 14 percent of Daimler-Benz. The transaction was valued at $300 to $400 million at the time.[9] Kuwait also acquired an estimated $500 million of London real estate around the same time. The United States and other developed markets, which were experiencing an economic downturn at the time, needed the cash infusion, and over time increasingly drew on Gulf capital for funding. By the early 1990s, the huge government fund managers of Saudi Arabia, Kuwait, Abu Dhabi, Qatar, Oman, and Bahrain were estimated to hold $200 billion in overseas investments.

In the private sector, Bahrain-based Investcorp (mentioned in Chapter 4) perhaps offers the best illustration of early private equity and direct investment activity. Established in 1982, Investcorp effectively facilitated the flow of capital from Gulf investors into attractive Western corporate assets. While a great deal of investing in US Treasury bills, large-cap stocks, and other traditional asset classes was already taking place, Investcorp offered an alternative investment option, along with the potential for excess returns. Since the early 1980s, it has completed transactions with a total acquisition value of approximately $41 billion. It has acquired and sold a multitude of well-known brand names, such as the luxury jewelry retailer Tiffany and soft drink company A&W in the United States, Gucci in Italy, and Ebel, the leading Swiss watch manufacturer.

Table 6.1 provides a snapshot of key Investcorp transactions from the early 1980s through 2007.

T A B L E   6.1

Investcorp Has a Sustained Record of Investing in Prominent Developed-World Companies

Time Period	Prominent Investcorp Investments
1980–1985	• First transaction: 50% purchase of Manulife Plaza, Los Angeles, USA • First corporate investment: A&W Brands, soft-drink company in the United States • Tiffany & Co., United States—acquisition • Jiffy Lube, United States—acquisition
1986–1990s	• Manulife, Jiffy Lube, and A&W Brands sold • Completed Tiffany IPO on New York Stock Exchange (NYSE) • Breguet, a Swiss watchmaker, and Chaumet, a French jeweler, acquired • Carvel, US ice cream company, acquired • Saks Fifth Avenue, United States—acquired 1990
1991–1995	• 50% acquisition of Mondi, a fashion group from Germany • Star Market, a US supermarket chain—acquired • Ebel, a Swiss watch manufacturer—acquired
1996–2000	• Saks Fifth Avenue listed on the NYSE • Jostens, United States—acquired • Avecia, a specialty chemicals business—acquired • Star Market sold
2001–2007	• Stahl, supplier of specialty chemicals, Europe—acquired • Jostens sold • Icopal, leading producer of roofing and waterproofing membranes—acquired • Moody International, provider of technical and inspection service, United Kingdom—acquired

Source: Investcorp corporate Web site, www.investcorp.com/ last accessed August 2009.

As is evident from the long list of transactions, Investcorp has a sustained history of investing in prominent companies in the United States, the United Kingdom, and Europe. Its track record provides a vivid example of the role that Gulf capital has played in Western markets for several decades. Investcorp's history also shows that the GCC region's appetite for developed-world corporate assets is by no means a new phenomenon, and in fact has been a reality of capital markets since the time when many of today's senior bankers were just starting their careers.

SHIFTS UNDERWAY

Even Investcorp, with its strong track record of OECD investments, has increased the amount of attention it has directed toward emerging markets in recent years. In 2007, the firm launched a growth capital fund focused on the Gulf and the wider MENA region. In citing its rationale for the fund, Investcorp observed that the MENA region has undergone an unprecedented economic transformation driven by strong oil revenues, is rapidly diversifying its economies, and is in the midst of a demographic transition that is creating strong growth opportunities.[10] Investcorp's shift toward emerging markets—not as a substitute for its core OECD portfolio, but rather as a complement to it—illustrates a posture found throughout the Gulf. Increasingly, GCC-based investors are seeing exposure to emerging markets as a crucial part of a holistic allocation strategy.

A 2008 assessment by the director-general of the Arab Monetary Fund yielded a significantly different picture of Gulf investors' geographic allocations from that painted in the 1975 US Treasury report cited previously. As is evident in the Figure 6.2, developed markets continued to represent the bulk of Gulf portfolios, but Arab and Asian countries have become significant investment destinations.[11]

The United States remained the dominant destination, and US investments are now believed to make up more than half of aggregate Gulf portfolios. European assets were estimated at around one-fifth of the total allocation—far below the 1975 estimate, in which the United Kingdom alone had a much larger share of OPEC outward investments. Arab, Asian, and other countries together made up about a quarter of Gulf portfolios, more than three times the allocation for "developing" countries in the 1975 study. It's important to note that

FIGURE 6.2

By 2008, Emerging-Market Investments Had Become a Sizable Part of Gulf Portfolios

Estimated Gulf Foreign Investment Allocation by Region, 2008

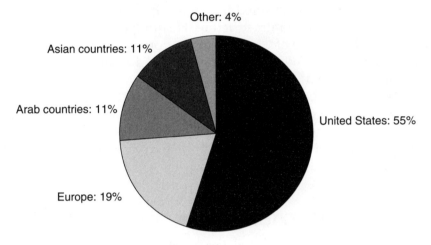

Other: 4%

Asian countries: 11%

Arab countries: 11%

United States: 55%

Europe: 19%

Source: Arab Monetary Fund, 2008.

the two studies (1975 and 2008) are not precisely comparable—the earlier research looked at OPEC members overall, and the later one only at the GCC. Nonetheless, the contrast is useful in assessing the general directional shift in investors' geographic allocations.

It is also interesting to note the evolution in terminology between the two studies, conducted 33 years apart. Whereas the term *developed* countries was previously synonymous with Western markets, by 2008 the Asian major economies were widely recognized as *developed* economies—Japan having long been a member of the Organisation for Economic Co-operation and Development (OECD) and South Korea having joined in 2006[12]—the club of developed nations. The differentiation between "Arab," "Asian," and "other" markets is a significant departure from the previous (unflattering) monolith of "developing" economies. The differentiation is much more meaningful now that the Arab and Asian regions each make up more than a tenth of total portfolios. The clustering of the United Kingdom into a broader "Europe" bucket (whereas previously it was a category on its own) reflects both the common market status of the EU and the decline of the United Kingdom's share of overseas portfolios as other markets have risen.

It's also striking that the Arab Monetary Fund does not use the terminology of "developed" and "emerging" markets in its 2008 analysis. At a Harvard Business School forum the same year, Jeff Immelt, the CEO of GE, observed that the classification of emerging markets may have outlived its usefulness, especially as certain emerging markets surpass the United States and Europe in areas like technology, health care, and infrastructure. He quipped that if one boards a direct flight from one of China's new airports and lands at the well-worn JFK airport in New York, it would be hard to tell which terminal was in a "developed" country.[13] Certainly the same could be said of the sleek airport in Doha or Dubai's new Terminal 3. That said, emerging markets share enough common characteristics (generally lower GDP per capita, rapidly evolving economies, lower historical levels of industrialization, and so on) to make the term useful for our current purposes.

DRIVERS OF CHANGE: EXTERNAL AND INTERNAL FACTORS

Greater attention toward emerging markets has been fueled by a number of factors. These drivers can be broadly divided into two categories: external factors related to global markets more generally, and internal factors that are specific to the GCC region. Table 6.2 summarizes four key factors within each category and sets the framework for our discussion.

T A B L E   6.2

External and Internal Factors Drive the Gulf's Interest in Emerging-Market Investments

External Factors	Internal Factors
1. Increased attractiveness of emerging markets	1. Changes in Gulf leadership and shifts in leaders' outlooks
2. Active promotion campaigns by certain emerging markets	2. Greater strategic alignment with certain emerging markets
3. OECD market crises	3. Cultural affinity with certain emerging markets
4. Increased scrutiny by OECD regulators and media	4. Rise of Islamic finance and investments

Attractiveness of Emerging Markets

The most powerful reason why Gulf investors have turned toward emerging markets is a simple one: emerging markets have become more attractive from a return on investment perspective. They represent pockets of growth and opportunities unavailable in more developed markets. China is a prime example: its growth has far outpaced global averages, and it is now the fourth-largest economy in the world. In the first half of 2009, China edged out Germany as the world's largest exporter, turning the tables on long-held assumptions regarding where the world's leading suppliers should be based.[14] It's no wonder that the Saudi king has made China such a priority—and that other Gulf leaders have done so as well.

In September 2006, the Kuwait Investment Authority (KIA) announced that it would be among the top investors in the Industrial and Commercial Bank of China (ICBC) IPO. The KIA would, according to the prospectus, buy shares in the bank valued at $720 million. Kuwait's desire to deepen its links with China was explicitly mentioned as a motivation for the transaction. "This participation demonstrates Kuwait's deepening economic ties with China as well as showcases the long-term strategic value of KIA as a core investor," said the managing director of the Kuwait Investment Authority, Bader al-Saad. "This participation also marks the beginning of KIA's long-term strategic investment plan in China, which the KIA hopes to extend to many other sectors."[15]

When the company went public on October 20, 2006, it raised $19 billion, becoming the biggest IPO in world history. Another Gulf investor involved with the deal was the Qatar Investment Authority (QIA), which was in to buy $206 million, according to the initial ICBC prospectus. ICBC's listing thus represented a relatively uncommon transaction in which sovereign investors from two GCC states were involved at the same time. In the future, we may see more such occurrences of multistate GCC sovereign participation in large, high-profile transactions. Commentators have noted that—in stark contrast to their welcoming stance toward Gulf investors and partners—Chinese oil-related firms have generally allowed the Western "majors" (BP, Total, and ExxonMobil) only limited, supporting roles. Thus is interpreted as a signal of China's strategic priority of ensuring its access to oil and therefore concentrating on relationships with the world's key producers.[16]

The development of Gulf–Asia trade flows and investment links is leading to what observers such as McKinsey & Co. are widely referring to as a "new Silk Road." This growing trade and investment corridor between the Middle East and Asia is seen as a revival of ancient trade routes between these two regions—routes that were a major driver of global economic activity for centuries. Today, the Silk Road is seen to span the major cities of the Gulf, South Asia, China, and the Association of Southeast Asian Nations region. Trade and investment among these regions has quadrupled in the past decade and will continue to rise dramatically through 2020.[17] This new Silk Road not only is boosting economies, but is changing the socioeconomic and geopolitical landscape of the East. Commercial ventures are increasingly focusing on fostering and profiting from these trade flows—there even is an investment firm named New Silk Route whose chairman is the former global managing partner of McKinsey.[18]

The broader "BRIC" (Brazil, Russia, India, and China) region has been taking steady measures to increase mutual cooperation and economic ties. The countries met for their first official summit in June 2009. A key focus of the summit was related to improving the current global economic situation and, importantly, discussing how the BRIC countries could be better involved in global affairs in the future. The ambition of the leading emerging-market countries to exercise greater influence on the world stage is a key long-term trend that is likely to play a part in shaping the future of international affairs.[19] Economic, competitive, and demographic realities certainly point to the increasing importance of emerging markets.

At the corporate level, the rise of emerging markets is manifesting itself as well. The Boston Consulting Group (BCG) has begun producing an annual study (authored by former colleagues of mine) called "The 100 New Global Challengers." In its 2009 report, BCG features companies from emerging markets that are increasingly contending for global leadership in their industries. As referenced in the report, in just the two years from 2006 to 2008, the number of companies based in Brazil, China, India, and Russia on the FT Global 500 list more than quadrupled, from 15 to 62. In addition to the BRIC economy companies that dominate the BCG list, other markets represented are Mexico, Indonesia, Malaysia, Turkey, and Thailand. In 2009, reflecting the emergence of the Gulf countries as emerging markets themselves, was the inclusion of companies from Kuwait (Agility) and the UAE (Dubai Ports World, Emaar Properties, Emirates Airlines, and Etisalat).[20]

The global trend of investment flows from one emerging market to another—dubbed "South-South" investment by some commentators—is by no means solely a Gulf phenomenon. China, for example, has launched a China-Africa Development Fund dedicated to investing in Africa. This vehicle, a government-owned investment entity, is valued at approximately $5 billion. This figure is a substantial sum in relation to asset values in Africa, giving China the muscle to make sizable, and potentially strategic, investments in the continent.[21]

This South-South global trend is resulting in the rise of foreign direct investment (FDI) from within developing countries. This kind of FDI reached a record level in 2005, with most of these investments ending up in other developing countries. In fact, many low-income countries now rely mainly on other developing countries for inward FDI, with outflows of $120 billion in such FDI now being recorded— the highest level ever. Asia accounted for almost 70 percent of these capital flows. The list of top developing-country sources in 2005 was led by Hong Kong (China), the Russian Federation, Singapore, Taiwan, Brazil, and China.[22]

Gulf investors—like institutional investors everywhere—have identified emerging-market opportunities as fundamentally attractive. The main driver of their increased attention to these fast-growing countries has been the potential for superior returns on their invested capital. Thus, the first key driver one must appreciate in understanding the GCC's shifting allocation is that greater emerging-market exposure has been seen as simply good for business.

Promotion Campaigns

In addition to the fundamental attractiveness of these markets, targeted trade and promotion initiatives have had a role in attracting Gulf capital. As discussed earlier, economic delegations at the senior-most levels have exchanged visits between key Gulf countries, China, India, and other emerging markets. Countries such as Malaysia have launched initiatives to attract foreign businesspeople in general and Gulf investors in particular through programs such as "Malaysia: My Second Home." The program facilitates visits to and residence in the country for 10-year periods, and even allows approved foreigners to bring children and elderly dependents into the country.[23] Making it easy for business leaders to travel, be stationed, and bring their families to another country is an important factor in encouraging trade and investments. The United Kingdom has undertaken a number of programs to continue attracting Gulf investors and their capital. One such measure is an annual gathering called the Islamic Finance and Trade Conference, a high-profile event at which a number of senior government officials have spoken. Gordon Brown addressed the forum in 2006 as chancellor of the exchequer and used it as a platform for communicating the United Kingdom's commitment to being a global hub for Islamic finance.[24]

In addition to having significant symbolic value, such events can often lead to legislative reform in the countries seeking investment and can also inspire Gulf investors to reciprocate through concessions and commercial partnerships. As we shall discuss in later chapters of this book, promotional events alone may not be enough to attract real investment flows and commerce. Coupled with fundamental economic attractiveness and genuinely enabling regulations, however, they can play an important role in catalyzing trade flows. For example, that certainly appears to have occurred between Saudi Arabia and China.

OECD Markets Shaken

One core appeal of the United States and other OECD markets over the years has been the safety of investments in those markets and the expectation of long-term market stability. The financial crisis of 2008–2009 has had a real effect, however, on investor perceptions regarding the OECD markets' safety and stability. Bank bailouts, deep and sudden declines in asset values, and fundamental questions of regulation and financial transparency are phenomena that investors consider possible in emerging markets but never expect in the OECD world. While the crisis does not erase a longstanding history of resilience, it certainly brings into question the assumption that the world's most developed markets are entirely safe and immune from major shocks and instability. Besides the question of stability, the sheer magnitude of the losses faced by institutional investors (including Gulf-based investors) has inspired them to more actively look for non-OECD alternatives.

According to the Monitor Group's report on sovereign wealth funds, "Recent behavior shows a marked shift toward domestic and emerging market deals." Monitor found that "in the third quarter of 2008, as the global financial crisis continued to worsen, sovereign wealth funds (SWFs) sought to limit their exposure to the riskiness of OECD markets while putting more capital to work in their domestic economies." Nearly half of the reported transactions in the third quarter of 2008 were domestic transactions, the highest percentage since 2003. Additionally, "54% of Q2 and Q3 deals by value ($23 billion out of $42 billion) were in emerging markets, the highest share of total deal value since 2005."[25] These data suggest that the financial crisis and global recession have accelerated the trend of institutional investors seeking greater exposure to emerging markets—a move to balance OECD exposure that has proven more risky than expected.

Volatility in OECD exchanges is also a factor pushing Gulf investors toward more sophisticated investment structures. As discussed in Chapter 4, some recent Gulf transactions have involved convertible structures in which debtlike returns are guaranteed and equity appreciation provides additional gains. Also, private equity and other forms of alternative investment are on the rise, giving Gulf investors greater influence over portfolio companies and more mechanisms to protect their capital. With "plain vanilla" listed equities proving volatile, leading institutions are looking toward structures and modes that spare them some of the uncertainties of choppy stock exchanges.

Increased Scrutiny

In the wake of the September 11, 2001, attacks and the subsequent "war on terror," international capital flows have faced a heightened level of scrutiny. This is especially true of investments by Gulf-based investors and Islamic institutions, which have been viewed with a heightened level of caution. As noted by Ibrahim Warde, "Following September 11, Islamic banks and financial institutions provided a logical target to those who were quick to associate anything Islamic with terrorism."[26] Warde points out regulatory events that triggered capital flight, observing that "a crucial development was the freezing of the assets of prominent Saudis, and the crackdown on Islamic financial institutions and charities, which led many Muslim investors to take a significant chunk of their assets out of the United States."[27]

The issue of increased scrutiny is most salient in relation to the United States. Congressional pressure used to block the acquisition by which Dubai Ports World would end up operating some American ports was a watershed event, sending strong negative signals to GCC investors. Gulf business leaders frequently recount negative personal experiences, such as at US airports, where immigration processes have been lengthy and (at times) have been perceived as degrading. For senior executives with choices regarding where to travel, the hassle of US airports has often proved to be enough to deter visits. While such inconveniences have by no means stopped the flow of Gulf capital, they have affected the degree to which GCC investors feel welcome in the United States. As we shall discuss at length in Chapter 11, regulators must strike a delicate balance between protecting national interests and not driving away much-needed capital. For many GCC observers, policies crafted during the "war on terror" have seemed unduly restrictive and unpleasant to deal with.

The posture of US President Barack Obama toward the Islamic world has, however, already begun to have an impact in reversing some negative repercussions of zealous regulation. Obama's comments regarding America's respect for the Muslim world, most notably at his historic Cairo address in 2009, have been well received by leaders in the Gulf and around the Muslim world. Although the scrutiny of investments is likely to remain high, Obama's comments help to remove a perception of negative bias toward Muslim investors. This is crucial for investors who are willing to comply with regulations when they are applied fairly but do not want to be singled out or viewed with undue suspicion.

Increased scrutiny in the United States and certain other OECD markets stands in stark contrast to the active investment promotion strategies of countries such as China, India, and Malaysia. As discussed earlier, these campaigns can help draw the attention of Gulf investors, who may prefer (all else equal) to place their capital in environments that welcome them rather than those that do not.

Internal Factors

In addition to the external factors just discussed, four unique internal Gulf drivers have also contributed to an increase in the focus on emerging markets. One such driver has been an increase in investment sophistication, led by a new generation of management and leadership. Previous generations were less familiar with complex investments and more focused on finding safe places for their surplus wealth. In addition, many previous leaders were unfamiliar with emerging markets, since their experience had been so focused on OECD investments. The increased sophistication of Gulf capital today, discussed in Chapter 4, has come with greater openness to emerging-market investments. As Gulf investors have become more willing to move beyond plain vanilla investments, opportunities in emerging markets are increasingly seen as being compatible with investors' objectives and risk appetites.

A second important internal driver has been an increasing alignment of GCC countries' national development agendas with the assets available in emerging markets. Infrastructure, for example, is a key priority for Gulf markets and is also a capability that is being actively developed in China, India, and certain other emerging markets. In addition, agricultural assets have become a strategic priority as Gulf states seek to secure their food supplies more strongly. Saudi Arabia, for example, has established an $800 million vehicle for investing in agricultural assets worldwide.[28] As emerging markets may offer substantial agricultural assets at favorable prices, one can expect a sizable portion of the entity's capital to end up in emerging economies.

At the same time, less developed markets are typically more willing to provide foreign investors—including those from the Gulf—with access to strategic sectors like telecommunications and financial services. Kuwaiti mobile telecommunications provider Zain, for example, has aggressively acquired companies in the Middle East and Africa, including in 2005 Celtel, once of the leading mobile providers in sub-Saharan Africa. Now it is a major presence in 15 countries in Africa and 7 more across the Middle East.[29] As noted in a *Harvard Business Review* article, Zain "has acquired 20 companies in the Middle East and Africa, growing from 600,000 to 45 million + customers. . . . Expanding steadily, it aspires to join the ranks of the top 10 mobile telecoms worldwide. Western majors like Vodafone have had to sit up and take notice."[30] Such ambitious acquisitions might well have been impossible in more developed markets, where telecom licenses are even more highly coveted and are often kept out of foreign investors' hands.

In the realm of financial services, Sudan has actively supported the establishment of foreign-owned Islamic banks within the country. Bahrain and Sudan jointly launched an Islamic reinsurance company in 2008. In addition, Qatar Islamic Bank has signed a memorandum of understanding with the government to set up a commercial and investment bank in Khartoum.[31] As highlighted in Chapter 3, Islamic banking conglomerates the DMI Group and Al Baraka Group have been able to establish substantial footprints across emerging Muslim markets. In OECD markets, such active invitation of foreign investors to establish banks is far less common.

Third, cultural affinity with certain emerging markets is proving to be a meaningful factor in shaping Gulf investment flows. Building trade links with Arab nations is a natural extension of cultural similarities and longstanding political ties. The emerging markets of Egypt, Jordan, Lebanon, Algeria, and Morocco have proved highly welcoming of Gulf capital and fertile ground for Gulf-based companies to expand. In numerous cases, trade flows have been enabled by the fact that expatriate executives working in the Gulf-based partner hail from the Arab country in which the investment or expansion is being made. This gives the GCC institution intimate knowledge of the target market and a high level of familiarity at the operating level. As noted in the *Harvard Business Review* commentary mentioned previously, "GCC investors are more comfortable than their Western counterparts with forging deals in emerging economies—partly because of their diasporic links and cultural ties to some of these countries and partly because they have fewer concerns than Westerners about whether these regions embrace democratic norms."[32] It should not, therefore, be surprising that "Damac, Dubai's largest private developer, has planned projects in Egypt worth more than US$20 billion and has said 20% of its revenue could come from Egypt by 2009."[33]

Another set of markets with close cultural affinity has been emerging markets in the 57 Organization of the Islamic Conference (OIC) member countries. These emerging markets include Turkey, Pakistan, Malaysia, and Indonesia, among others. During the period 2003–2007, three of the largest OIC markets—Turkey, Saudi Arabia, and Malaysia—have shown a significantly greater growth in trade with OIC member countries than with the rest of the world. This trend shows the measurable impact of cultural affinity driving increased commerce.[34]

As noted in the Malaysian press, "Middle Eastern investors have been snapping up properties in Malaysia. . . . [T]he country's young population, large projects, stable government and economy, relative transparent laws on property ownership and availability of Islamic financing are all factors. In addition, many are already familiar with Malaysia as a popular Arab vacation destination."[35] As noted in the preceding commentary, these capital flows have been fostered by government initiatives linked both to property laws and to the promotion of Islamic finance. By developing its Islamic finance sector, Malaysia has steadily made itself more attractive to Gulf investors.

Turkey holds unique appeal for Gulf investors because of its unique status as a country that is, at the same time, both part of the Muslim world and globally regarded as a founding member of the OECD. As pointed out by the *Economist*, "growing numbers of Arab investors have flocked to Turkey, because they see it as part of Europe, not the Middle East."[36] Turkey is home to a number of world-class operating companies and conglomerates, yet it is relatively accessible to GCC investors. According to the Turkish Treasury's report, foreign direct investments from the Gulf region and Middle Eastern countries have jumped from $495 million in the January–October 2007 period to $1.9 billion in the January–November 2008 period.[37]

Pakistan, despite its serious security and governance issues, has seen steady investment flows from the Gulf. In its very attractive telecommunication sector, Etisalat (UAE) bought a 26 percent stake in Pakistan Telecommunication Company for $2.6 billion in 2005. In May 2007, Qatar Telecom (Qtel) acquired the Pakistan-based telecom service provider Burraq Telecom. Abraaj Capital, one of the leading private equity firms in the Gulf, launched a $300 million fund targeting buyout opportunities in the country.[38] Pakistan benefits from both a level of cultural affinity with the Gulf and the strong presence of Pakistani professionals based in the Gulf and aware of opportunities in their native country.

Finally, the rise of Islamic finance and investments has acted as a catalyst for GCC investments in other Muslim countries. As we shall discuss extensively in the next chapter, Gulf investors' interest in Shariah-compliant investment opportunities has grown substantially in recent years as a result of a variety of factors. Gulf-based Islamic banks find natural growth opportunities in expanding into other Muslim markets. Additionally, the structuring and Shariah requirements associated with Islamic investments—especially in the context of private equity transactions—are often better understood by potential portfolio companies when they come from the Muslim world. Although the bulk of high-profile Islamic private equity transactions have occurred in the OECD world, Muslim markets are often more inclined to meet the structuring and Shariah requirements associated with such investments.

DEVELOPED MARKETS REMAIN PRIMARY OUTLET

As we have seen, emerging markets are becoming increasingly important investment outlets for Gulf capital. It is, however, crucial to remember that emerging-market investments act as complements to Gulf investors' OECD holdings and are not the main focus for most investors. While developing-world investments are clearly becoming more central, developed markets are likely to remain the primary outlet for GCC capital for the foreseeable future.

Even as emerging markets draw increased attention, the developed markets retain key advantages that justify their continuing centrality. Some of these advantages include

- Unmatched depth and breadth of capital markets
- Dollar denomination of assets, which is compatible with GCC revenues
- The availability of safe, conservative investments (despite recent crises and volatility)
- Greater compatibility with investors' general preference for small stakes in strong companies
- The availability of strategic technology and capabilities
- The availability of "prestige" investments sought by certain Gulf investors
- A strong fit with vital OECD political and security alliances

The increased appetite for emerging-market investments should therefore be seen as an evolution in the development of Gulf capital and not as a revolutionary shift. Emerging-market investments have things to offer—high economic growth potential, access to strategic assets, welcoming supervisory regimes, genuine affinity with the Gulf region, affinity to Islamic finance, and other benefits—that OECD markets often lack. At the same time, the world's most developed markets have much to offer—unmatched depth and breadth, proven track records, superior security, and the whole host of attributes listed earlier—that emerging markets simply cannot match. For savvy Gulf investors, the question will not be whether to forgo one set of markets in favor of the other, but rather how best to optimize their exposure to both.

KEY LESSONS

- Gulf institutions have long *invested heavily in the United States and other OECD markets*, where the bulk of their overseas investments have been made.

- A number of *external market factors*, including the fundamental attractiveness of emerging markets, active trade promotion initiatives, crises in OECD markets, and increased scrutiny from developed-world regulators, have contributed to a shift toward greater investment in emerging markets.

- In addition, several *internal factors*, including shifts in GCC leadership, increasing alignment of economic strategies, cultural affinity with certain markets, and the rise of Islamic finance and investments, have further driven increased interest in emerging-market investments.

- Despite the increased focus on emerging markets, the world's most *developed markets remain the primary outlet* for Gulf capital. Shifts in geographic allocation seek to complement existing portfolios rather than revamp them.

7

CHAPTER

Principled Principals: The Increasing Shariah Affinity of Gulf Investors

A few years ago, I started a presentation to a group of students at an Ivy League law school with a question: "How many of you were raised in a Muslim country?" A significant number of hands shot up. Next, I asked how often, while living in the Muslim world, they enquired as to whether the food they were served was halal *(permissible by Islamic law). Their responses were uniform—they hardly ever posed such queries. Muslim societies, despite their differing levels of religious observance, overwhelmingly conform with Islamic practice when it comes to preparing food. It would seem out of place for one to ask whether a dish was* halal *or for a food merchant to position herself as an "Islamic" food shop. Consumers take it for granted—unless they're seeking something that is explicitly prohibited by the Shariah—that the products being offered are "Islamic."*

I then challenged the audience to think differently about the phenomenon of Islamic finance in the Muslim world. Perhaps, I suggested, it was not surprising that Shariah-compliant financial services have taken root and are growing rapidly. On the other hand, perhaps it is more surprising that conventional banking and investments became so dominant in Muslim markets in the first place.

A major trend in the evolution of Gulf capital is the increasing Shariah affinity of Gulf investors. Make no mistake about it: conventional investments, like conventional banking, continue to make up the bulk of Gulf investors' financial activity. There has, however, been a sharp and steady rise in GCC-based (Gulf Cooperation Council) investors' interest in (and at times insistence on) Shariah compliance as a condition for investments. Observers of the region and those who wish to collaborate with Gulf investors must be aware of this trend and be sensitive to its unique requirements.

In this chapter, we discuss the increasing Shariah affinity of Gulf investors from a number of perspectives. We begin by exploring the causes of this increased appetite for Islamic investments and assessing the drivers that support this ongoing trend. We then explore how investment firms and other market actors have been serving this demand to date. While significant progress has been made in recent years, significant gaps in the product sets and capabilities of Islamic investment firms remain—gaps that must be borne in mind when assessing the industry. In addition, as we then review, increased Shariah affinity has begun to affect asset prices in the GCC region and capital-raising strategies internationally. In closing, we will consider the potentially transformative impact of institutional demand for Shariah-compliant investments—a new frontier that could fundamentally change the trajectory of the Islamic investment industry and shape Gulf capital more broadly. Though they are a small part of the overall Gulf market today, Islamic investments represent a dynamic market segment of increasing significance and impact.

DRIVERS OF DEMAND

The trend toward greater Shariah affinity is driven by a number of factors at play within the Gulf. As illustrated in Figure 7.1, three core drivers may be identified as fueling the ongoing interest in Islamic investments.

Rise of Islamic Liquidity

Over the past decades, there has been tremendous growth in what could be characterized as Islamic liquidity. Two fundamental causes of this growth have been (1) the increased prosperity of the Gulf region (increasing the total pool of GCC liquidity) and (2) the resulting accumulation of savings and wealth by Shariah-inclined customer segments within the market. Prior to the oil booms of the 1970s, wealth

FIGURE   7.1

Increased Shariah Affinity Is Driven by Multiple Factors

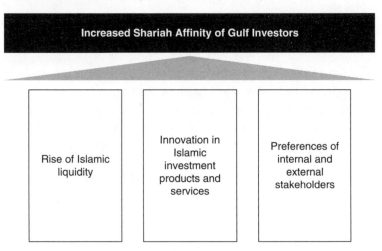

in the Gulf was fairly limited, and thus the total savings pools were relatively small. Savings were particularly scarce within the mass market, a segment of the population with relatively high Shariah affinity. Wealthier segments of the population used conventional banks, either accepting interest-based terms or limiting themselves to Shariah-neutral transactions. Although some leading business families refrained from using banks altogether, a common approach was to keep savings entirely in non-interest-bearing current accounts. In fact, HSBC's former chairman Sir John Bond traced the origins of the bank's Islamic financial services not to the launch of HSBC Amanah in 1998, but rather to the bank's servicing of Muslim clients in the 1800s who specifically instructed the institution not to credit their accounts with interest, since interest was against their religious values.[1] The level and sophistication of financial services in the Gulf was historically quite low—a reflection of the scarce underlying wealth of the region.

Things changed rapidly, however, as the GCC boomed in the 1970s. Those who had previously had some level of savings suddenly found themselves with sizable amounts of wealth—wealth that triggered rapid changes in the financial services sector (including the introduction of a requirement in Saudi Arabia that banks must be Saudi-owned[2]) and fueling the development of Bahrain as a thriving offshore banking hub.[3] Those who had previously had no savings soon found themselves accumulating money and needing a place to keep it. Historically "unbanked" customers, many of whom were strictly Shariah-compliant in their personal lives and wished to be so in their financial activities as well, all of a sudden entered the market.

Driven mainly by increased retail demand for Islamic financial services, the share of Islamic assets as a percentage of the total banking market has increased steadily in the Gulf over the years. The exact size of the "Islamic" asset base is difficult to estimate, since it should rightly include the assets of Islamic banks, the Islamic assets of conventional banks, and assets held in Shariah-neutral vehicles by customers whose preferences are shaped by Shariah considerations. Nonetheless, signs of growing Shariah affinity by banking customers are apparent throughout the region:

- HSBC analysis found that the Saudi banking market became majority Islamic (in terms of assets) in 2005, fueled principally by retail demand.[4]
- A number of financial institutions in the Gulf have converted entirely from conventional to Islamic finance, including the National Bank of Sharjah (UAE) (now called Sharjah Islamic Bank), Dubai Bank, Kuwait Real Estate Bank (now called Kuwait International Bank), and Bank Al Jazira (Saudi Arabia).[5]
- The bulk of the major new banking initiatives in the region, including Al-Rayan Bank (Qatar), Al Hilal Bank (UAE), Noor Islamic Bank (UAE), and Bank Alinma (Saudi Arabia) are fully Islamic banks.
- Conventional banks have been steadily increasing their Islamic banking activities, with market leaders such as the National Commercial Bank (Saudi Arabia's largest by market share)[6] and the Saudi British Bank converting branches and retail operations to be fully compliant with the Shariah.

Some observers have suggested that the GCC banking market will be predominantly Shariah-compliant within a decade[7]—a projection that (except for Saudi Arabia) seems overly aggressive, considering the current rates of adoption of Islamic banking in the region.[8] Nonetheless, signs point to sustained interest in Islamic financial services for the foreseeable future.

The rise of Islamic banking has gathered pools of wealth—customer deposits, bank treasuries, and fiduciary accounts—that need to be gainfully mobilized in Shariah-compliant ways. While a considerable amount of this Islamic liquidity can typically be lent out in the form of Islamic financing (personal loans, home financing, and so on), much of it needs to be put to work through Islamic investments. This requirement has led to more and more interest in Shariah-compliant investments.

Innovation in Islamic Investment Products and Services

In the early stages of their development, Islamic financial institutions had a limited set of savings and investment offerings available for customers. There were few Islamic asset management firms, and those that existed generally were not suitable for the retail investor. At the same time, Islamic banks had fairly few savings products. The 1978 liability allocation of Kuwait Finance House, a pioneering Islamic financial institution, illustrates the types of savings vehicles available (see Figure 7.2).

More than two-thirds of the bank's liabilities (roughly speaking, customer deposits) were in the form of savings accounts, through which the depositor was entitled to a share of the profits from the bank's activities. Another 15 percent of liabilities were

F I G U R E   7.2

Kuwait Finance House Had Three Liability Products in 1978

Kuwait Finance House Liability Allocation, 1978

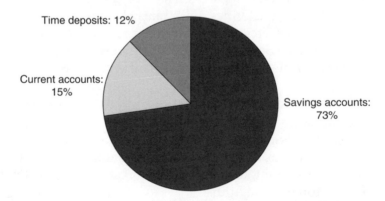

Source: Adnan M. Abdeen and Dale N. Shook, *The Saudi Financial System* (New York: John Wiley & Sons, 1984) and research team analysis.

simply current accounts—accounts from which the customer received no return and no risk of loss was incurred. The last category, making up 12 percent of liabilities, was time deposits—deposits that were less liquid than the other two categories but were also entitled to higher returns based on the investment activity undertaken by the bank. While these three core products may have been sufficient for the majority of mass-market customers, investors with more substantial amounts of wealth required a broader range of options for deploying their savings.

In the 1970s and 1980s, a number of Islamic investment companies [for example, the DMI Group and the Islamic Investment Company of the Gulf (IICG)] took root, offering financing to corporations and other institutions on the one hand and raising funds from banks and high-net-worth individuals on the other. The appearance of such investment companies gave wealthy Islamic investors a few more choices, but they still faced a highly constrained set of options. Besides placing deposits in an Islamic bank, investors could buy shares in Islamic financial institutions, invest directly in assets or companies that operated fully according to the Shariah, or participate in custom-made or syndicated investment opportunities (if the investors were sophisticated enough to do so). The vast array of investment outlets available to conventional investors was not accessible by Islamic ones.

Major breakthroughs occurred in the mid-1990s that dramatically expanded the universe of options available to Islamic investors. As illustrated in Figure 7.3, the number of Islamic equity funds introduced in the period 1996–2000 was more than triple the number introduced in the previous period, and after 2000 the number and variety of new funds continued to grow several times over.

The key breakthrough that enabled this expansion of investment options was a landmark set of Shariah rulings regarding investing in publicly listed companies. Prior to the mid-1990s, the consensus view of Islamic scholars was that investing in publicly listed companies that themselves used conventional financing (for example, a furniture manufacturer that had conventional debt on its balance sheet) was not permissible. The rationale for this was consistent with one of the Islamic finance principles discussed in Chapter 3 of this book: if undertaking an activity is considering immoral, investing in it should likewise be considered immoral. Equity investments by Islamic investors were therefore limited to companies that fully complied with the Shariah in their activities.

FIGURE   7.3

Breakthroughs in the 1990s Dramatically Increased the Options
Available to Islamic Investors

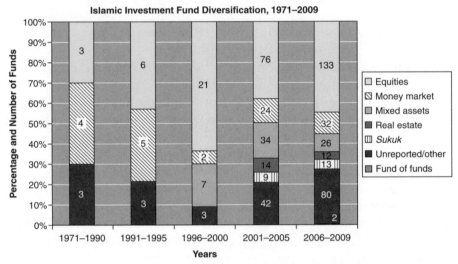

Source: Islamic Financial Information Service and research team analysis.

In the mid-1990s, based on an understanding that fully Islamic
companies "are very rare in contemporary stock markets" and that
"almost all the companies in the public markets are in some way
involved in an activity which violates the injunctions of [the]
Shariah,"[9] jurists began permitting investment in listed companies.
This permission, however, came with a number of conditions that had
to be met in order for the investment to be allowed. First, the company's core business had to be permissible—investing in a company
whose core business is gambling, for example, is not allowed.
Additionally, the company's use of conventional debt (as evidenced
by the debt-to-equity ratio of its balance sheet) must be within a
certain limit. Investing in a real estate company that relies heavily on
conventional debt, for example, would be considered impermissible
despite the fact that its core business was permitted by the Shariah.
Third, the company must not derive a significant portion of its income
from interest. Therefore, investing in an early-stage software company that has not begun generating sales revenue but collects significant interest from its bank deposits might be deemed impermissible.
Fourth, it is incumbent on the investor (or the investment manager) to

ascertain what portion of the company's income has been derived from impermissible sources and give away a corresponding portion of the investment income in charity. This process is referred to as "purification" in the Islamic investment industry, and it is a critical component of the role of an Islamic asset manager.

A Closer Look: The Spirit Behind the Ruling

The four guidelines pertaining to the Shariah screening of listed equities have become common practice in the Islamic investment industry, and are applied (in one form or another) by hundreds of equity funds and indexes like the Dow Jones Islamic Indexes. The 230 or so Islamic equity funds launched since 1995 have essentially been built on the ruling just discussed. Although the core guidelines previously outlined are widely communicated within the Islamic investment industry and beyond, some of the more subtle aspects of the rulings that allowed for listed equity investments are rarely discussed. These subtle aspects are, however, important in understanding the spirit behind the landmark rulings.

Justice Taqi Usmani, one of the most influential jurists in the Islamic finance sector, noted in his writings on the matter that a "Muslim shareholder should raise his voice . . . in the annual general meeting of the company" if the company in which he invests uses conventional leverage or collects a small amount of interest income.[10] This guideline reflects a spirit that the Islamic investor should (ideally) not be content with Shariah filters and "purification" of impermissible income alone—he should seek to influence companies to conform to higher ethical standards. In this sense, Islamic investors are expected to be ethical activists. Similarly, jurists insist that Islamic private equity investors who take significant stakes in companies (and are generally represented on portfolio companies' boards of directors) take greater responsibility for influencing the companies' activities. Commentators have noted that Islamic scholars allowed investing in listed companies as a stepping-stone—a measure that was necessary for the industry to develop—but intended to encourage a migration toward more Islamic balance sheets in investment-worthy companies.[11]

The ruling permitting investment in listed companies served as a major catalyst for the Islamic investment industry, and has had tremendous commercial benefit. That this ruling came with conditions and was intended (at least by some jurists) to be a stepping-stone rather than a destination is a prime example of a recurring theme: the delicate interplay between Shariah authenticity and commercial considerations.

Expanding Options

The wide range of listed equity funds now available to Islamic investors spans a broad range of strategies, including global funds, regionally focused funds, single-country funds, and sector-specific funds. In addition to the array of listed equity funds (which number well above 200 now[12]), the Islamic asset management industry also offers more than 25 real estate funds, more than 20 *sukuk* (fixed-income) funds, and 50 "money market" funds that offer liquidity along with Shariah-compliant returns. This proliferation of options is both a result of increased Shariah affinity (visible in the form of customers demanding Shariah-compliant equivalents to conventional funds in the market) and, in turn, a driver of enhanced interest in Islamic investments. As illustrated in Figure 7.4, there is a "virtuous

F I G U R E   7.4

Product Innovation and Customer Demand Form a "Virtuous Circle" for Islamic Investments

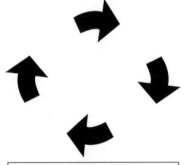

Product Innovation

• Expansion into new asset classes, regions, and modes of investment

• Critical mass formed to justify launching new products

• Enhanced value proposition and relevance to customers

Customer Demand

• Greater interest in Shariah-compliant investments

circle" by which product innovation and customer demand reinforce each other.

As managers expand into new asset classes, regions, and investment modes, their value proposition and their relevance to customers' needs increase. This builds confidence and acceptance among Shariah-inclined investors that Islamic alternatives do indeed exist and that they can prudently allocate some of their wealth to such assets. As customers grow more comfortable with Islamic investments, a critical mass of customer interest is formed to justify managers' devotion of additional time and effort to product innovation. For example, as a pool of customers became comfortable with Islamic listed equity funds, they naturally became more open to the idea of Islamic real estate funds. Many of them were already investing in real estate, but did not have Shariah-compliant vehicles for doing so. The interest of an early set of customers gave asset managers the confidence to launch Islamic real estate funds, which have now become common in the market.

As the cycle has continued, asset managers are continuing to push the boundaries of innovation. A number of fully Islamic private equity funds, managed by firms such as Arcapita and Unicorn Investment Bank of Bahrain, have been in operation for years and have been capitalizing on the region's growing interest in alternative investments. The US-based firm Shariah Capital has partnered with Barclays to launch a vehicle called Al Safi Trust, a platform that pursues an investment strategy akin to that of a hedge fund using Shariah-compliant methods to replicate the effect of short selling.[13] With each passing year, the range of options available to Islamic investors is becoming wider.

Stakeholder Preferences

Along with the rise of Islamic liquidity and increased product innovation, a third key driver that has fueled the trend toward Shariah affinity is the shifting preferences of a wide range of stakeholders. As families have grown and a new generation of leaders has emerged, there is a growing expectation (at least among some younger leaders) that there need not be a trade-off between financial returns and conforming to the Shariah. A generation that has grown up witnessing the rise of Islamic finance increasingly expects to be able to conduct its financial matters with world-class results without having to compromise on its ethical values. As this generation assumes greater authority in family businesses and investment vehicles, one can expect to see an ongoing shift toward Islamic investments at the family level.

Ernst & Young (E&Y), in a 2008 study of the Islamic investment sector, sought to quantify the preferences of Muslim customers for Shariah-compliant investment products. Its analysis found that only 20 percent of the market is willing to accept substantially lower returns in exchange for a product's being Shariah-compliant. A full 40 percent of the market, however, was found to prefer Shariah-compliant products if they perform equally as well as conventional ones. Given the choice between two otherwise identical offerings, these investors will choose an Islamic one. Another 30 percent of the market was found to be (in E&Y's terms) "value-seekers" who will choose the asset with the highest return without a preference for Shariah compliance. Only 10 percent was found to actually prefer conventional finance as a matter of principle.[14]

For institutions that are public-facing or otherwise have a broad range of stakeholders, moral pressure to shift toward Islamic finance and investments can be substantial. Increasingly, decision makers and business owners in the Gulf are asked "awkward" questions by customers, staff, and other stakeholders: Is your company Shariah-compliant? If it isn't, why not? Aren't there Islamic alternatives available for what you currently do conventionally?

Years ago, the chief executive of a major Gulf institutional investor confided to me his experience with these pressures. In his personal life, he was a practicing Muslim and supported Islamic finance. In his fiduciary role, however, he invested a massive pool of assets in conventional instruments. He, like other leaders of institutional investors, was not yet convinced that Islamic alternatives could meet his institution's investment needs. He reported, however, that beneficiaries of the assets he managed—the general public of his country—were increasingly asking whether the institution was investing in line with the Shariah. These questioners wanted assurance that they were not benefiting from investments that violated their personal ethics. The executive was struck by these questions, and expected that they would increase in number over time. Hence, his institution might face more and more pressure to make Islamic investments.

As Islamic financial services become increasingly common in the Gulf, stakeholders' comfort with them is likely to grow. As suggested by E&Y's analysis, a full 60 percent of Muslim customers either insist on Islamic investments or prefer them when given the option. For a business owner, this could mean that 60 percent of her customers, staff, and suppliers increasingly favor Islamic finance and investments. This shift in preferences could lead more and more institutions to replace their conventional investments with Islamic equivalents (where such equivalents are available).

MEETING THE DEMAND

The demand for Islamic investments has been met by a wide range of financial institutions, asset managers, and investment firms. It has now become commonplace in the Gulf (especially in Saudi Arabia) for conventional institutions to offer Islamic investment products to their customers. Often these are created to match conventional offerings in the same or a similar asset class. In addition, conventional firms are often opting to launch only an Islamic version of a new fund, recognizing that Shariah-inclined customers will not accept a conventional fund, whereas conventional investors will typically accept attractive Islamic products.

The region's increasing affinity for Shariah-compliant investments has spawned the creation of a number of fully Islamic investment management and principal investment firms. Table 7.1 provides a sampling of a few of these fully Islamic players.

Fully Islamic investment firms face a set of advantages and drawbacks similar to that faced by fully Islamic banks when competing with conventional institutions. Islamic firms enjoy specialist capabilities, access to Shariah-inclined shareholders, and greater perceived authenticity in the marketplace. They can, at times, also enjoy an advantage when sourcing investment opportunities from strongly Shariah-inclined sellers. Conventional firms, in contrast, often enjoy more established brands and track records, have easier access to world-class talent, and have access to global networks of affiliated institutions.

REALITY CHECK: SIGNIFICANT GAPS REMAIN

Although the Islamic investment industry has made significant progress in its development, it's crucial to note that significant gaps in the industry's offerings and capabilities remain. As illustrated in Figure 7.5, its relative maturity is much greater in certain asset classes than it is in others, and not all asset classes have fully arrived.

Listed equity and real estate are two asset classes in which the Islamic investment industry can claim substantial depth: as noted earlier, there are hundreds of Islamic equity funds and dozens of real

TABLE 7.1

Selected Fully Islamic Investment Firms

Firm	Country	Year Established	Area of Focus
Arcapita (formerly First Islamic Investment Bank)	Bahrain	1997	Principal investments in developed markets
Global Investment House	Kuwait	1998	Asset management, investment banking, and brokerage in GCC and wider MENA regions
International Investment Bank	Bahrain	2003	Private equity, real estate, and asset management in regional and international markets
Unicorn Investment Bank	Bahrain	2004	Investment banking and private equity in wider MENA and international markets
Al Imtiaz Investment	Kuwait	2005	Investment advisory, asset management, and private equity in Kuwait and MENA region
Ryada Capital Investment Co.	Kuwait	2005	Asset management and advisory services in GCC and international markets
Venture Capital Bank	Bahrain	2005	Venture capital–based investment bank in GCC and MENA markets
Jadwa Investment	Saudi Arabia	2006	Advisory and principal investments in GCC and global markets
Seera Investment Bank	Bahrain	2006	Equity investment management in GCC region and global markets
Prosperitus Capital Partners	London	2007	Private equity and alternative investments advisory services in emerging-market real estate and infrastructure projects

estate funds available. For the portion of an investor's portfolio that is allocated to listed equities (which can be substantial) and to real estate (which is typically fairly limited), a reasonably full set of Islamic options can be found.

Structured products and cash management are asset classes in which the industry has substantial experience but is still maturing. Term deposits that replicate short-term Treasury bills have long been used as a simple technique for cash management. Islamic institutions often also provide their private banking and corporate clients with structured products with a bit more complexity to meet specific needs.

F I G U R E   7.5

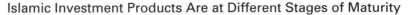

Islamic Investment Products Are at Different Stages of Maturity

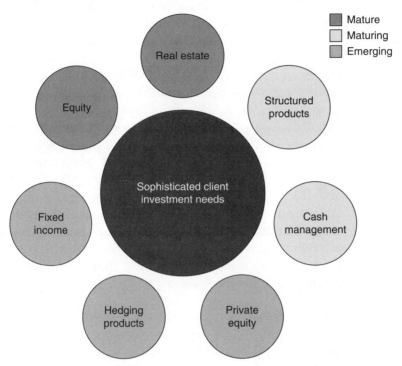

Compared to their conventional counterparts, however, the Islamic equivalents would rightly be considered far less mature. First, the depth and breadth of the offerings is far less than can be found at conventional institutions. In addition, the complexity involved in these transactions (as well as the need for certain processes to be conducted manually by bank staff) makes them markedly more cumbersome than their conventional equivalents. The basic need may be met today, but more sophisticated solutions are in order as the industry develops.

Alternative asset classes (other than real estate), such as private equity and hedging products, are emerging today. An increasing number of offerings exists, although many of them have yet to experience a full cycle of capital raising, investment, and realizing returns. As they do so, customer confidence in these asset classes can be built and further development can be enabled.

A final—and quite substantial—gap in the Islamic investment universe is the scarcity of fixed-income equivalents. This is a major challenge for the industry, especially since sophisticated investors customarily have significant allocations in their portfolios for fixed income. Although the Islamic Financial Information Service (IFIS reports that more than 20 *sukuk* (bond-equivalent) funds have been launched since 2001,[15] this is a relatively small number in light of the potential demand for such instruments. In addition, the scarcity of *sukuk* issuances has prevented the development of substantial secondary markets for these securities. *Sukuk* investors typically hold on to their securities, since they do not see many alternatives in the market. Another complication arises from differing Shariah standards regarding *sukuk* transactions—differences that cause many Gulf investors to deem the majority of Malaysian *sukuk* impermissible.

One trend that is helping to expand the *sukuk* market is increased interest by Gulf institutions in including *sukuk* tranches in their large-scale debt-raising initiatives. In 2006, the Saudi industrial giant SABIC had an $800 million *sukuk* issuance. The transaction was a major landmark both in its size and in the fact that the *sukuk* certificates were tradable and therefore set a benchmark.[16] The Al-Waha Petrochemical Company, another major Saudi enterprise, included significant Islamic tranches in debt facilities for two major projects called Rabigh and Yansab. Together, the projects included nearly $15 billion in total debt, of which a sizable portion was Islamic.[17] Project finance lends itself to *sukuk* and Islamic facilities, since Shariah guidelines call for the identification of specific assets like the ones required in the context of major projects.

Recognizing the current gaps in the Islamic investment industry provides an important reality check for both observers and participants. Today, it is difficult for the Islamic investment industry to assert that it can fully meet all the needs of sophisticated investors. Until this assertion can be credibly made, the industry will find it challenging to attract the large pools of institutional capital that can propel the Islamic investment space forward.

IMPACT ON ASSET VALUES AND CAPITAL STRATEGIES

Although Islamic investments continue to be a minority of total assets, the rise of Shariah-compliant investments has started to have a measurable impact on asset values in Gulf markets. In 2007, a study by the government of Qatar found that companies that were publicly deemed impermissible by Islamic jurists suffered an appreciable disadvantage in market capitalization.[18] By not having access to Islamic investors, these companies had fewer sources of equity and thus lower valuations.

The Saudi IPO market provides concrete examples of how Shariah compliance can have an impact on retail investor demand. When a joint venture between Saudi Telecom and the UAE's Etisalat had an IPO in 2004, the offering was 51 times oversubscribed and attracted nearly 4.3 million retail investors—about a quarter of the entire Saudi population.[19] This offering was deemed Shariah-compliant by the population, and therefore there were no Shariah barriers to participation.

When the National Company for Cooperative Insurance (NCCI), a conventional insurance company, had its IPO, the offering was also oversubscribed—but only 11.5 times. When asked about the general public's hesitation to participate in the insurer's IPO, NCCI's chairman noted that "insurance is a matter of controversy among *ulema* [Islamic jurists]," and therefore it was not expected that as many Saudis would feel comfortable participating in the investment.[20] It has become widely acknowledged that noncompliant offerings will not find as broad a base of retail investors as Islamic offerings will.

This is not, however, to say that noncompliant issuance has been abandoned. Despite statements deeming its shares impermissible, Kingdom Holding Company held an IPO to which 1.3 million Saudi retail investors subscribed (about a third of the number that subscribed to the Saudi Etisalat IPO).[21] The experience of Shariah-compliant offerings merely suggests that far more investors will participate if they know that an IPO complies with Islamic law.

The Gulf's appetite for Shariah-compliant offerings is also affecting the capital-raising strategies of companies outside the region. The US-based firm East Cameron Partners became the first US company to issue *sukuk* when it issued an Islamic bond offering in 2006. An advisor from a firm that helped arrange the deal alongside Merrill Lynch explained the rationale for the offering as follows: "An Islamic bond would be easily placed with conventional investors, which can widen the investor base, whereas the opposite isn't true."[22] Just as Gulf firms are leaning toward Islamic structures to fully tap into the GCC market, companies outside the region see Shariah compliance as an important feature in developing offerings in which they hope to include Gulf investors.

INSTITUTIONAL APPETITE: A POTENTIAL TRANSFORMATION

Although the Islamic investment industry has achieved meaningful scale, large institutional investors remain a major untapped market. As discussed in Chapter 2, four key segments of the institutional landscape can be identified in the Gulf: generalist sovereign wealth funds (better characterized as "trusts"), specialist government investment vehicles, private institutions, and private investment houses. Of these categories, two have begun showing a significant interest in Islamic investments: private institutions (especially a set of leading business families) and private investment houses (especially those created specifically for Islamic investments). While the precise proportion of sovereign wealth funds and specialist investment vehicles placed in Islamic assets is not public information, these institutions are understood to hold predominantly conventional portfolios, with relatively few Islamic investments.

The executives leading these large institutional investors have had good reasons for not limiting themselves to Islamic investments. As we have discussed, the Islamic investment industry has not yet developed the breadth and depth of options required by sophisticated investors. Furthermore, even when launched by well-established firms, Islamic funds customarily lack the kind of long track records that institutional investors demand. In addition, senior leaders of these institutions may personally have little direct experience with Islamic investments and probably built their careers at a time when the Islamic financial services industry was very much a niche player. As I have repeatedly seen in discussions with senior leaders, the ethic of upholding a fiduciary responsibility—to use the best means available to protect and grow national assets—has overridden concerns related to Shariah compliance.

As Islamic investments have grown more sophisticated, however, their applicability to major institutional investors has grown. A number of governments and sovereign entities in the region have directly invested in Islamic financial institutions (through Shariah-compliant structures, of course), recognizing Islamic finance as a growth area. As stakeholders and the general public become more comfortable with Islamic finance, they are likely to exert greater pressure on sovereign institutions to explore Islamic investments. One key trend to watch will be whether the expansion of consultative bodies, chambers of commerce, and parliaments (like those of Bahrain and Kuwait) will influence policy makers' perspectives on Islamic investments. If popular sentiment continues to incline toward Shariah compliance and this sentiment is carried forward by representatives, we could witness increased institutional attention to Islamic investments.

In contemplating Islamic investments, it is crucial that decision makers and observers keep in mind that Islamic investments are not an asset class of their own. They are not like equities, fixed income, alternative assets, and other asset classes, which are mutually exclusive and require an adjustment of other asset classes' allocations in order to fit. Shariah compliance is merely a filter than can be applied to all these asset classes. There need not be, for example, a separate allocation for "Islamic listed equity funds" as distinct from "listed equity funds" in general—rather, a portion of the listed equity allocation can be transferred into Islamic holdings. The same applies for all other asset classes; managers can work within the existing allocation models and simply scan for Islamic investments as alternatives to conventional ones. Therefore, making the transition to more Islamic portfolios may not be as disruptive as one might otherwise imagine.

The transformative impact that a shift in institutional preferences would have on Islamic investments is tremendous. To appreciate the magnitude of such a shift, consider the relative size of the Islamic investment industry compared to the scale of Gulf institutional investors. Standard & Poor's (S&P) has estimated the global Islamic asset base to be about $700 billion[23]—less than the estimated assets of the Abu Dhabi Investment Authority (ADIA) alone. Based on McKinsey Global Institute estimates and other analyses, we might estimate that Gulf sovereign wealth funds hold roughly $1.5 trillion in assets—twice the size of the entire Islamic industry. Therefore,

- If Gulf sovereign wealth funds were to place a modest 10 percent of their assets in Islamic investments, the Islamic investment asset base could grow by more than 20 percent.
- If they were to shift to 25 percent Islamic, the asset base could grow by more than 50 percent.

It would require Gulf sovereign wealth funds to invest only half their assets in Islamic vehicles (a figure that appears highly unrealistic today but that is useful for illustration) for the Islamic asset base to double. The fact that GCC sovereign assets will continue to grow as a result of both capital appreciation and infusions of new funds generated by budget surpluses could accelerate the growth of Islamic investments significantly.

Cultivating an institutional appetite for Shariah-compliant investments by the largest Gulf investors is a daunting challenge for the Islamic investment industry, and will remain so for the foreseeable future. The potentially transformative impact of capturing even a small piece of that enormous pie, however, makes this challenge a top priority for the industry.

KEY LESSONS

- While Gulf investments remain predominantly conventional, *increasing Shariah affinity* is a key trend among the region's investors.

- The *rise of Islamic liquidity, innovation in Islamic investment products, and shifting preferences of Gulf stakeholders* have been the key factors contributing to the trend toward Shariah-compliant investments.

- Islamic investment products have matured substantially, but *asset classes are at differing stages of maturity*, and meeting all the needs of sophisticated investors is a challenge.

- The preference for Shariah compliance has begun to *have an impact on asset prices in the region and capital-raising strategies beyond it.*

- The GCC's largest *institutional investors remain a mainly untapped market for Islamic investments* and could have a transformative impact on the industry.

8

CHAPTER

Lifting the Curtain: Heightened Visibility and Transparency of Gulf Investors

In American politics, we have an expression that's used in discussing highly confidential matters: "Those who know aren't talking, and those who are talking don't know." When it comes to highly sensitive information, those who are entrusted with it are careful not to disclose it publicly, despite the speculation and commentary of analysts. Sometimes the analysts get it right and sometimes they don't, but they rarely have full information.

A culture of "portfolio privacy" reminiscent of the spirit just described has been the norm for Gulf investors and advisors for decades. Executives leading the region's institutional investors, especially the largest ones, have diligently guarded the privacy of their portfolios. Asset managers and advisors have similarly protected client confidentiality, being well aware that if they disclosed private information, they would run the risk of spoiling valuable relationships. The world, and especially its most sophisticated financial players, has long understood that Gulf investors hold substantial portfolios and exercise substantial muscle. The details of their activities, however, have generally not been shared publicly.

As Gulf capital has evolved, however, there has been an increasing shift toward visibility and transparency. Partly, this shift has been driven by the evolution of Gulf portfolios to include asset classes and investment modes in which greater disclosure is the norm. In addition, the institutional attributes of Gulf investor bodies—especially newly created government investment vehicles and private investment houses—increasingly lend themselves to disclosure and transparency. Third, external pressures (both formal and informal) have called for increased disclosure, and these pressures are being taken seriously in the region. Together, these factors contribute to the trend toward heightened visibility and transparency.

This chapter begins with an assessment of the core reasons why Gulf institutions have historically preferred privacy, and why many still do so today. Next, we turn to the fundamental forces driving toward higher profiles and greater disclosure for Gulf investors. We then explore the example of the Abu Dhabi Investment Authority (ADIA) and the measures it has taken in recent years (including the multilateral "Santiago Principles" adopted by a set of sovereign funds) to enhance transparency and disclosure on its own terms. In closing, we assess the outlook for ongoing increases in openness, as certain factors driving this trend may continue for the foreseeable future.

Gulf investors have long guarded their privacy; today, a number of them are becoming more transparent. The level and pace of this shift, though substantial, may not satisfy the desires of certain overseas observers. They may, however, take comfort in the overall trend toward openness and the fact that the drivers of this trend appear to be solid and sustained. One can also expect ongoing disparity between the disclosure practices of various categories of Gulf investors—a disparity driven by the institutional realities of these different types of firms.

ATTRIBUTES OF OPENNESS

To understand the culture of portfolio privacy that has historically marked Gulf institutions, it's worthwhile to explore, in general, the attributes that cause institutions to disclose their investment activities and the associated results. As highlighted in Table 8.1, in the past, these attributes have generally had limited applicability in the Gulf Cooperation Council (GCC) context, but they are becoming more relevant today.

T A B L E   8.1

The Core Attributes Promoting Disclosure Have Historically Had
Limited Relevance to the Gulf Context

	Relevance in GCC Context	
Attribute	**1970s–Mid-2000s**	**Mid-2000s and Beyond**
Dependence on a broad base of stakeholders	Low	Moderate
Competition for additional capital	Low	Moderate
Competition for target assets	Low	Moderate
Requirements of home regulators	Low	Moderate
Requirements of portfolio companies' regulators	Moderate	High

A first and highly fundamental attribute that generally drives investors toward disclosure is dependence on a broad base of stakeholders. Investing entities must of necessity report their activities and results to the parties that make their investments possible—shareholders (in the case of companies) or investors (in the case of funds and other investment vehicles). In the case of government-related entities, there are parliaments, oversight bodies, and other governing agencies. When the set of stakeholders is large, information that is reported to shareholders or investors inevitably becomes public information, making public disclosure a natural (and efficient) way to reach the stakeholders.

Consider, for example, the case of famed investor Warren Buffett. Buffett's investment approach and philosophy are well chronicled and widely followed, inspiring books with titles like *Warren Buffett Speaks: Wit and Wisdom from the World's Greatest Investor*[1] and *The Warren Buffett Way.*[2] The annual letter that he writes to investors is read worldwide, and the core investment principles that he espouses have become the bedrock for the "value investing" philosophy. Investors flock to the annual general meeting of his company, Berkshire Hathaway, which has become such an elaborate event that the company issues a full Visitor's Guide, complete with seating rules (for example, guidelines on saving seats for others and on a newly established "Student Section" for observing the goings-on).[3] Buffett's investment activities are public information no more than a quarter after they occur.

There is, however, a key structural reason why Buffett is so open: Berkshire Hathaway is a publicly traded company with 1.5 million shares outstanding and a share price (as of mid-2009) of well above $100,000 per share.[4] Even if Buffett wanted to keep Berkshire's portfolio details private, he could not do so—disclosure requirements for public companies are too stringent. In addition, his often unconventional approach (for example, not allowing splits in Berkshire's Class A shares and therefore keeping the price of one share so high) requires explanations to shareholders if he is to keep the shareholders' confidence.

Historically, GCC-based investors have had only a small number of stakeholders on whom they have relied for support. Sovereign entities rely on government support, and decision making has generally been limited to a small circle of participants. In the private sector, family entities have generally protected their privacy carefully. Investment houses have had relatively small circles of investors behind them and therefore have been able to keep their performance information relatively private. Thus, the attribute of multiple stakeholders has often not been applicable to Gulf institutions.

Recently, however, stakeholder bases have been expanding. This is especially true in the case of entities that have raised (or prepared to raise) equity or debt from external sources. Prince Alwaleed Bin Talal's Kingdom Holding, for example, has taken on a significant burden of disclosure by floating 5 percent of the company in a 2007 IPO. Although it is still controlled by Alwaleed, the entity might (based on the 1.3 million Saudis who subscribed to the IPO) have more than 1 million minority shareholders today—all of whom are entitled to a significant amount of information about the company under Saudi capital markets laws.[5] In 2008, the UAE government-linked investment vehicle Mubadala secured a credit rating[6]—an important step toward being able to raise external debt funding directly. If and when Mubadala decides to float bonds or commercial paper, it will necessarily face more disclosure requirements than it will if it does not seek capital from stakeholders other than the Abu Dhabi government. Developments like these suggest that the stakeholder bases of Gulf investors may continue to broaden—a trend that will bring with it a higher level of disclosure.

A second attribute that typically leads institutional investors to disclose their portfolios and activities is competition for additional capital. The US investment house Fidelity Investments, for example, provides a virtual database of mutual funds on its public Web site—including more than 175 funds that it manages directly and more than

4,500 external funds that are available through Fidelity.[7] This information is critical to helping investors assess Fidelity's performance and the strength of its management capabilities—criteria that will drive investors' decisions as to whether or not to provide Fidelity with more capital to manage. Disclosure, therefore, is essential to securing more funds.

In the case of major Gulf investors, competition for additional funding has historically been more subtle. As discussed in Chapter 2, each Gulf state has its own process through which wealth generated by budget surpluses is allocated to different investment entities. "Generalist" sovereign wealth funds have been the default use of surplus funds after budgetary needs, central banks, and other bodies are adequately funded. If a generalist fund was seen as underperforming, the response of decision makers would be to adjust the fund's investment strategy or potentially make changes in its management; however, ceasing to allocate capital to the fund was generally not an option. In the case of private investors, the bulk of the surplus wealth was generally being created not through passive investment gains, but rather through businesses that were directly owned and that continued to deliver streams of profits. Thus, the investment arms of leading families were growing as a matter of course, not because they were winning the confidence of their shareholders—who were a limited set of family members in any case.

The rise of specialist investment vehicles (in the public sector) and investment houses (in the private sector) has had a major impact on the level of competition for additional capital. For Gulf governments, there is a wider set of investment options—generalist sovereign wealth funds are not the only choice. Specialist vehicles that perform strongly and exceed their strategic objectives may seek fresh infusions of capital as a consequence of their good work. When there are multiple specialist vehicles with similar objectives, a spirit of competition is likely to emerge. As discussed in Chapter 2, government-linked specialist investment vehicles are culturally more like private firms than they are like government entities. One way in which this culture manifests itself is in a competitive drive to demonstrate success.

Private investment houses in the Gulf—not unlike Fidelity—need to communicate their successes to the market continuously. It is, therefore, not surprising that firms like Investcorp, Abraaj Capital, and Arcapita speak publicly about their successful track records.[8] The details of how past funds have performed may not be publicly available, but this information can probably be acquired under confidentiality agreements if an investor is seriously considering placing funds with one of these managers. As competition among investment houses in the region intensifies, the need for them to disclose their track records and portfolio strategies—at least to limited audiences—will only grow. If investment houses begin seeking capital from public markets through listing on stock exchanges, disclosure requirements will rise dramatically.

A third reason why investors make disclosures about themselves is to stand out in the competition for attractive assets. Strong portfolio companies typically have multiple suitors who are ready to inject capital, and the highest bid is not necessarily the sole criterion for choosing an investor. The strength of the investor, its ability to add value to the portfolio company (particularly if a board seat is being given), and the overall impact of being associated with the investor are all factors that are considered when a portfolio company assesses the case for accepting the capital infusion. Unknown, mistrusted, or incompatible investors may have their offers rejected even if the price they offer is highest; conversely, capital with a strategic fit may be welcomed even if the investors' bids are somewhat lower than those of other potential buyers.

When Gulf institutions focused their investments almost entirely on Treasury bills, listed equities, and other "plain vanilla" securities, competition for attractive assets was not an issue. These securities are readily available on exchanges, and investments in them (when made in reasonably modest increments) have little or no impact on the market price. The price moves with demand, and strategic fit is not an issue. Since plain vanilla investments give the investor little influence over the direction of the company (unless a common stockholder accumulates a very large stake), portfolio companies need not be very discriminating in whose capital they accept. Gulf investors pursuing small stakes and conservative investments have not, therefore, needed to compete for prize assets.

As Gulf investments have become more sophisticated, however, competition for good assets has risen. To win out in private equity transactions, bidders often need to make known their strength and suitability as a partner. Although some Gulf entities (most notably Investcorp, which was making investments in US firms like A&W Brands and Tiffany & Company in the early 1980s)[9] were competing for prized assets long ago, many are only now throwing their hats into the ring in competitive situations. This trend is likely to lead more investors to speak about their strategies and track records in public, and it poses a particular challenge in the case of tight-lipped sovereign wealth funds that are seeking to engage in direct private equity investments (such as ADIA's investment in Citigroup). Specialist entities with more focused portfolios and shorter histories (and, therefore, fewer sensitive matters to disclose) may prove more effective in making high-profile investments going forward.

A fourth factor that has generally driven investors to disclose their activities is the regulatory requirements of home regulators. Publicly listed companies, for example, are required by their home regulators and the exchanges on which they are listed to provide thorough and timely reports on their business activities and results. In the case of investment companies, this naturally includes portfolio composition, investment positions, and gains or losses. Privately held companies and investment vehicles have generally been spared such detailed requirements, although income must be reported (on a confidential basis) to tax authorities, and the credentials and backgrounds of authorized investment managers are also made known. In the wake of the global financial crisis, calls for greater transparency of hedge funds and private investment vehicles have abounded and gained some momentum. The degree to which additional disclosure will be required remains an open question.

In the Gulf context, home regulators have historically had less of a need for disclosure by investors. First, the majority of the investment activity was being undertaken by sovereign entities that were directly controlled by governments. Governments were therefore been able to access whatever information they needed at will, without formal disclosure processes in the public domain. Second, even private investments had principally been undertaken by sophisticated investors and high-net-worth individuals—the retail investors who customarily require disclosure laws for their protection were not very active until the boom of the 2000s. Third, the bulk of the investments being made were either in overseas assets that were not governed by GCC regulators or in domestic companies and assets (e.g., real estate) that were already well in sight of regulators. Hence, specific investment disclosure laws were less necessary.

Recent developments, however, have heightened home authorities' interest in regulating investment activity. As more investment companies have gone public, reporting requirements on public exchanges have become applicable to them. Overall, Gulf regulators have found the booms and busts that were seen on local exchanges in the 2000s troubling and have instituted rules to help protect small investors. At the height of the IPO boom in the mid-2000s, for example, UAE regulators introduced requirements that companies have established track records before they could list on public exchanges.[10] This applies to both operating firms and listed investment companies. The more broadly investment firms draw on retail investors or shape the local economies, the more home regulation they can expect.

A final consideration, one that has typically been more stringent than the requirements of GCC home regulators, has been the requirements of regulators in portfolio companies' home markets. This has long been a significant concern—shaping, for example, Gulf institutions' preference for keeping their stakes in listed companies below the threshold at which they must report their shareholdings to local exchange commissions (often this threshold is 5 percent). Private equity institutions such as Bahrain-based Arcapita, whose investments are necessarily high-profile since they are controlling stakes, have long been mindful of how regulators overseas will perceive them. For example, Arcapita's 2005 rebranding (it was formerly called First Islamic Investment Bank) was reportedly motivated by a desire not to have its activities seen as having religious overtones.[11]

As the rules of overseas regulators evolve, Gulf investors will need to adapt their disclosure practices accordingly. As we shall discuss in a later chapter, however, regulators need to strike a delicate balance. Too little regulation may expose sensitive sectors to risk; too much may drive away much-needed capital and have a negative impact on asset values. Already a key concern of Gulf investors, the requirements of lawmakers in the countries where they invest will naturally have an impact on the extent and nature of GCC institutions' public disclosures.

INCREASING RELEVANCE TO THE GULF

As outlined in the preceding discussion, factors that generally influence institutions toward greater investment transparency are increasingly relevant to the GCC context. Figure 8.1 illustrates the three types of shifts that are driving a culture of greater disclosure among Gulf investors.

As GCC portfolios have expanded to include higher-profile assets, the need for disclosure has grown accordingly. This is particularly true for direct investments in Organisation for Economic Co-operation and Development (OECD) companies—investments like Mubadala's

FIGURE 8.1

Three Types of Shifts Are Driving Greater Disclosure by Gulf Investors

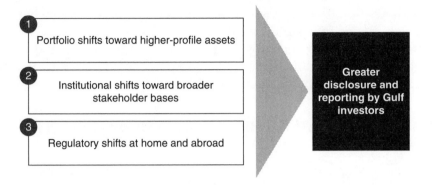

8 percent investment in US chipmaker AMD,[12] and two Kuwaiti firms' buyout of Aston Martin.[13] Gulf buyers and their portfolio companies, when announcing such investments, can expect significant attention and scrutiny from all sides. Increasingly, Gulf investors will need to exercise media savvy when positioning their investments in overseas companies. AMD's press release related to the Mubadala investment is a telling example—the company emphasized its ongoing US focus, describing its November 2007 deal as a "strategic transaction with the Advanced Technology Investment Company (ATIC) and Mubadala Development Company of Abu Dhabi, setting the stage for the formal launch of the world's only U.S.-headquartered semiconductor foundry."[14] Such positioning made it clear to observers that AMD would not be unduly influenced by Abu Dhabi and that it would continue contributing principally to the American economy.

The second type of shifts (toward broader stakeholder bases) is a natural evolution for many Gulf institutions. As families grow, more family members take on leadership roles in managing private assets, and information sharing becomes more formalized. In some cases, private institutions become interested in partial IPOs (like that of Kingdom Holding) as mechanisms for generating additional capital and also achieving a measure of liquidity for family members. In others, there is interest in raising debt capital through bonds, *sukuk*, or commercial paper—all of which require some level of disclosure. In addition, there continues to be an increase in the number and reach of private investment houses that rely on third-party funds and therefore need to make their objectives and successes known. Their increased market share may contribute to a culture of greater disclosure.

Third, regulatory shifts at home and abroad will continue to influence how Gulf-based entities report. As discussed elsewhere, at the international level, such shifts may be a delicate balancing act between attracting capital and enabling free markets, on the one hand, and ensuring the protection of strategic assets, on the other. Within the region, their scope is likely to relate to how broadly investing institutions affect the mass population.

ADIA AND THE SANTIAGO PRINCIPLES: TRANSPARENCY ON ITS OWN TERMS

A prime example of the migration toward greater transparency is the shift in disclosure practices by ADIA. In recent years, ADIA has undertaken both unilateral and multilateral measures to make its objectives and guiding principles better known. A close look at these measures can provide perspective on how other leading investors in the Gulf may position themselves in the years ahead.

In a March 2008 letter to the finance ministers of the Group of Seven (G7) industrialized nations, the IMF, the World Bank, the OECD, and the European Commission, ADIA outlined nine principles that guide its investment approach. These include acting as "predominantly passive investors" that take on "small stakes in companies that involve no control rights, no board seats, and no involvement in the management or direction of firms." The letter asserted that the emirate "has never and will never use its investments as a foreign policy tool," but rather that its investments "have always sought solely to maximize risk-adjusted returns." At the same time, ADIA made known its expectation of not facing discrimination: its letter stated that it was Abu Dhabi's intent "to ensure that financial markets remain open, that investors that play by the rules are not discriminated against, and that the regulatory process remains transparent and predictable."[15]

For those familiar with ADIA, the letter contained no surprises. The principles of passive investment, minority stakes, and noninterference were evident in ADIA's decades-long track record. The remarkable aspect of the message was not its contents, but the fact that it was sent—and that it was sent in such a public fashion. The act of sending the letter signaled that ADIA was taking the matter of public perception seriously, and that it wished to address it head-on.

Another sign of the priority given to the matter is that the person who signed it—Yousef Al Otaiba, then Abu Dhabi's director of international affairs—was later appointed the UAE's ambassador to the United States.[16]

Later in 2008, a multilateral working group of sovereign wealth funds (cochaired by an ADIA director) developed a set of 24 voluntary guidelines referred to as the "Santiago Principles."[17] Some of the key "Generally Accepted Principles and Practices" (GAPP), selected and categorized by our research team, are provided in Table 8.2.

With regard to disclosure, the Santiago Principles speak of "key features" and the "general approach," adopting the posture that the general public should know why a sovereign wealth fund (SWF) exists and what its general purpose is. More detailed reporting ("to the owner," importantly, with no reference to the general public) is also called for, but there is no explicit requirement that annual reports be made public. A number of the Santiago Principles (not included in Table 8.2) discuss the internal management of SWFs and their adherence to the best practices of institutional investors.

Investment objectives are generally expected to be maximizing risk-adjusted returns (a familiar theme from the ADIA letter discussed earlier), with an important caveat: investments can be made for other reasons as long as there is public disclosure of the underlying objectives. There is also a broad expectation that SWFs will act in a manner consistent with the norms of asset management.

In cases where there is significant economic impact on the market in which a SWF invests, the principles call for coordination with domestic authorities so as to serve the host country's policy objectives. The principles also call for SWFs to refrain from using privileged information to compete with private entities—a principle that presumably applies to both private investors at home and private operating companies in the host country.

Importantly, the Santiago Principles affirm SWFs' interest in exercising the ownership rights associated with equity investments. The principles see such rights as an integral part of the value of an SWF's investment, and they call for the SWF to exercise such rights in line with its investment objectives. Disclosure of general policies toward voting rights in public companies is called for, but there is no requirement that SWFs speak publicly about their specific stances on individual matters.

Based on the ADIA letter and the Santiago Principles, five salient observations may be made regarding the posture that sovereign

TABLE 8.2

Highlights of the Santiago Principles for Sovereign Wealth Funds

Topic	Principle Number	Principle
Disclosure of key features	GAPP 1.2	"The key features of the SWF's legal basis and structure, as well as the legal relationship between the SWF and other state bodies, should be publicly disclosed."
	GAPP 2	"The policy purpose of the SWF should be clearly defined and publicly disclosed."
	GAPP 4.1	"The source of SWF funding should be publicly disclosed."
	GAPP 4.2	"The general approach to withdrawals from the SWF and spending on behalf of the government should be publicly disclosed."
Quantitative reporting	GAPP 5	"The relevant statistical data pertaining to the SWF should be reported on a timely basis to the owner, or otherwise required, for inclusion where appropriate in macroeconomic data sets."
	GAPP 11	"An annual report accompanying financial statements on the SWF's operations and performance should be prepared in a timely fashion and in accordance with recognized international or national accounting standards in a consistent manner."
Investment objectives	GAPP 19	"The SWF's investment decisions should aim to maximize risk-adjusted financial returns in a manner consistent with its investment policy, and based on economic and financial grounds."
	GAPP 19.1	"If investment decisions are subject to other than economic and financial considerations, these should be clearly set out in the investment policy and be publicly disclosed."
	GAPP 19.2	"The management of an SWF's assets should be consistent with what is generally accepted as sound asset management principles."
Impact on host countries	GAPP 3	"Where the SWF's activities have significant direct domestic macroeconomic implications, those activities should be closely coordinated with the domestic fiscal and monetary authorities, so as to ensure consistency with the overall macroeconomic policies."
	GAPP 20	"The SWF should not take advantage of privileged information or inappropriate influence by the broader government in competing with private entities."
Ownership rights	GAPP 21	"SWFs view shareholder ownership rights as a fundamental element of their equity investments' value. If an SWF chooses to exercise its ownership rights, it should do so in a manner that is consistent with its investment policy and protects the value of its investments. The SWF should publicly disclose its general approach to voting securities of listed entities, including the key factors guiding its exercise of ownership rights."

Source: International Working Group of Sovereign Wealth Funds, press release, April 6, 2009; categorization by research team.

investors (and, to a degree, other Gulf investors) are likely to take in the coming years regarding public disclosure and openness:

- *A self-governing approach is preferred over external regulation.* ADIA's proactive approach in issuing its letter and the multilateral approach to the Santiago Principles signal clearly that sovereign entities seek to set their own policies. To them, this self-governing approach appears far preferable to external regulation.

- *A principles-based approach is preferred over a rules-based approach.* The Santiago Principles are not rules—they are guidelines. In a posture more akin to European reporting practices than to American Sarbanes-Oxley-type regulation, sovereign wealth funds seek to lay out a set of principles and a basic intent rather than precise and detailed rules. This approach gives them greater flexibility, and good faith is expected from all involved.

- *Investors expect accommodation of owners' stated objectives.* Sovereigns expect to have the right to set their own investment objectives. At the same time, the Santiago Principles commit them to stating their general objectives and investing in accordance with those objectives. In the event that an investment is made for noneconomic reasons, specific disclosure is expected.

- *Investors must show sensitivity to the impact of their investments on the countries in which they invest.* In the event that an investment has a significant impact on a host economy, investors appear to be committed to communicating the impact and working with the local authorities. This type of action is likely to be expected by local regulators in any case, and investors are well served by accommodating these expectations proactively.

- *Investors insist on protection of their decision rights.* Both the ADIA letter and the Santiago Principles reflect a willingness to engage in greater disclosure of objectives and collaboration with local regulators. At the same time, they insist that decision rights remain with investors. While they are willing to give out information, it is unlikely that major institutions will be open to ceding their right to make decisions about the entities in which they invest.

DIVERGING OUTLOOKS BY INVESTOR CATEGORY

As the practices of Gulf-based investors evolve, the prospects for greater disclosure and openness vary substantially among the different categories of investor. The greatest transparency can be expected from private investment houses. These firms have an incentive to make their successes known (in order to attract more capital), and many of them invest in asset classes like private equity, in which disclosure is necessary. In addition, as they draw more on public capital markets and retail investor funds, their home regulators will expect a higher level of reporting and public disclosure.

The next most open category of investors may well be government-linked specialist investment vehicles. These institutions tend to invest in high-profile asset classes in which disclosure is important. A number of them have prepared for raising debt (and perhaps, one day, equity) from external sources, which will require them to provide a reasonable level of information. In addition, subtle competition for capital allocations from governments may feed a desire to attract publicity and recognition as accomplished investors.

The greatest diversity in levels of disclosure may be among private institutions. Some will continue to guard the privacy of their portfolios, and the nature of their investment strategies may not mandate much public disclosure. Others will venture into asset classes that require a higher profile or even raise external funding, and therefore will need to reveal more about their activities.

Disclosure levels of generalist sovereign wealth funds, at least for the foreseeable future, may well be guided by the Santiago Principles discussed earlier. The Sovereign Wealth Fund Institute, a research body focused on the topic, issues a ranking of SWF transparency called the Linaburg-Maduell Transparency Index. In its January 2009 rankings, the top five SWFs in terms of transparency were Singapore's Temasek, Ireland's NPRF, the sovereign fund of Alaska (US), Norway's GPF, and the sovereign fund of New Zealand. Of the Gulf's sovereign entities, the UAE's Mubadala was ranked highest (ADIA and other UAE entities were further down the list), followed by the sovereign fund of Bahrain and the Kuwait Investment Authority.[18]

A review of these transparency rankings shows a correlation between well-institutionalized democracy and SWF transparency. The top five entities are all democracies, with institutions in place that publicly question public policy and the use of public resources. In such contexts, it is only natural that sovereign investment vehicles will need to report their activities and face scrutiny from numerous stakeholders. It's also noteworthy that Bahrain and Kuwait, the GCC states with the most active parliaments, are also the ones with the most transparent generalist sovereign wealth funds.

Therefore, the reporting practices of sovereign investors may well track the development of parliamentary, consultative, and other democratic institutions in the region. While each Gulf state has introduced such institutions in one form or another over the past years, their influence and decision rights vary substantially. The openness of sovereign wealth funds is not a question to be taken in isolation, but rather is linked to broader structural matters in the region.

Overall, the pattern of Gulf investors has consistently been toward greater transparency. The degree, however, to which particular institutions disclose their objectives, activities, and results will certainly vary based on a wide set of institutional and external factors.

KEY LESSONS

- Gulf institutions have generally maintained a *high degree of privacy in their portfolios*, as the characteristics of these institutions did not require much openness and disclosure.

- *Shifts in Gulf portfolios, institutional dynamics, and local and global regulation* have supported a trend toward greater disclosure among institutional investors in the region.

- Gulf institutions (particularly the largest ones) are likely to *adopt greater transparency based on a set of identifiable principles*. Importantly, they are likely to continue to seek to adopt disclosure norms on their own terms.

- Among GCC investors, the *outlook for transparency varies significantly* among the different categories of institutions based on the circumstances facing each category and organization.

PART III

GLOBAL IMPLICATIONS

9

CHAPTER

Tapping the Flow: Strategies for Attracting Gulf Investors

Sometimes we meet senior people who come in and think that at the end of a one hour meeting they will walk away with $1 billion. They underestimate our sophistication.[1]

— An executive director of the Abu Dhabi Investment Authority (ADIA), as quoted in *BusinessWeek*

In the latter half of 2008, a storied venture capital fund in Silicon Valley was struggling. After two cycles of dismal returns, and with the financial crisis having taken its toll on its usual limited partners, the fund was struggling to raise capital. In a conversation, one of the general partners remarked, "Well, how hard can it be? We have a 20-year track record; we should be able to get some money out of those Arabs." Not surprisingly, the fund failed to raise any Gulf capital and was shortly out of business.

Part I of this book provided a background on Gulf capital and Islamic finance and their rise to global prominence. Part II explored key trends that are shaping these phenomena and are likely to continue to influence their evolution. In Part III, we turn our attention to the implications of the rise of Gulf capital and Islamic finance for global firms—companies, organizations, and enterprises that may not be actively engaged with Gulf counterparties or

Islamic finance today. As these new global players have increased in importance, they have begun to influence global markets in ways that affect both firms that work directly with the region and firms that do not. As Gulf capital and Islamic finance develop as global players, their behavior will influence global markets and have an impact on a wide range of participants. One area in which the rise of the Gulf is playing a salient role is the field of raising capital.

Since publishing Dubai & Co., *I have frequently been contacted by non-Gulf companies that are seeking to raise capital from Gulf Cooperation Council (GCC) investors. Sometimes their strategies for doing so were thoughtful, well considered, and strategically sound. Other times, however, their postures have been like the Silicon Valley fund just discussed—brashly assuming that "Arab" investors would be soft targets for ill-conceived investment pitches. In reality, raising capital from the Gulf, like raising capital from any market, requires sound strategies and careful planning. This chapter provides frameworks and principles for crafting such strategies— and thereby avoiding the fate of countless firms whose propositions to GCC investors have fallen flat.*

We begin by reviewing the fundamental reality that Gulf investors are not monolithic, and therefore no "one-size-fits-all" approach to attracting capital from the region can work. Next, we provide a core framework for thinking through capital-raising strategies involving Gulf counterparties by understanding these investors' objectives, priorities, and portfolios as well as developing substantial and genuine relationships. In closing, we discuss a number of key principles related to fostering institutional relationships, building in-market presence, and engaging advisory firms with grounding in the region.

BEYOND "ONE SIZE FITS ALL"

In Chapter 2, we discussed the landscape of Gulf investors, dividing institutional investors into four broad categories. A key theme of our discussion was that Gulf capital is not monolithic, but rather that there is a rich and dynamic landscape of investors with varying objectives, sizes, and maturity. Considering the diversity of Gulf institutions, it is only natural that a diversity of approaches is required to attract Gulf capital. A "one-size-fits-all" approach will not work when the landscape is so varied and evolving.

Table 9.1 takes the framework that we discussed in Chapter 2 and extends it to the realm of "customary investment partners." Each category of Gulf institution has traditionally worked with different

T A B L E   9.1

Customary Investment Partners Vary by Category of Institution

Category	Objectives	Customary Investment Partners
"Generalist" sovereign wealth funds	Preserve and grow national wealth	• Massive global asset managers • Leading global investment banks
"Specialist" government investment vehicles	Grow national wealth through strategic investment	• Leading global investment banks • Well-established alternative investment asset managers • Select few regional and emerging-markets institutions
Private institutions	Preserve and grow private wealth	• Both global and regional investment banks • Well-established and promising new alternative investment asset managers • Range of regional and emerging-markets institutions
Private investment houses	Maximize financial returns for third-party investors	• Partners vary based on house objectives and region of focus • Most open to multifaceted partnerships with financial institutions • Possibility of conflicts of interest and competitive issues

types of external partners in identifying investment opportunities and making investment decisions. The differences in their chosen partners reflect differences in their overall investment objectives.

Generalist sovereign wealth funds (SWFs), as stewards of massive amounts of capital, are charged with the task of preserving and growing national wealth. As we have discussed earlier, these institutions can more accurately be called "national trusts" because of their wealth-preservation objectives and their conservative investment style. These sovereign entities have long partnered with the world's largest asset management firms—companies like UBS, Barclays Global Investors, Fidelity, Northern Trust, State Street Global Advisors, and other massive firms whose assets under management can often exceed $1 trillion. To put the matter of scale in perspective, if the Gulf's total foreign investments were managed by a single entity, that entity's assets under management would be as large as those of State Street or Fidelity and about three times those of Goldman Sachs.[2]

Partnerships with the giants of asset management are not surprising given the relative scale of SWFs. Only the world's largest asset managers have the capacity to absorb sizable chunks of a leading SWF's portfolio and manage the inflows and outflows of capital. Smaller firms simply lack the depth to take on meaningful portions of a SWF's portfolio. To put things in perspective, the largest SWFs in the region often will look at a public transaction only if they can invest a minimum of $500 million. At the same time, the SWFs themselves prefer to work with partners whose global reputations, strong track records, and stellar client bases are sources of comfort. Making safe investments is the most important job of a large sovereign wealth fund; finding safe asset management firms to support them is consistent with this goal. As well as introducing higher levels of risk, working with smaller and newer asset management firms would involve an administrative burden for sovereign wealth funds that might not be worth the effort for only a small piece of the overall portfolio.

Generalist sovereign wealth funds, by virtue of their size and importance, also have access to the world's leading investment banks and financial advisors. Investment banks with sizable asset management arms, such as Deutsche Bank, Citigroup, and JPMorgan Chase, are often able to expand their relationships with SWFs to span both asset management and other investment banking services such as advisory services. Besides generating substantial direct revenue, working with sovereign entities allows global banks to deepen their relationships with senior government officials and decision makers. This, in turn, can help the banks win lucrative mandates for government projects, privatizations, sovereign debt, and other financial initiatives.

For firms wishing to attract capital from generalist sovereign wealth funds, the most practical way to do so is likely to be through large asset management firms or leading global investment banks. Direct investment review by the principals of these SWFs is hard to come by, and the external relationships they have built are strong and well guarded. Rather than trying to break into the fortresses directly, it may often be more advisable to build ties with the relevant doorkeepers. Companies that do so may be more likely to attract a piece of generalist sovereign wealth funds' massive portfolios.

Two exceptional cases in which generalist funds have taken direct stakes in companies are the 2008 investments in Barclays by the Qatar Investment Authority (QIA) and in Citigroup by ADIA. In both cases, the funds invested directly rather than through asset managers or agents. Tellingly, however, both cases involved investments in global financial institutions that presumably already had substantive relationships with the sovereign wealth funds. In a way, the fact that these exceptional investments were made is further evidence of how important are the ties between the largest global banks and generalist sovereign wealth funds.

"Specialist" government investment vehicles may often have broader (although also highly selective) sets of investment partners with whom they collaborate in making investments. Like generalist sovereign wealth funds, they enjoy access to the world's leading investment banks for advisory support and a wide range of services. Leading investment banks see their relationships with specialist vehicles as highly strategic for largely the same reasons as they value SWF relationships: lucrative direct business and access to public-sector decision makers. At the same time, senior leaders of specialist government investment vehicles often have professional backgrounds in generalist sovereign wealth funds and therefore are able to carry over some of the external relationships that they built while working at the large generalist organizations.

More than the generalist funds, specialist vehicles are also likely to build relationships with leading alternative asset managers such as private equity firms, real estate investment firms, and other direct investment advisors. This is because the mandate of the specialist vehicles—to grow national wealth through strategic investments— inherently lends itself to alternative investment modes and direct investment. Diversifying local economies, building national capabilities in underdeveloped sectors, and serving other strategic objectives often require private equity investments, joint ventures, project finance, and other alternative investment modes. To execute these investment styles successfully, specialist government vehicles often partner with world-class alternative investment managers. The external partners provide government vehicles with access to investment opportunities, technical collaboration on due diligence and investment terms and conditions, and co-investment opportunities on large, capital-intensive transactions.

Reflecting this extensive collaboration with alternative investment managers, Dubai International Capital (DIC) reportedly placed about $400 million with firms such as Carlyle Group and Kohlberg Kravis Roberts (KKR). Investing in the funds of these seasoned pros was, according to the chief executive of DIC, "the quickest and most efficient way to be part of the club."[3] Abu Dhabi's Mubadala has taken its level of partnership further by buying a stake in Carlyle itself.[4] These measures show specialist government investment vehicles' serious commitment to building ties with leading principal investment firms—ties that entail more than just direct financial returns, but also involve the indirect benefits associated with being close affiliates.

Specialist vehicles may, depending on their mandates, also develop ties with a few select regional and emerging-market institutions. Vehicles created expressly for investing in local markets (such as a number of funds created for entrepreneurship or for small and medium-sized enterprises) find value in partnering with local banks and advisory firms that have access to local business owners. Similarly, vehicles that are making strategic investments in Asia, Turkey, and Africa often find merit in establishing ties with leading banks and investment firms in their target markets. In fact, one potential strategic benefit associated with the participation of Kuwait and Qatar in the IPO of the Industrial and Commercial Bank of China (ICBC) may be the access that a financial services asset firm provides in making other investments in China.[5] Although the investment in ICBC was made by generalist funds, they have paved the way for specialist vehicles to take strategic stakes in other sectors.

As with generalist funds, one way to access specialist vehicles' capital is through investment banks and other asset managers who partner with these vehicles. Doing so can add significant credibility to an investment proposal. Specialist vehicles do, however, also have internal investment teams that can assess proposals that are sent directly to them. In this respect, they are more accessible to corporations seeking funding. Crafting a winning proposal is possible if the proposal fits well with the vehicle's strategy and investment style. As we shall discuss shortly, an understanding of these matters is crucial to developing a robust capital-raising strategy for the region.

The category of investors that we have called "private institutions" is the most diverse category and has the largest range of institution types, objectives, and levels of sophistication. Broadly speaking, these institutions seek to preserve and grow private wealth and are generally family-based organizations. Some of these institutions' operating models blend elements of generalist sovereign wealth funds and specialist government vehicles, allocating a major portion of their assets to wealth preservation and stable growth and holding another portion of assets for strategic investment and above-market capital appreciation. Typically, the strategic elements of the portfolios did not come about through an asset allocation model, but rather consist of the core businesses through which the family has generated its wealth. In this sense, private institutions often act both as investors and as operators of family conglomerates.

This hybrid model calls for a relatively broad range of investment partners. Both global and local investment banks can serve as important partners, with the asset management and private banking arms of global banks often acting as the agents for diversified, passive international investments. As discussed in Chapter 4, private institutions in the Gulf are believed to be some of the most important limited partners (investors) in major global private equity firms. In fact, a number of global private equity firms are increasing their in-market presence in order to court Gulf investors more actively.

Local investment banks provide services to operating companies within the family conglomerates and therefore develop strong ties with the families themselves. Principals will often place a portion of their private wealth in local institutions that serve the businesses they own as means of gaining local and regional investment exposure and building deeper ties with service providers. Private institutions are also often themselves owners of local financial institutions—in the GCC, as elsewhere, major business families view ownership of a financial institution as an important element of their conglomerates' strategies. In Saudi Arabia, for example, major business families such as the Al-Olayan family and the Al-Hugail family take prominent roles in local banks. Reading the rosters of boards of directors for local banks, in fact, provides a fairly good indication of who Saudi Arabia's leading business families are.[6] In addition to owning banks, private institutions and families have been catalysts in establishing the region's private investment houses, investing in asset managers like Investcorp, Arcapita, Abraaj Capital, SHUAA Capital, Global Investment House, and others as well as investing in these institutions' funds. This leading role of private institutions in investment houses creates partnerships between the two categories, often making it possible to build ties with leading families by working with the investment houses they support.

In sourcing capital from private institutions, it is crucial to understand the decision-making processes and influences that shape investment decisions. While this is of course true for all categories of investors, private institutions may often have the most complex and multifaceted decision-making procedures. In extended family organizations, it is vital to understand the roles of the various generations and branches of the family. Since external advisors often play a key role, knowing who these advisors are and what their perspectives are is likely to be very important. An investment proposal that may seem to fit squarely with a private institution's apparent strategy and investment style may fail if it is offered through the "wrong" part of the organization or if the support of key decision makers is not solicited in advance. Similarly, proposals that may seem out of scope could indeed find success if they are championed by appropriate stakeholders in the institution or the family.

Private investment houses, the fourth category of Gulf institutions, also have a range of investment partners that varies widely depending on the house's strategy and region of focus. Managers of global equity funds will require relationships with international trading firms, custodians, and the like. Private equity firms with an Organisation for Economic Co-operation and Development (OECD) focus, such as Investcorp and Arcapita, develop deep ties with investment banks in the United States to secure access to deal flow and, where relevant, local financing. Arcapita has long maintained an office in Atlanta, Georgia, as a base for originating transactions and assessing US opportunities. The choice of a midsize city has proved to be prudent for Arcapita, enabling it to be a meaningful player in the Atlanta market rather than being considered a relatively small outfit in New York or London. By locating its US office in Chicago, Illinois, Bahrain-based Unicorn Investment has also chosen a city with broad coverage in which it can have an impact.[7] Investment houses that focus on the GCC and the Middle East and North Africa (MENA) region or on other emerging markets will build ties with local investment banks in their target markets. Especially for countries where corporate data are scarce and analyst coverage is relatively sparse (Central Asia, for example), relationships with investment banks are vital for getting an accurate reading of the market and of potential acquisition targets.

For private investment houses, relationships with financial institutions can be multidimensional and somewhat complex. Banks serving these firms are generally happy to provide market research, commentary, and analysis in hopes that this will lead to fee income through the support of due diligence and investment transactions. At the same time, investment houses are able to direct significant income to banks and other financial institutions through M&A advisory fees, transaction support, financing at the portfolio company level, and other such methods. Having preferred access to leading banks can help an investment house identify acquisition targets and add value to its portfolio companies more effectively, thereby delivering stronger results to its investors. It thus makes sense for investment houses and financial institutions to have multifaceted and deep relationships.

That said, there are also areas in which conflicts of interest or competitive tensions between investment houses and the financial institutions that serve them can potentially arise. Banks and other advisors may serve multiple clients with similar investment objectives, and they need to strictly guard each client's confidentiality. There also need to be fair and equitable procedures for determining which investment opportunities to share with which client, so that the investment houses feel that they receive adequate priority from the banks. More subtle, however, is a conflict that may arise because investment houses and banks are often pursuing the same institutions and families in raising capital for their funds or services. An investment house can, for example, be actively marketing a fund to a certain family while the private banking unit of the financial institution is actively marketing other funds and investment options to the same family. Conflicts and competitive tensions may, therefore, be an inevitable cost of the overall beneficial relationship between the two institutions. Anticipating, recognizing, and managing the conflicts are important to keeping the relationships healthy and transparent.

A CORE FRAMEWORK FOR DEVELOPING CAPITAL-RAISING STRATEGIES

Developing a robust strategy for raising capital from Gulf investors requires careful consideration along a number of dimensions. Figure 9.1 illustrates a core framework for developing strategies that are well grounded and more likely to succeed:

First and foremost, the proposition must be consistent with the core objectives of the institution being targeted. A highly compelling pitch for a fixed-income fund—no matter how strong the proposition is—is likely to fall on deaf ears if it is made to a specialist government investment vehicle or private investment house that is charged with making private equity and direct investments in companies. Once, for example, I was involved in marketing a direct investment (investing in a corporate entity) to the private equity team of a major generalist SWF. Though they were impressed by the proposition, the principals informed us that it simply did not fit with their mandate—all their

FIGURE   9.1

Robust Capital-Raising Strategies Must Address Four Dimensions

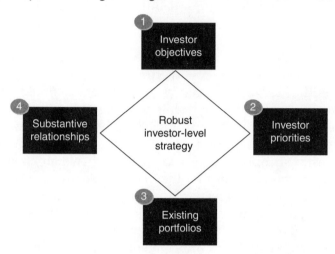

evaluation criteria related to fund structures rather than corporate vehicles. In situations like these, the best one can hope for is a friendly referral to another fund that might be a better fit.

Assessing counterparty objectives is a basic first step that one would expect any sophisticated firm to take. Surprisingly, however, companies often fail to undertake this research when seeking Gulf capital. Even if the publicly available information on an investor's objectives is limited, a simple first step is to understand which category of institution (per our Chapter 2 framework) the investor belongs to. Knowing the general characteristics of the category can enable a company to make more intelligent assumptions than lumping institutions together by region or by country. A private investment house from Kuwait, for example, may have more in common with the private investment houses of Bahrain than it does with the Kuwait Investment Authority (a generalist SWF).

A second crucial dimension to consider is the priorities of the investing institution. Although these are related to the investor's core objectives, they are not the same thing—it is possible for two institutions to have similar core objectives but very different priorities. The financial crisis of 2008–2009 has illustrated this nuance nicely. Certain specialist government vehicles (especially some Dubai-based ones) needed to shift their priorities to manage the consequences of having highly leveraged positions. Balance sheets needed shoring up through additional capital, consolidation, or the liquidation of certain assets in order to fund others. At the same time, other specialist government vehicles, especially those that continued to receive capital infusions in 2008 and 2009, have been able to use the downturn to actively invest in now-cheaper assets. Analysis by the Monitor Group suggests that during the crisis, the priorities of SWFs shifted toward emerging-market and nondollar investments[8] even though their core objectives have not changed. One reason why certain Gulf investors have chased "trophy" assets in recent years may have had less to do with their basic investment objectives than with an immediate priority on making high-profile acquisitions and thereby building their global profiles and reputations. Knowing what matters most at the moment can thus be invaluable intelligence for firms seeking to source capital.

Finding out an institution's current priorities—which are always shifting—can be more challenging than assessing the institution's overall investment objectives. The ideal method for doing so—when possible—is through direct communication and meetings with the investor. For firms that lack such access, public reports and interviews with the press can be a useful indication. Abu Dhabi, for example, has published *The Abu Dhabi Economic Vision 2030*, a comprehensive plan for the diversification of the Emirate's economy by the year 2030. In this document, the government identifies its immediate economic priorities and sets concrete goals in strategic sectors. For instance, the document expressed interest in strategic partnerships in pharmaceuticals, biotechnology, and life sciences: "This sector is still nascent in Abu Dhabi and to further grow it, the Emirate . . . would need to leverage its strong and diverse international relationships to attract the world's best partners."[9] Such statements are a clear cue to companies in these industries—and the advisors who serve them—to polish their investment proposals and bring them to Abu Dhabi's specialist government investment vehicles. Recent transaction activity is another key source for understanding shifting priorities.

Third, a robust capital-raising strategy must consider investors' existing portfolios and how the assets being pitched might fit with them. Hospitality companies seeking to raise capital, for example, can consider Kingdom Holding Company a likely fit based on Kingdom's existing investments in the Four Seasons Hotels, the Fairmont Hotels, Disneyland Paris, and other such assets. Offering assets that complement these companies—for example, a services firm that targets high-end business travelers—could also prove effective. Luxury retailers seeking growth capital can find a tried and tested partner in Investcorp, whose investments in Gucci, Tiffany, and Saks Fifth Avenue have been mentioned earlier in this book.

In the Gulf context, gaining clear visibility into investors' portfolios can be especially challenging. As discussed in Chapter 8, disclosure has historically been limited. The best way to overcome this challenge is through direct relationships with the institutions, through which selective information about portfolios may be shared. As GCC operating companies—especially those listed on public exchanges—raise their reporting standards, more information about their investment practices and shareholding can be obtained. Although business families will often guard the details of their investment activities carefully, they frequently insist on representation on the boards of portfolio companies in which they have stakes. Looking at the directorships held by a particular family can therefore serve as a rough proxy for understanding the family's corporate investment portfolio. In the case of investment houses, disclosure standards are much higher, since success stories are key to raising additional capital going forward.

Finally, a well-considered approach to building relationships with the investor is vitally important. For an investment proposal to succeed, it typically needs support at three levels of the organization: the principal/leadership level, the professional management level, and the analyst level. Principals and leaders are the ultimate decision makers and are largely concerned with matters of policy and strategy rather than the details of specific investment proposals. They can, however, choose to closely examine a specific opportunity and look at it in much detail. This is often the case in family institutions where the principals are savvy businessmen who built the family fortune through careful management of operating companies. I have, at times, been surprised by family leaders' appetite for detail on investment proposals, even when their management teams hold primary responsibility for due diligence.

The professional management level often includes a mix of local and expatriate executives charged with implementing the institution's investment strategy. Building relationships at this level is often comfortable for international firms, since their professional counterparts come from familiar backgrounds and similar business cultures. An investment bank that is pitching a proposal, for example, will often find an ex-banker sitting across the table at management-level discussions. In building relationships with these professionals, it's helpful to understand the executive-level goals and performance targets against which they will be measured. If a manager's incentives are linked to the number of successful transactions he leads, one can expect a fast pace of activity. If, instead, his main responsibility is to enhance the returns on existing investments, his enthusiasm for new deals may be limited unless the new assets help the existing portfolio perform better. Absolute return is generally an objective for all professionals; strategic objectives below that, however (such as opening up new markets or sectors), are important to keep in mind when interacting with them.

Analyst-level professionals (the ones charged with the detailed assessment of proposals) are often overlooked but are vitally important. Remember this: while analyst support can rarely ensure that a proposal will be approved, analyst opposition generally guarantees that a proposal will fail. Making the effort to understand analysts' perspectives, questions, and priorities can be very helpful in developing a winning proposal. If analysts vouch for an investment's merits, senior executives and principals are far more comfortable about allocating the capital to it. This level of staff should not be left out in building an institutional relationship strategy.

The four-dimension framework we have presented is by no means limited to attracting capital from Gulf investors. These principles are relevant in all capital-raising initiatives. In the Gulf context, however, each element of the framework has its own unique challenges and opportunities. Understanding both the conceptual framework and the realities of the Gulf are important for successfully engaging GCC-based institutions.

RELATIONSHIP BUILDING: FROM CORDIAL TO SUBSTANTIVE

Relationship building—something that is essential in nearly all business environments—is particularly crucial when it comes to attracting Gulf capital. First of all, interpersonal trust is paramount in encouraging principals to put their faith in an investment proposition. Furthermore, relationships are crucial for gaining insights into markets, organizations, portfolios, and priorities that are simply not discussed in public. In the Gulf more than elsewhere, market intelligence initiatives cannot be complete without relationships through which information can be freely exchanged.

In relationship-building efforts, it's important to avoid a common pitfall: misinterpreting Gulf hospitality as evidence of a substantive business relationship. Muslim and Arab culture—and particularly Gulf norms—considers hospitality to be a key part of good character. In a famous saying, the Prophet Muhammad is reported to have said, "Let he who believes in God and the Last Day [meaning the Day of Judgment] honor his guest."[10] There is a well-known expression (which rhymes in Arabic) that the essence of Islam is "good speech and feeding food" to guests and others.[11] In a word: hospitality.

Receiving hospitality is not, however, the same thing as having a real business relationship. Table 9.2 provides some general indicators of cordial ties—an important first step in relationship building—as opposed to substantive business relationships in the region:

On countless occasions, I've heard international businesspeople claim to have strong Gulf relationships based on being invited to dinners and gatherings in locals' homes (referred to as *majalis* in Arabic), having general business discussions, or receiving holiday cards. While all these things are good signs, they are more often reflections of Gulf hospitality and cordiality than signals of genuine business relationships.

Substantive business relationships include these courtesies plus more. One strong sign of a substantive relationship is the ability to discuss the challenges and issues facing the host's businesses or investments—such information is usually private and is shared only

T A B L E   9.2

Distinguishing between Cordial Ties and Substantive Relationships

Cordial ties	• Dinner invitations
	• Invitations to homes and evening gatherings (*majalis*)[1]
	• Discussion of market trends and general business environment
	• Written greetings on holidays and special occasions
Substantive relationships	*All the above, plus:*
	• Discussions of challenges and issues facing their businesses and investments
	• Disclosure of nonpublic information regarding their businesses and investments (e.g., portfolio allocations)
	• Requests to visit your office and participate in events that you host
	• Phone calls and visits on holidays and special occasions
	• Transactions and commercial agreements

[1] *Majalis* is the plural form of the word *majlis*, the term commonly used for evening gatherings in local homes.

when the host trusts you and believes that you can be of real help. When Gulf business leaders start sharing nonpublic information about their businesses, this is another signal that they consider your business relationship to be a real one and thus worthy of such disclosure. A third sign that a relationship has become substantive is when Gulf counterparties express interest in visiting your offices and participating in events that you host. This signals that they see value in an ongoing relationship and merit in the information and resources that you have to offer. Finally, when transactions and commercial agreements are entered into, a relationship is clearly substantive.

Migrating from cordial relationships to substantive ones can require a great deal of effort and persistence. Without sincere interest in—and genuine concern for—the counterparty, moving up the spectrum may prove difficult. The fruits of doing so, however, can be substantial. Furthermore, it's hard to move up the ladder if one does not realize that she is on a lower rung; thus, an honest assessment of cordiality versus substance is needed.

INCREASINGLY STRATEGIC TIES

In Chapter 4, we discussed how certain Gulf investors have increasingly sought strategic equity investments to complement their passive holdings in OECD assets. This trend reflects a general shift toward greater sophistication as well as a priority—especially among specialist government investment vehicles—to diversify national economies and develop expertise in key strategic sectors.

This trend has important implications for firms that wish to receive Gulf capital. For those GCC firms that are seeking to make strategic investments, nonfinancial benefits such as knowledge transfers, skill development, and benefits to the national economy need to be a key component of the investment proposal. Sometimes these benefits can capture the attention of senior leaders more than mere promises of high financial returns. As Gulf investors often see themselves as stewards of public or private assets, they are increasingly concerning themselves with the full range of benefits available to the stakeholders they serve.

Another manner in which the desire for strategic investments manifests itself is in an increased appetite for co-investment arrangements and the right to invest alongside world-class partners. This drive reflects Gulf institutions' eagerness to further develop their alternative investment capabilities and improve the range of investment opportunities available to them. In crafting proposals to Gulf investors, co-investment privileges in future transactions can be an important selling point.

POSITIVE EXAMPLES: AMD AND GE

In sourcing a minority investment from Mubadala in late 2007, US chipmaker AMD adopted an approach that reflected a number of the principles that we have articulated. In Chapter 8, we discussed how the press release and other public statements offered a high degree of transparency and reassurance that the transaction posed no security threat and was helpful to the US economy. From a capital-sourcing perspective, however, there are a number of other good practices that one can draw from the transaction:

- *Alignment of objectives.* AMD's partner was Mubadala, the specialist investment vehicle charged with alternative investments that diversify Abu Dhabi's economy and build strategic capabilities.
- *Fit with investor priorities.* Within the broad mandate of strategic capabilities, high-tech expertise is a key priority for both Abu Dhabi and Mubadala. Hence, AMD was a good fit with the investment vehicle.
- *Fit with existing portfolio.* Mubadala already had similar-sized stakes in leading OECD companies such as Ferrari. The Ferrari transaction—like the AMD one—sought to bring expertise and other strategic benefits to the UAE in addition to delivering a strong financial return.
- *Deep relationships.* In the announcement of the transaction, it was clear that the partners had carefully thought through the messaging in order to address the sensitivities of all stakeholders.[12] Such collaboration reflects holistic relationship building.

A more farsighted example of relationship building was the investment of $50 million by General Electric (GE) in 2005 to build a Technology and Learning Center in Qatar's Science and Technology Park. The center was envisioned as offering training to GE customers in the Middle East, Africa, Europe, and Asia, as well as undertaking research and development in key areas like oil, gas, and water.[13] At the center's announcement, Sheikha Mozah Bint Nasser Al Missned, head of the Qatar Foundation and wife of the country's ruler, noted the fit of the center with Qatar's development strategy. "Transferring the expertise and technology of leading companies to the Qatar population is an important part of our strategy and GE is showing that it embraces this vision."[14]

In *Dubai & Co.*, we noted that GE's investment seemed highly prudent, both for the direct output of the center (in the form of training and research) and—perhaps more important—for the goodwill it built with the government of Qatar. By 2008, GE's annual Middle East revenues had reached $6.6 billion.[15] While it's impossible to precisely trace the link between investing in relationships and generating revenue, one can expect GE's commitment to building goodwill to be a significant enabler of regional earnings.

IN-MARKET WHILE WORLD CLASS

As Gulf prosperity has grown, so has the presence of firms seeking to tap into the flow of GCC investments. Bahrain, the region's offshore banking hub for decades, has long been home to dozens of international banks. In the boom of the 2000s, global banks and financial institutions flocked to the Dubai International Financial Centre (DIFC) and the Qatar Financial Centre (QFC), free zones dedicated to financial services and offering access to the lucrative UAE and Qatar markets. As Saudi Arabia has made it easier for foreign institutions to own nonbanking financial institutions, a number of foreign financial conglomerates have deepened their presence there.[16] As noted earlier, the private equity firms KKR[17] and the Carlyle Group[18] have both opened offices in Dubai, and other investment firms are likely to establish bases in the region.

As more firms have set up shop locally, Gulf institutions increasingly expect to be serviced by professionals who are based in the region and have local expertise. Market developments in recent years suggest that servicing Gulf clients entirely from afar (which long was the norm when London-based teams typically covered the region) is no longer a viable approach in many industries. Besides banks, management consulting firms such as McKinsey, the Boston Consulting Group (BCG), Booz & Co., and others have established significant presences in the GCC. Thus, a degree of local presence is often expected in order to demonstrate adequate commitment to—and expertise in—the region.

That said, it is also crucial for global firms to continuously position themselves as being world class and able to bring in leading best practices from the world's most sophisticated markets. As an executive from a multinational bank once told me, the same Gulf-based clients would sometimes react more positively when he called them from his London office than when he called them from his offices in Dubai or Bahrain. Especially when the investment products or services being offered are related to global markets and overseas counterparties, a presence in the world's most respected financial centers is key. The challenge is to both signal commitment to the region and simultaneously show a level of world-class expertise that typically demands ongoing ties with centers like New York, London, and Hong Kong.

KEY LESSONS

- In raising capital from Gulf-based investors, *a "one-size-fits-all" approach will not work*—customized strategies are required.

- Various categories of Gulf investors have *different sets of customary investment partners* depending on their objectives and their regions of focus.

- In developing institution-level capital-raising strategies, *firms must consider four dimensions:* investor objectives, investor priorities, existing portfolios, and substantive relationships.

- One should *not confuse cordial ties with substantive relationships:* substantive relationships take time to build, are far deeper, and are marked by different types of interaction.

- While an *in-market presence is increasingly essential,* signaling world-class expertise and ties to leading financial centers are often also important.

10 CHAPTER

Follow the Leader: The Impact of the Gulf on Investment Strategies

Large sovereign wealth funds have become major players in private equity, not only as investors, but also as competitors.[1]
—David Rubenstein, a founder of the Carlyle Group

As discussed in the previous chapter, one way in which Gulf capital affects global firms' strategies is as a source of funding. In recent years, more and more companies—either deliberately or otherwise—have found themselves tapping into Gulf Cooperation Council (GCC) investors for funds.

The impact of Gulf investors, however, extends well beyond the specific companies in which they directly invest. Consider, for example, the transformative impact that a set of Gulf investors had on the valuations and partnership strategies of stock exchanges in 2007–2008. In 2007, an equity investment in OMX, a Nordic exchange, had been hotly pursued by both Borse Dubai and US-based Nasdaq. In a surprise move, however, a different Gulf-based buyer, the Qatar Investment Authority (QIA), acquired 10 percent of OMX and 20 percent of the London Stock Exchange (LSE).[2] The QIA deal had the potential to derail both Nasdaq's and Borse Dubai's chances of acquiring OMX. Borse Dubai responded by cutting a complex deal with Nasdaq in which the Gulf exchange would buy a 20 percent stake in Nasdaq and almost all of Nasdaq's 31 percent stake in the LSE. In return, Borse Dubai transferred all of its OMX shares to Nasdaq, allowing the much-anticipated merger between Nasdaq and OMX to finally proceed.[3]

By February 2008, when the dust from the deal had settled, the stock exchange industry had been significantly reshaped. The merged Nasdaq-OMX group, now the world's largest exchange company, operated eight major stock exchanges, with total assets in excess of $12 billion.[4] The merged group also included Borse Dubai as an important strategic investor. In London, more than 50 percent of the London Stock Exchange was now owned by Borse Dubai and the Qatar Investment Authority.[5] In the Gulf, as part of the strategic partnership, the Dubai International Financial Exchange (DIFX) was expanded and rebranded as the Nasdaq Dubai. Stock exchanges that had no direct involvement in the transactions nonetheless found themselves facing an evolved industry landscape and significantly changed valuations for the assets they had long operated. This complex web of transactions reflects the broad global impact of Gulf investment activity.

This chapter explores how the activities of Gulf-based investors are relevant to the strategies of firms other than those that deal with the region directly. First, we discuss how Gulf investment can signal a "rising tide" of capital flows through which asset values throughout a sector or a market are increased. Next, we discuss the growing role of Gulf institutions as co-investors alongside global principal investment firms as well as the competitive tensions that are introduced as Gulf investors place capital at multiple levels in the private equity industry. These developments have real implications for principal investment firms and companies seeking funding as they formulate their capital strategies. Third, we explore how operating companies in a wide range of sectors (especially those that are capital-intensive) are affected by the activities of Gulf investors as these investors fund companies operating in the same sectors. Understanding the activities of Gulf investors, we argue, is important for developing robust corporate strategies in certain sectors, even if a company conducts no business in the Middle East. Major operating companies, particularly in the banking, travel, infrastructure, and logistics sectors, need to be aware of the positions of Gulf investors in order to optimize their strategies.

EQUITY MARKETS AND ASSET PRICES: A RISING TIDE

The flurry of transactions among the QIA, Borse Dubai, Nasdaq, the London Stock Exchange, and OMX did more than just affect the industry structure; it also had a material impact on the valuations associated with these assets. When Nasdaq bought into OMX, it paid a price of Skr212 per share. When Borse Dubai made its investment in OMX, it paid Skr230 per share; and the QIA's price of entry was Skr260.[6] This represents a jump of 23 percent in value overall and—importantly—a 13 percent jump between the price paid by the first Gulf investor and the second. This rapid appreciation took place in a matter of months. The QIA's acquisition of 20 percent of the LSE for £633 million in September 2007 and the subsequent "bid fever" drove up shares in the LSE by more than 20 percent that very month and an additional 14 percent by October.[7] In the case of both exchanges, investments made immediately following the inflow of Gulf capital would have appreciated rapidly, if only because of the expectation of increased demand by similar investors.

The telecom sector is ripe with examples of ambitious Gulf expansion driving up asset prices across the industry. Three of the GCC's largest telecom operators—the UAE's Etisalat, Kuwait's MTC Zain, and Saudi Arabia's Saudi Telecom Company (STC)—have all undertaken extensive expansion plans that entailed pricey acquisitions. In May 2005, MTC Zain acquired 85 percent of African telecom operator Celtel for $2.84 billion,[8] giving the firm a substantial footprint in the region. Zain later expanded its African presence in 2005 and 2006 through further purchases in Madagascar, the Sudan, and Nigeria. Etisalat also has a major presence in the Africa through its acquisition of stakes in Zantel and Atlantique Telecom in West Africa. In March 2006, Etisalat acquired 26 percent of Pakistan Telecommunication Company Limited (PTCL), Pakistan's leading fixed and fixed-wireless operator, to strengthen its presence in populous markets close to the Gulf.[9] These transactions not only delivered value to the sellers but also increased asset values in the broader marketplace.

The race for acquisitions between Etisalat and MTC reached a high point in July 2006 during the auction of Egypt's third mobile license, for which Etisalat ultimately outbid MTC in the final round of the auction. Tellingly, no fewer than five Gulf telecom operators participated in the auction. As a result of this intense competition, Etisalat was forced to raise its initial bid of LE10.9 billion to a final price of LE16.7 billion, 17.6 percent higher than MTC's final offer. The "unprecedented cost"[10] of the license and Etisalat's commitment to pay double the required share of revenues to the Egyptian state led analysts to comment that "Etisalat has overpaid, leaving its newest subsidiary with more financial ground to make up . . . [and] years before it starts seeing profits."[11] Established international providers including Norway's Telenor and South Africa's MTN chose not even to exceed the LE10 billion ceiling with their bids, reflecting a crowding out of non-Gulf players from Middle Eastern and African telecom markets as a result of license and asset price inflation.

In some cases, Gulf buyers have had an impact on valuations across multiple sectors in a country. In Turkey, for example, GCC investors have been observed undertaking a widespread "investment hunt."[12] The flow of capital into the market began with corporate acquisitions. In 2005, Dubai-based Oger Telecom (owned by the Hariri family and Saudi Telecom) won the privatization bid for 55 percent of fixed-line operator Türk Telekom for $6.55 billion,[13] at the time the largest ever foreign direct investment into Turkey. Capital flows from the Middle East into Turkey increased from $43 million in 2004 to $1.8 billion in 2006,[14] and before the financial crisis, Dubai-based developer Emaar had planned to inject $5 billion of investment into Turkey by 2010.[15] This flow of investment has created an increase in asset prices in the Turkish market as a surplus of Gulf oil wealth chases a limited number of Turkish assets.

The impact on asset prices is most strikingly visible through the acquisition by the Saudi National Commercial Bank (NCB) of a majority stake in Türkiye Finans, an Islamic-style "participation bank" with $3.5 billion in assets. Following 11 other acquisitions in the Turkish banking sector between 2004 and 2007, including Arab Bank's acquisition of MNG Bank and Citi's acquisition of Akbank, NCB paid $1.08 billion for 60 percent of Türkiye Finans in July 2007.[16] At 5.9 times book value, the price "set a milestone in the Turkish banking sector by achieving the highest price-to-book value multiple ever,"[17] evidence of asset price inflation and multiple expansion in the Turkish market.

Arguably, observing the activities of Gulf investors can provide a clearer indication of a "rising tide" than comparable observations of other investors. This is due to two primary factors. First, Gulf investors tend to move in clusters, with one institution's moves closely following another's. To a large degree, the clustering reflects the reality that Gulf economies—and especially those of the UAE, Qatar, and Kuwait—share common characteristics and therefore common national and corporate development strategies. In light of these commonalities, interest in similar assets seems natural. The clustering is also, however, driven by Gulf institutions' close monitoring of one another and keenness to stand out within the peer group, leading at times to rivalries for the same or similar investment opportunities.

The second key factor enabling the rising tide effect is the volume of liquidity available to Gulf investors. Unlike other institutions with comparable wealth, GCC-based entities often have highly liquid port-folios that can easily be sold to provide funding for acquisitions. Gulf-based corporations (such as the telecom providers discussed earlier) tend to offer all-cash bids for stakes in companies, whereas Organisation for Economic Co-operation and Development (OECD)–based firms may be more inclined to make bids through a combination of cash and shares in the buyer. Sellers generally prefer all-cash transactions, giv-ing Gulf buyers a better chance of successfully completing the acquisi-tion. Thus, not only do Gulf institutions like to follow one another into sectors and markets, but they also have the means to do so in ways that influence asset prices meaningfully. Investors that are active in global markets, and especially those that are active in niche areas, would be well served to carefully observe the actions of Gulf-based investors as a signal of potential changes in valuations.

Gulf investors are rarely first movers in driving investment trends: Macquarie and Nasdaq both made offers for the London Stock Exchange before either Borse Dubai or the QIA, Citigroup had invested in the Turkish banking sector long before NCB, and Cerberus had started a trend of large capital investments in automakers before Aabar or the QIA. However, when Gulf investors do enter a market, they do so in clusters and with scale. The result of these clusters, "investment hunts," and strategic motivations has been a rising tide in asset prices in many of the countries and sectors entered by Gulf investors. This trend has the potential to benefit other investors who are positioned to take advantage of this rising tide where it is manifested in public equities markets and stock prices, but it may also crowd out interna-tional investors who are unwilling to pay the "Gulf premium" created by the clustering of Gulf investors in a particular market.

MULTILEVEL INVESTMENTS: STRATEGIC AND COMPETITIVE IMPLICATIONS

As discussed in Chapter 4, GCC-based investors have steadily increased their exposure to alternative investments as their level of sophistication has risen. This exposure has been expanded, especially over the past decade, using a number of different methods and investment approaches. Gulf investors' first forays into private equity have generally been as limited partners (LPs) in the funds of established private equity funds. The Abu Dhabi Investment Authority (ADIA), for instance, has by public accounts been an investor in Advent Central & Eastern Europe II (1998), Carlyle Asia Real Estate Fund (2005), and 3i Europe Partners V (2006), among a slew of other investments in private equity funds.[18] More recently, however, large Gulf-based investors have adopted a multilevel approach to private equity investments. This approach, illustrated in Figure 10.1, has strategic and competitive implications for other principal investors worldwide.

At the first level of investment, participation as limited partners in funds, Gulf investors have gained exposure to private equity returns while playing a passive role. As an LP, an investor typically makes no direct decisions about a fund's investments—such decisions are the sole right of the fund manager in its capacity as the general partner (GP). GPs customarily take advice from major investors through advisory panels, investor events, and other informal channels, but they reserve the right to make investment choices as they deem fit, limited only by the parameters defined in the offering documents to which LPs have subscribed. Investing as an LP is the standard method by which institutions—Gulf-based or otherwise—participate in private equity.

F I G U R E   10.1

Gulf Investors Have Adopted a Multilevel Approach to Private Equity Investment.

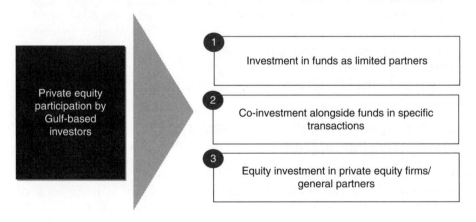

The next level of participation is through co-investment alongside funds in specific transactions. In an example of such activity, the Kuwait Investment Authority (KIA) is believed to have invested $300 million alongside Kohlberg Kravis Roberts (KKR), TPG Capital, and Goldman Sachs in the 2007, $45 billion mega-buyout of Texas utility TXU Corp.[19] Co-investment can often be advisable for Gulf-based investors and other large institutions for a number of reasons. First, participating as a co-investor enables an institution to benefit from the due diligence and investment analysis process undertaken by the GP and thereby reduces the level of effort and expertise required in choosing the investment. Second, the capital injected through co-investment is customarily not subject to the 2 percent management fee applied to the LPs' commitments to funds, potentially making co-investment more efficient for the LP. Third, acting as a co-investor allows institutions to "cherry-pick" the portfolio companies in which they wants to increase their exposure (beyond the exposure to the asset that they receive in proportion to their participation in the overall fund). This option value creates an incentive for institutions to commit to private equity funds (and thereby secure co-investment rights) while also reviewing specific transactions in which the fund participates.

The scale of GCC-based institutions' co-investment activity cannot be precisely stated, since most transactions are outside the public domain. A 2008 survey by the UK-based law firm Norton Rose, however, suggests that co-investment activity is likely to grow: a survey of key players in private equity and the sovereign wealth fund (SWF) sector found that 40 percent of respondents believed that SWFs would increasingly co-invest directly. By contrast, only 15 percent believed that investment as limited partners would continue to be the dominant trend in the industry.[20] It was reported that PCP Capital Partners—which had been due to supply 10 percent of the capital behind BlackRock's $13.5 billion acquisition of Barclays Global Investors—was a special-purpose vehicle designed to shield the identity of Gulf-based co-investors.[21] Indeed, even after PCP's role in the deal fell through, the KIA, QIA, and ADIA were all reportedly interested in injecting equity into BlackRock directly to finance the transaction.[22] Tellingly, when KKR appointed its office head for the Middle East, a core responsibility cited was "to explore global co-investment opportunities with MENA [Middle East and North Africa] institutions."[23]

A third level of participation in private equity that has arisen in recent years is equity investments in private equity firms that act as general partners for multiple funds. In 2007, ADIA accumulated an 8 percent stake in regional investment bank EFG-Hermes,[24] and in 2007 Mubadala took a strategic 7.5 percent stake in the Carlyle Group for $1.35 billion in cash[25] in addition to a $500 million commitment to a Carlyle fund. In contrast to investing in funds or in specific portfolio companies, investing in the GP provides exposure to the lucrative management economics of private equity. This approach is, however, less focused than choosing a fund or a company in which to invest.

Multilevel participation by GCC entities has noteworthy fundamental implications for other principal investors. Their role as LPs has long made the GCC entities an attractive set of target investors for private equity funds. Their increased role as co-investors creates an incentive for fund managers to actively incorporate Gulf preferences into the design of fund strategies: knowing that GCC-based LPs are likely to co-invest if a transaction fits their needs can make the overall investment case for that transaction (from the fund's perspective) more compelling. Having Gulf investors take equity in the GP adds another layer of incentives (or, possibly, a requirement) to incorporate their preferences into the funds and other activities of the GP.

Some people in the private equity world have seen the increasingly active roles of Gulf investors as a competitive threat. In the words of one executive cited in the press, "They will be the industry, we will be working for them."[26] Clearly, there have been—and will continue to be—situations in which Gulf-based principal investors and global private equity firms find themselves competing for the same assets or opportunities. There will, however, also be situations in which Gulf institutions will provide co-invested capital, exit opportunities for portfolio assets, investment in GPs, and much-needed lifelines for portfolio companies. If strategies are adequately adapted to fit the evolving context, private equity firms could in fact stand to gain significantly from increased direct investments by GCC entities.

OPERATING COMPANIES: DEALING WITH DEEP POCKETS

Operating companies that compete in global markets can, in certain circumstances, be deeply affected by the actions of Gulf-based investors even if the companies don't deal directly with the region. If a Gulf institution makes a major investment in a competitor or funds the launch of a rival firm, a multinational company can find itself waking up to a new strategic challenge. Facing off against a well-capitalized rival with access to deep pockets, especially in volatile times, can prove a daunting task for many global firms.

The airline sector is ripe with examples of strong, Gulf-funded new entrants. Abu Dhabi's six-year-old airline Etihad drew attention in 2009 when it placed a $7 billion engine order at the Paris air show, aiming to expand its fleet from under 50 planes to over 150 within the next decade.[27] Etihad, like Qatar's national carrier Qatar Airways, has yet to make a profit and does not plan to do so until 2010 at the earliest, but government backing allows both airlines to make large capital investments in order to acquire some of the most modern fleets in the industry. These airlines are insulated against fuel price rises by the natural hedge of oil production, operate in favorable domestic markets, and indirectly benefit from government financial support in order to fulfill the strategic objective of establishing their capitals as global transport hubs. GCC governments will, for example, invest in upgrading airports and infrastructure, whereas many US and European cities are struggling to fund such projects.

These edges have enabled Gulf carriers to become some of the world's leading airlines, competing against legacy carriers such as British Airways, Air France, and KLM, all of which have been forced into alliances as economic conditions have tightened. Faced with a need for additional capital, Australian carrier Virgin Blue was even reported to be courting a Gulf airline as a strategic investor in 2009.[28]

Besides funding new entrants, GCC investors have also provided an important source of capital for international companies during the financial crisis. The Qatar Investment Authority's investment in Porsche has facilitated a merger between Porsche and Volkswagen by 2011,[29] and the white knight investments of the KIA and ADIA in Daimler AG have allowed the German carmaker to show resilience relative to its bankrupt American rivals. In the banking sector, where capital sufficiency has been crucial to survival, ADIA provided a lifeline to Citigroup by becoming its largest shareholder,[30] and the KIA's investment in Merrill Lynch allowed the bank to raise enough capital to survive until its acquisition by Bank of America.[31] The sale by Abu Dhabi's International Petroleum Investment Co. (IPIC) of 10 percent of its Barclays stake (an investment discussed in Chapter 4) resulted in the bank's stock price falling by 15 percent in a single day, reflecting the impact of IPIC's initial investment on investor confidence and the reversal of that confidence on its withdrawal.[32] For several of the world's largest banks and automakers, infusions of Gulf capital have represented a route to survival.

Overall, international operating companies and anyone who invests in them should be aware of the positions of Gulf investors. Gulf capital has the ability to create deep-pocketed regional champions that are more than capable of competing in international markets from scratch. Gulf investors have also helped to reshape the domestic structure of national and regional markets within the Gulf—at times, introducing formidable local rivals to multinational businesses. Finally, Gulf investors have had a significant impact on the survival of firms in the banking and automotive sectors, two of the United States' largest industries. This unexpected turn of events underscores how Gulf capital has indeed become a global player.

KEY LESSONS

- The entry of Gulf investors into a sector or national market can *create and signal a rising tide* that increases asset prices in that market, as Gulf investors cluster together and enter a market with scale. Savvy institutional investors can benefit from this tide if they recognize it and act in time.

- Gulf investors have increasingly adopted a *multilevel approach to private equity investment*, investing as limited partners, co-investing alongside funds, and directly investing in general partners. This shift has meaningful implications for the strategic landscape of private equity.

- Gulf capital is *increasingly funding global operating companies*, at times reshaping industry dynamics and providing deep pockets of capital and a significant competitive advantage to those companies in which they invest.

11

CHAPTER

Rules of the Game: Policy Perspectives for Regulating Investments

The newspaper article began with an attention-grabbing headline: "Agency to check Arab investment."[1] As the article explained, "Huge oil revenues received by Arab nations and other members of the Organization of Petroleum Exporting Countries (OPEC) have aroused concern about investment of their surpluses to take over key US companies." A senator from the Northeast criticized the administration for what he believed to be a lax approach, calling it "myopic" for failing to appreciate "the danger of Arab investors using their US investments for political purposes." Perhaps he had in mind a recently proposed transaction—the year before, a major defense contractor had turned down a major proposed investment by an Arab entity.[2] Meanwhile, the administration was calling for a more nuanced approach to investments by foreign entities, assessing individual transactions on a case-by-case basis.

Observers of Gulf capital will find this story a familiar one. One might assume that it relates to the controversy that arose in 2006 when Dubai Ports World (DPW) acquired a company that operated ports in the United States. In that case, the Bush administration had approved the acquisition, but prominent members of Congress questioned and debated it. The deal was ultimately restructured in such a way that DPW would not operate US ports.[3]

In fact, the story is from 1975, and the administration being criticized was that of President Gerald Ford. It reflects a previous oil boom and an era of unprecedented Gulf wealth, budget surpluses, and foreign investment. The question of what—if anything—regulators should do about Gulf investment in the United States is by no means a new one, as 35-year-old headlines attest.

The regulation of Gulf investments has long been a delicate matter, fraught with sensitive political and economic considerations. Many of these considerations are based on a broader—and classic—debate regarding the balance between free markets and the protection of domestic assets. A number of the issues raised in the public discourse, however, appear to specifically target Gulf or Arab investors, sending a signal that not all overseas capital is equally "foreign." Thus, Gulf investors perceive (and, at times, experience) barriers that don't apply to other institutions that are making investments beyond their borders.

This chapter explores the theme of approaches for regulating Gulf investments, offering a perspective on various potential stances. Some parties to the public debate have called for heavy restrictions and blanket prohibitions, rooted in a set of concerns regarding the Gulf and its investors. This stance, however, appears excessively cautious and runs the risk of driving away much-needed capital. We will also explore how regulators outside the United States—especially in the United Kingdom—have adopted a more welcoming stance toward Gulf capital and Islamic finance, and consider the implications of these varying approaches for countries' global competitiveness. While our discussion is largely rooted in a US perspective, a comparative view is in order and may have added relevance for non-US readers. In addition, we observe how regulatory considerations regarding investment flows are becoming a two-way street, with Gulf governments beginning to show an ability to reciprocate a spirit of protectionism—especially as parliaments in the region gain clout. We then offer a perspective on transaction-specific regulation as being potentially the most practical solution for balancing the concerns involved in regulating Gulf investments.

UNPLEASANT TRUTH: FACING "PROTECTIONISM PLUS"

Many of the concerns cited regarding investments by foreign institutions are standard protectionist stances related to globalization and the cross-border flow of capital. In addition to these standard arguments, however, there are a set of concerns that are frequently discussed

TABLE   11.1

Gulf Investments Face Concerns beyond General Protectionist Arguments

General protectionist concerns	Protection of US jobs and American workers
	Retaining control of firms that are vital for national security
	Protection of industries that are of strategic importance to the national economy
	Protection of private and confidential data
Gulf-specific concerns	Perception that "Arab" institutions will act contrary to US interests
	Association of the Middle East with conflict and violence

when Gulf investments are involved, but that are not part of the customary protectionist debate. Table 11.1 provides an illustrative set of concerns, divided into general protectionist concerns and Gulf-specific issues.

A chief concern of protectionists, particularly in difficult economic times, is protecting US-based jobs and preventing American workers from losing their employment. In the case of investments by overseas buyers, there is particular sensitivity to the possibility that jobs may be transferred overseas, especially to the buyer's home market. While this concern is a legitimate one and keeping workers employed is a laudable policy objective, it is not clear that foreign buyers will necessarily be more inclined to move jobs overseas. In fact, the outsourcing of manufacturing and routine business processes to lower-cost countries is a far broader trend than foreign investment and is being fueled by efficiency drives within major corporations. It may be a fallacy to assume that a foreign buyer will necessarily be more inclined to transfer jobs outside the United States than an American owner—especially when comparing short-term private equity and hedge fund buyers with longer-term institutional investors.

Another important concern relates to the control of firms that are vital for national security. Even if there may be a short-term financial argument for allowing the sale of such companies, in the longer term, such transactions may be seen as compromising the state and thereby affecting the economy. National security arguments are reasonable and should be respected, particularly when they relate to military matters like defense manufacturing. Although the "national security" argument is sometimes applied too broadly, it is a fundamentally sound and important one.

A third area of concern for protectionists is the protection of certain "strategic" sectors of the national economy that are seen as pivotal for economic competitiveness. It was this perspective (along with a deep concern for protecting jobs) that motivated the government-led bailout of US auto manufacturers.[4] A perception among many policy makers was that the automotive sector has long been a pillar of the US economy and a source of competitive advantage. It should, therefore, not be allowed to wither away.

While there is merit to the concept of fostering strategic industries (doing so, for example, is a common strategy among developing nations[5]), it is also important to take into consideration the signals being sent by the global marketplace. If a country has long considered a certain industry to be a strategic one, but the world increasingly prefers products that were made elsewhere, it may be time for that country to reassess what its genuine strategic investments truly are. Garment manufacturing, for example, was long a strategic sector in the United Kingdom before cost and quality dynamics made manufacturing in Asia more competitive.[6] That said, the perspective that certain sectors are strategic to a national economy is a well-grounded one and is worthy of consideration by leaders and policy makers.

Fourth, there are concerns—especially in the digital era, with information flowing so readily across borders—regarding the protection of private and confidential data. Such concerns have been raised, for example, regarding Research In Motion (RIM), the Canada-based manufacturer of BlackBerry devices that store millions of confidential e-mails.[7] These types of concerns are also important, and can be addressed through policies that do not prevent transactions or excessively encumber business operations. In the financial services sector, for example, there are often stringent laws regarding the storage and transmittal of confidential customer data across borders—laws that can be obeyed while still pursuing active outsourcing strategies as a way of increasing efficiency.[8]

If these were the only the concerns raised when Gulf investors seek to buy US assets, their challenges would in many ways be the same as those faced by any foreign buyer. The unpleasant truth, however, is that Gulf-based institutions face an added layer of issues because of perceptions of the Middle East region. One such issue is the perception that "Arab" institutions will act contrary to US interests, or at least are more likely to do so than other foreign entities. For some, this perception of conflicting interests is rooted in deep-seated memories of the 1970s: oil embargos, long lines at the gas pump, and the general feeling of energy insecurity. Added to this, of course, are the terrorist attacks of September 11, 2001—attacks in which the vast majority of the identified hijackers were Gulf Cooperation Council (GCC) nationals.[9] Thus, the perception that Arabs will act in opposition to US interests has some basis in history.

In the case of Gulf investors, however, such a perception is an oversimplification that overlooks a number of important realities. First, it is important to remember that all the GCC member states are staunch military allies of the United States and provide a significant level of direct military support to the United States. America's Central Command for the wars in Iraq and Afghanistan, for example, has been stationed in Qatar. Longstanding US business partners France and Germany, by contrast, opposed the war. The United States has long had military bases in Saudi Arabia, and Saudi Arabia was America's key ally in the first Gulf War in the early 1990s.[10] Bahrain is home to a US naval fleet.[11] Another important reality—a reality that is highly visible when one visits the Gulf but harder to appreciate from a distance—is that Gulf governments (especially that of Saudi Arabia) are themselves prime targets of terrorist attacks. While some of the most visible signs of antiterrorist force (such as policemen with machine guns in New York City subways) are no longer needed in America, it remains common for hotels in Riyadh to have metal detectors and barricades to protect against terrorist attacks. Terrorism is thus a common enemy of the US and GCC regimes, not a cause that is being promoted by state actors. It's also noteworthy that although Osama bin Laden is indeed a Saudi, he was exiled by his government long before 2001 and organized Al Qaeda's attacks from the mountains of Afghanistan. Not only is Afghanistan well outside the GCC, but it's not even part of the Arab world.

When many Americans think of the "Middle East," the immediate images that come to mind are those of war and conflict. Indeed, the Middle East has seen a great deal of conflict in recent decades. These conflicts, however, have been almost entirely concentrated in the Levant region of the Middle East, including the conflict between the Palestinians and Israel, civil wars in Lebanon, and two wars in Iraq. The notable exception was the first Gulf War, in which Kuwait was invaded by Iraq and the GCC member states were key allies of the United States.

Regardless of these facts, negative public perceptions regarding Middle East investors are a reality in the US market. These perceptions inspire feature stories like a 2008 *BusinessWeek* piece entitled "Who's Afraid of Mideast Money?"[12] and other such commentaries. As long as such perceptions remain, lawmakers will be inclined to apply a standard to Gulf investors that could be described as "protectionism plus"—a standard dose of skepticism topped off with additional questions that are specific to the region.

In addition to offending Gulf investors and encouraging them to take their capital elsewhere, there is another major drawback of taking a protectionism plus approach: it violates the principles of the World Trade Organization (WTO) and the General Agreement on Tariffs and Trade (GATT). One core principle of the WTO—of which the United States and all GCC member states are members—is the principle of "most favored nation" status. This principle requires each member state to treat entities from all other member states equally—for example, France should not discriminate between a Japanese company and a Brazilian one, since all three countries are WTO members.[13] Since the Gulf states are members of the WTO, for the United States to treat GCC entities differently from the entities of other WTO member countries is—strictly speaking—contrary to the "most favored nation" principle.

The Gulf's own gradualism in adopting the principles of the WTO makes it difficult, however, for GCC members to actually complain about the matter. In signing up for the WTO, member states have negotiated different timelines and exceptions for the implementation of its principles. Restrictions on foreign ownership in key Gulf sectors prevail to this day, as do other protectionist measures related to commercial activity and employment.[14] Thus, while Gulf states may rightly be irked by the level of protectionism plus that they face, their own economic policies make it difficult for them to publicly cry foul for the time being.

CASE IN POINT: DUBAI PORTS WORLD

A prime example of how protectionism plus has been applied to Gulf entities is the case of the Dubai Ports World acquisition of P&O. The 2006 controversy related to the acquisition, which would have resulted in DPW operating ports in the United States, was aptly dubbed a "debacle" by a Harvard Business School case[15] and has had serious ramifications for how both US and GCC stakeholders view the prospects for cross-border acquisitions.

At the time of the P&O acquisition, DPW was already the sixth-largest port operator in the world. In addition to ports in the Middle East, DPW was successfully operating ports in China, Australia, Germany, and (in the Americas) the Dominican Republic and Venezuela. DPW's port security technology was widely admired, and the company had built a reputation as a world-class institution.[16]

The Bush administration, for which homeland security policies were a top priority, duly reviewed and approved the deal. The Committee on Foreign Investments in the United States (CFIUS), a 12-agency panel chaired by the deputy secretary of the treasury, unanimously approved the DPW transaction. Tellingly, CFIUS was itself established in 1975 by the Ford administration "to placate Congress, which had grown concerned over the rapid increase in Organization of the Petroleum Exporting Countries (OPEC) investments in American portfolio assets."[17] Dubai Ports World had unanimously passed through the oversight body set up to guard against potentially compromising investments—a body created with exactly DPW-like transactions in mind.

Congressional objections to the deal reflected the reservations about the Middle East that are a hallmark of protectionism plus. Senator Charles Schumer of New York argued that "foreign control of our ports, which are vital to homeland security, is a risky proposition." (This part of his statement reflects general protectionist concerns.) Targeting the Gulf, he added, "Riskier yet is that we are turning it over to a country that has been linked to terrorism previously."[18] It is this additional scrutiny that is a unique challenge for Gulf-based institutions, especially Saudi entities.

In the public debate about DPW, a number of crucially important details were often overlooked. One of these details is that DPW was already operating a number of ports in international markets, and had developed the appropriate security protocols. In addition, the US government would still have had complete customs authority and inspection rights at the ports. As pointed out by a member of Congress, DPW's role would have been "like the person in the control tower at the airport. It has nothing to do with security."[19] Furthermore—and most fundamentally—P&O, the firm that was already operating the US ports in question, was itself a foreign company. It was, in fact, a UK firm.

The DPW affair thus clearly demonstrated that not all overseas capital is considered equally "foreign" and that Gulf entities can expect to be held to a higher standard. Popular opinion supported this stance: polls showed that Americans had more problems with an Arab firm running US ports than they had with a British one doing so.[20] This position (which is, at root, a discriminatory one) sent strong signals to international investors in the Gulf and beyond.

REAL CONSEQUENCES OF ZEALOUS PROTECTIONISM

In addition to causing offense to Gulf and Middle East investors and conveying to them that their capital was less welcome than that of other investors, the DPW affair and similar forms of zealous protectionism have a real economic impact. One clear example was the breakdown of negotiations between the UAE and the United States regarding a bilateral trade agreement. Discussions regarding such a pact fell apart as an immediate consequence of the DPW debacle: talks were formally postponed on March 10, 2006—the day after DPW restructured its deal to avoid managing US ports.[21] This setback was particularly awkward for the Bush administration, since it had approved the transaction already, only to have its judgment challenged by Congress. A year later, it became clear that a bilateral trade agreement would not be reached in the near term: there were too many issues outstanding, and the UAE's own protectionism had become a cause of concern.[22] The economic benefits that might have accrued from a bilateral trade pact with the UAE were lost (at least for the time being) as a result of a protectionist posture that made UAE parties feel singled out.

The DPW affair also prompted Congress to pass more stringent regulation of foreign investment in the form of a bill called the Foreign Investment and National Security Act of 2007. This legislation, according to congressional papers, broadened the definition of national security to extend to "those issues relating to 'homeland security,' including its application to critical infrastructure, and critical technologies."[23] The legislation's impact was far broader than the Gulf; it affected all overseas investors seeking US assets. If an asset is deemed "critical" for homeland security, rigorous review by CFIUS will occur, and CFIUS will be required to report back to Congress. In its commentary on the bill, the *Wall Street Journal* issued harsh criticism, dubbing it "The Don't Invest in America Act."[24]

Although reasonable protection of strategic assets makes sense, overzealous protection can indeed have the impact feared by the *Wall Street Journal*—it can drive investors not to invest in America. An SEC official echoed a similar sentiment [specifically related to sovereign wealth funds (SWFs)] in 2008 testimony before Congress, noting that "if we were to prohibit sovereign wealth funds from investing in our markets for fear they might introduce market distortions, there is a risk we might actually end up doing precisely this to ourselves."[25] Put differently, by depriving ourselves of SWF capital, we could distort asset prices and disrupt the free flow of capital. Failing to accept equity investments runs the risk of discouraging much-needed Treasury bill and debt investments. In seeking excessive protection, legislation can in fact cause much damage.

In a comprehensive report on the actions of sovereign wealth funds—aptly titled "Assessing the Risks: The Behaviors of Sovereign Wealth Funds in the Global Economy"—the Monitor Group found that sovereign entities "do not appear to be investing for political reasons. Some funds are making strategic investments to hasten economic development in their home country, but they do not appear to be active in ways that threaten the economic or national security of foreign countries where they invest."[26] It is critical that regulators bear this in mind, lest they unnecessarily deprive their home markets of capital. Monitor's assessment is broadly consistent with the guidelines of the Santiago Principles for SWF behavior (discussed in Chapter 8), especially with regard to the objectives of sovereign investment vehicles. The Santiago Principles, which emphasize public disclosure of fund objectives and collaboration with local regulators in cases where there is a significant economic impact, propose a framework for disclosure and transparency. The Monitor report was empirical, looking at sovereign investors' track records and actual behaviors.

Gulf investors have strong structural reasons for investing in US dollars and American assets—reasons that are likely to remain in place for the foreseeable future. For the parts of Gulf portfolios that are dedicated to alternative investments, however—such as direct investments (buyouts) in companies, significant real estate purchases, and the like—Gulf investors naturally assess the regulatory environment and potential hurdles to the transaction. If regulation is seen as onerous, sentiment-driven, or unpredictable, even an otherwise attractive investment may be declined. This can have real implications for domestic firms' ability to attract funding—particularly at a time when countries are competing to attract scarce capital for investment.

MORE WELCOMING COMPETITORS

Not all countries have shown the same level of reluctance to accept high-profile Gulf investments. In fact, several countries have actively pursued regulatory and trade strategies to attract GCC capital to their shores. Recognizing that Gulf investors have choices, these countries have worked to position themselves as particularly accommodating of Gulf capital and its needs. One mechanism for doing so is through events like state visits and trade delegations—even without introducing formal regulation, such measures convey enthusiasm and acceptance of investment flows and trade ties.

In recent years, for example, there have been multiple delegations sent between China and GCC countries. In early 2009, Chinese president Hu Jintao traveled to the Gulf and met with senior leaders, including the king of Saudi Arabia. In the meetings with King Abdullah, Hu reportedly "proposed that the two countries maintain high-level visits, establish a high-level consultation mechanism, take advantage of their own resources and markets, promote an all-around energy partnership, and expand two-way investment."[27] This multifaceted agenda indicates to both GCC and Chinese institutions that the two countries view their economic interests as aligned and that they see value in collaboration. The sprit of balanced engagement is also reflected in trade figures—in 2007, trade volume from the GCC to China was $30 billion, and the flow from China to the GCC was $28 billion.[28] Hence, it should not be surprising that Gulf investors have played central roles in a number of Chinese IPOs and investment opportunities. China's interest in "two-way investment" is also a key signal of partnership—not only does China want to tap into the Gulf's surpluses, but it also wants to invest in the region and benefit from its ongoing growth. Such reciprocation is a message that is well received by Gulf decision makers.

Another way in which governments signal their interest in attracting Gulf capital is by enabling Islamic finance. Regimes that accommodate Shariah-compliant financial structures and investment can hope to tap into growing pools of Islamic capital based mainly in the GCC region. The United Kingdom has been particularly active in promoting its ambition to act as a global hub for Islamic finance. Initiatives by the Ministry for Trade and Investment, the Financial Services Authority (FSA), and other bodies have conveyed a consistent message of seeking to accommodate Islamic finance. In 2007, the chairman of the FSA articulated the United Kingdom's stance, saying, "It is important that we showed we were able to accommodate Islamic banking practices alongside traditional non-Islamic banking, for reasons of both principle and practical importance."[29] The UK authorities have removed double-taxation provisions and double-stamp-duty provisions in order to ensure that Islamic finance operates on a level playing field. UK regulators have even permitted the establishment of fully Islamic banks, including the Islamic Bank of Britain, signaling their commitment to Islamic financial services, and have established advisory bodies that are consulted by the government on matters of Islamic finance.

As indicated in the FSA chairman's statement, the UK's promotion of Islamic finance is for both principled and practical reasons. Since it has a substantial and growing Muslim population, it is important that the United Kingdom ensure that the financial system is equally accessible to all. Aspirations for being a global hub, however, indicate the United Kingdom's keen interest in remaining a leading destination for Islamic capital from the Gulf and the broader Muslim world. Having long been a leading destination for Gulf investors (who frequent London for both business and recreation), the United Kingdom does not want to miss out on outward GCC investments. The enthusiasm for Islamic banking shown by Malaysia, Singapore,[30] and even France is often motivated (at least in part) by a drive to attract Gulf investors. French Finance Minister Christine Lagarde has promised to make adjustments to the regulatory and legal arsenal to enable Paris to become a major marketplace in Islamic finance.[31]

In the context of US financial regulation, such active support of Islamic finance has not been present. In large part, this is due to systemic characteristics of the US regulatory system. Unlike the United Kingdom, the United States adheres to a strict separation of church and state, so that any "promotion" of a faith-based investment mode may be seen as religious favoritism. In fact, some have gone so far as to sue the US government, now a major shareholder in insurance giant AIG, because that company offers Shariah-compliant insurance products.[32] At the same time, religious accommodation is a key principle of US law. Therefore, all (including religious Muslims) can argue that access to capital and financial services that are in line with their beliefs should not be unduly withheld. More fundamental, however, is the fact that US financial regulation takes a market-based approach, reacting to the requests and actions of market actors but not actively promoting any particular approach. US financial regulators would, for example, react to a request for a banking license from someone who was seeking to establish an Islamic bank but would not proactively offer such a license.

The guiding philosophy is that the regulator's role is to respond to actors rather than initiate new practices. An official at the Federal Reserve Bank of New York reflected this spirit in 2006 remarks, stating, "We have dedicated ourselves to keeping our ears to the ground on this issue by co-sponsoring and/or attending a number of conferences and meetings on Islamic banking, but we have not seen anything concrete manifest itself yet."[33] A US regulator would prefer to see market action before taking a formal stance. Hence, broad statements about the future role of Islamic finance are not consistent with the prevailing style of regulation.

Proactive efforts to attract Gulf capital may seem less necessary for major markets like the United States and Western Europe, which are familiar environments for GCC-based institutions and the people who lead them. Less familiar destinations and emerging markets typically need to exert more marketing efforts in order to attract attention and become known. At the same time, however, complacency on the part of leading countries is a high-risk approach. As other countries court Gulf capital and build trust, increasingly sizable portions of GCC portfolios may be directed to these markets. Recapturing these allocations, especially if investments in new markets deliver superior returns, may prove daunting.

When it comes to the United States and other leading markets, the role of trade delegations and other promotional events would not be to emphasize the basic merits of the Organisation for Economic Co-operation and Development (OECD) investments. Gulf investors are already focused on these developed markets and know them well. What Gulf investors will require, however, is a sense that their capital is welcome and that it will not face undue discrimination. Today, there is no such message—and the consequences are detrimental.

BECOMING A TWO-WAY STREET

Countries' regulation of Gulf investments has implications for more than the role of Gulf capital in their home markets. Increasingly, such regulation may affect how Gulf states themselves regulate investments and initiatives by foreign investors and companies within the Gulf region. This phenomenon is beginning to manifest itself, with the most vivid example being the high-profile breakup of a proposed joint venture (JV) between Kuwait Petroleum Corporation (KPC) and US-based Dow Chemical. The proposed JV was referred to as "K-Dow."

Announced in late 2007, K-Dow appeared to be strategically sound and beneficial for both parties. In a comment published in the *Financial Times*, I commended the initiative as "enabling Dow and KPC to build a stronger business than either could do on its own."[34] Cheaper access to raw materials would give the relevant Dow business unit a competitive advantage, and KPC would benefit by expanding its range of activities. The journal *Middle East Economic Survey* noted, "It is hard to find anyone at all connected with Kuwait's oil industry who thinks the K-Dow deal was bad for the country."[35]

A year later, however, Kuwait pulled out of the transaction unilaterally. The reason cited in reports was that the Kuwaiti press and certain parliamentarians had voiced concerns about the deal, and were intent on probing the transaction with an eye to potentially blocking it. Although the deal had been carefully assessed, reviewed, and approved by the prime minister, the public controversy was sufficient to stop the partnership. The breakup is strikingly reminiscent of the Dubai Ports World controversy in the United States—except in reverse. In the case of K-Dow, the questioning regulator is from the Gulf.

This turn of events signals that, at least for transactions related to Kuwait and Bahrain (the Gulf states with the most activist parliaments), consideration of legislators' concerns is becoming more of a two-way street. Whereas Gulf investors have become accustomed to factoring in the sensitivities of US and EU legislators and media, multinationals dealing with the Gulf have not had a similar challenge. Foreign companies have been able to rely on their Gulf counterparts to fully manage the local politics. Almost none would have imagined that a deal that had been approved by a Gulf prime minister would subsequently face hurdles. Going forward, global firms sourcing capital from certain Gulf states will be well advised to consider potential legislative and media controversy as a possible risk factor.

For Gulf investors, the key implication is that they will need to assure global partners that postagreement controversies will not force deals to fall apart. After the K-Dow affair, international partners may insist on stronger breakup penalties and other measures of assurance. This may mean outreach and consultation with a broader set of local stakeholders.

As Gulf governance models evolve, so will the requirements to manage regulatory and public perceptions of business transactions. Countries that are seen as welcoming of (or at least fair to) Gulf counterparties may expect better public perception when their own companies seek to strike deals in the Gulf. Firms that seek to partner with Gulf institutions should therefore be mindful of both the way the Gulf regulates foreign companies and the way their home countries view Gulf business interests.

DEAL-SPECIFIC REGULATION AS THE PATH FORWARD

In the sensitive matter of regulating investments, there may not be any easy answers. It does, however, appear clear that neither blanket prohibitions on foreign investment nor a completely laissez-faire approach is appropriate. Figure 11.1 illustrates three broad approaches, along with the benefits and drawbacks of each.

Blanket prohibitions (prohibiting, for example, equity stakes above a certain threshold or any investments by certain types of institutions) have the benefits of clarity and uniformity. The rules would be well understood and clear to enforce. The drawbacks, however, seem to outweigh these benefits. Most important, blanket prohibitions run the risk of driving away much-needed capital. This, in turn, has a negative impact on asset values and growth. In the words of the Monitor report on sovereign investment, "Foreign direct investment is beneficial both for national economics and international relations."[36] Cutting it off is unnecessarily detrimental, both economically and politically. In addition, barriers to investment may well be inconsistent with the WTO and other international treaties or agreements.

At the other end of the spectrum, complete laissez-faire (nonregulation of the markets) does not seem prudent either. Nonregulation

F I G U R E   11.1

Deal-Specific Review Seems Most Optimal Stance

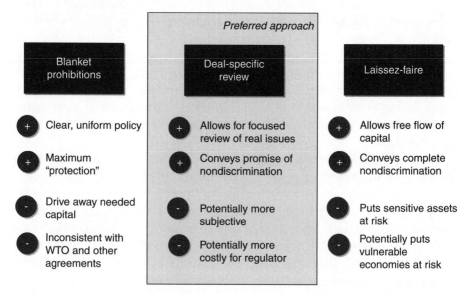

does, of course, allow for the free flow of capital and signal complete nondiscrimination. At the same time, however, it puts a country's sensitive assets at risk. In the US context, one example from the 1970s is that of defense contractor Lockheed Martin. Lockheed reportedly turned down a $100 million investment offer from an Arab group in 1974.[37] Considering the sensitive nature of Lockheed's work and its integral role in national security, turning down a major foreign investment (from any overseas buyer, irrespective of its origin) seems entirely reasonable. In the context of small countries that receive massive direct investment, their overall economies could possibly be put at jeopardy by excessively unregulated markets.

The optimal path forward, therefore, seems to be to review transactions on a case-by-case basis. This allows regulators to focus their reviews on the most relevant transactions and the most critical elements of those transactions, determining the appropriate depth based on the circumstances. Importantly, a case-by-case approach can signal that transactions will be assessed on their merits and properly investigated—the political biases of a parliamentary debate are not expected. Parties to the transaction can take comfort that if their proposal adequately addresses potential areas of concern, they can expect the deal to be approved. Thus, both the regulator and the parties involved may find that a transaction-specific approach is more suitable for both protecting national interests and guaranteeing a fair investigation.

Deal-specific review does, however, have certain drawbacks. One is that, at least when compared to the extremes of blanket prohibitions and complete laissez-faire, a transaction-specific approach necessarily introduces a level of subjectivity into the review process. America's interdepartmental CFIUS process (especially with its expanded "homeland security" mandate) needs to make judgment calls regarding what issues are indeed sensitive enough for investigation. Once this is done, the actual assessment of risks is a matter of administrative judgment. Thus, a fair degree of discretion acts as a drawback of the approach as well as a core benefit. Another drawback is the cost of conducting such reviews—typically minor compared to the economic value of the transactions, but nonetheless a concern for government agencies.

A final benefit of deal-specific reviews is that they are broadly compatible with the direction in which major overseas investors and home regulators are both moving. The Santiago Principles for sovereign wealth investments, collectively developed by a set of sovereign investors in late 2008, acknowledge the need for transaction-specific disclosure when deals are made for noneconomic reasons. Furthermore, they call for collaboration with domestic regulators on deals that have significant economic impact.[38] In the United States, meanwhile, the Foreign Investment and National Security Act of 2007, while broadening the scope of deal reviews, is fundamentally compatible with a transaction-level approach to reviewing investments. As the world's economies and capital markets become increasingly interdependent, it seems that there is no substitute for careful analysis of each transaction's unique circumstances.

KEY LESSONS

- Gulf investors *have long faced protectionism plus* with regard to their overseas investments because of negative perceptions of the Middle East.

- The *Dubai Ports World controversy of 2006* is a prime example of GCC-targeted protectionism that was not applied equally to other foreign investors and did not fully consider the key facts of the investment proposal.

- Countries worldwide have adopted *differing postures toward Gulf capital*, with several adopting active strategies to attract GCC and Islamic investors. Such measures bring comfort to Gulf-based investors and should not be underestimated.

- In a recent trend, *parliamentary pressures within the Gulf have begun to affect transactions*, most notably the broken-up joint venture between Kuwait and Dow Chemical. Regulatory and public perception concerns are becoming a two-way street.

- *Deal-specific review of foreign investments* appears to be the optimal approach for regulators to adopt, as it offers flexibility, rigor, and well-considered protection.

An Essential Toolkit: Islamic Finance Capabilities

HSBC Amanah, the global Islamic finance unit of the HSBC Group, has long made Shariah training a priority for its executives. Every executive in the business has been required to take a focused training course on the aspects of Shariah that are essential to financial transactions. The course, historically taught by a member of HSBC Amanah's Shariah committee, includes lectures, case studies, and an exam. In 2006, the highest score on the exam was earned by an analyst in the private equity group. This analyst was bright, diligent, and motivated—and, as it turns out, he was also not a Muslim.

As Islamic finance has become an increasingly important and global phenomenon, Islamic finance capabilities have become increasingly essential. These capabilities are an essential toolkit for servicing a growing number of customers in the Muslim world, especially in the Gulf Cooperation Council (GCC) region, whose business interests extend worldwide. Few investment bankers covering the US auto sector, for example, would have expected Islamic structuring capabilities to be a relevant skill set. That changed, however, when the most attractive buyers of Ford's Aston Martin business line turned out to be two Kuwaiti institutions that insisted on Shariah-compliant structuring.[1] As GCC and Islamic capital expand worldwide, so does the need for financial institutions to be able to meet their unique requirements.

In this chapter, we begin with an overview of the three principal business models that global financial institutions have pursued to meet the needs of Islamic customers. The most basic of these is the product model, where conventional banks offer a handful of Islamic products as part of their overall proposition to customers. A step beyond this is the window model, where institutions develop Islamic business units while continuing to offer Shariah-compliant products and services through the same distribution channels as conventional ones. A third approach is the subsidiary model, where institutions establish separate entities for their Shariah-compliant business and service customers through dedicated channels. Each model, as we shall see, has its benefits and its drawbacks.

Next, we explore the range of skills required to offer a winning proposition in Islamic finance. Shariah structuring and product development are a core set of skills, without which an Islamic financial services organization cannot function. In addition to structuring capabilities, however, proposition design and distribution skills, though often overlooked, are also critical for long-term success. To win, organizations require strength across the spectrum of capabilities.

In closing, we discuss another set of capabilities that Islamic financial institutions often need: the ability to shape their broader environments. These capabilities are especially important for entities that are (or aspire to be) leaders in their home markets or that operate in environments where Islamic finance is less familiar. Breakthrough success may often rest on an organization's ability to shape the environment around it to better enable Islamic financial services and make them more competitive.

No financial services institution can be truly global without Islamic finance capabilities. This chapter is your guide to the capabilities required and to thinking through what approach best suits your institution and its customer proposition.

CORE BUSINESS MODELS

In offering Shariah-compliant financial services, conventional institutions have pursued a range of approaches over the past decades. These approaches can be summarized as three core business models, illustrated in Figure 12.1.

Product Model

The customary approach that conventional banks entering the Islamic financial services space often take is the *product* model. Under this model, institutions offer Shariah-compliant products and services

F I G U R E   12.1

Conventional Institutions Have Pursued Three Models for Islamic Finance

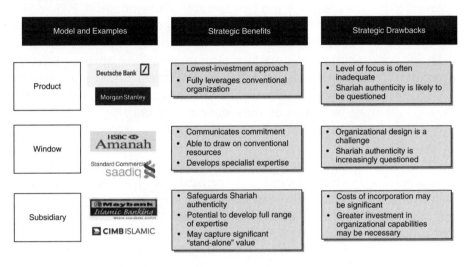

Model and Examples	Strategic Benefits	Strategic Drawbacks
Product — Deutsche Bank, Morgan Stanley	• Lowest-investment approach • Fully leverages conventional organization	• Level of focus is often inadequate • Shariah authenticity is likely to be questioned
Window — HSBC Amanah, Standard Commercial saadiq	• Communicates commitment • Able to draw on conventional resources • Develops specialist expertise	• Organizational design is a challenge • Shariah authenticity is increasingly questioned
Subsidiary — Maybank Islamic Banking, CIMB ISLAMIC	• Safeguards Shariah authenticity • Potential to develop full range of expertise • May capture significant "stand-alone" value	• Costs of incorporation may be significant • Greater investment in organizational capabilities may be necessary

alongside conventional ones and through their conventional distribution channels. Institutions that pursue the product model need only add Islamic products and services to their existing set of offerings. The personnel who work on the Shariah-compliant offerings are not necessarily specialists, and do so in addition to their conventional responsibilities.

A number of leading global financial institutions today employ the product model to serve Islamic customers. Deutsche Bank, for example, launched an Islamic investment platform called Al Mi'yar in early 2009. The platform, which complies with Islamic accounting standards, offers access to a range of investment options to meet the needs of Shariah-inclined investors.[2] Deutsche Bank's global Islamic finance business is led by Hussein Hassan, whose title at Deutsche Bank is "head of structuring MENA [Middle East and North Africa] and head of Islamic finance."[3] The executive leading Islamic finance therefore bears the responsibility for both Islamic and conventional finance, giving Deutsche Bank the flexibility to allocate resources with maximum fluidity. Morgan Stanley also participates in Islamic finance (through, for example, a family of Islamic indexes[4]) without having established a dedicated Islamic finance unit.

The chief benefit of the product model is that it requires the least investment in building specialist capabilities. Organizations that use this model need not build fully Islamic teams—they can use the resources that they already have in hand. In addition, there is no need for a distinct Islamic brand or separate marketing materials beyond the materials specifically used for Shariah-compliant products. Firms that are seeking to test the Islamic finance market and explore its potential fit with their existing business find the product approach to be a logical first step. If Islamic products prove successful, further investment may be made. If they do not, it's easy to just drop the products without significant implications for the organization or the brand.

While the product approach has the lowest risk, it also has significant limitations in terms of potential rewards and market share. A lack of focus in the organization can mean that the market opportunity is not adequately captured. A product approach can work well when an institution's goal is to react to the needs of existing customers—private bankers, for example, have long used such an approach when their clients specifically ask for Islamic products. The approach is less suitable, however, when an institution aspires to actively build Islamic market share and bring in new business. In such cases, not having a dedicated team for Shariah-compliant business can mean that the business is not developed to its full potential.

Another drawback of the product approach is that customers are more likely to question its Shariah authenticity than they would be if they saw an Islamic brand or entity. This is particularly true of retail customers and less sophisticated investor segments who do not probe into the details of product structuring and features. For institutional customers and private banking clients, however, there is often an adequate opportunity to communicate the Shariah compliance of the product through direct customer interaction. Institutions pursuing the product model may rely on the Shariah supervisory capabilities at the product or fund level (e.g., the Shariah committee of the fund) rather than undertaking their own institution-level Shariah governance.

Window Model

In the 2000s, an increasing number of global banks adopted the *window* model for providing Islamic financial services. In this model, the financial institution creates a specialist Islamic finance team and develops a distinct Islamic finance brand while continuing to distribute products and services through the global (conventional) channel infrastructure. Customarily, banks adopting the window model will also have institution-level Shariah governance mechanisms, including a Shariah committee that oversees the full range of operations.

HSBC was a pioneer of the window model, creating HSBC Amanah in 1998. HSBC's investment in Islamic finance, like that of Citigroup before it, sent a strong signal to the world of finance that Islamic finance was a substantial opportunity that was worth pursuing. To many observers of Islamic finance, this was an important validation that the industry had demonstrated its viability. Over time, HSBC Amanah has expanded into a full range of financial services offerings, including retail, commercial, investment, and private banking as well as private equity. According to a 2006 publication, HSBC Amanah was at that time serving more than 300,000 customers worldwide and had ambitious plans to expand further.[5] Standard Chartered, which has launched the Saadiq brand for Islamic financial services, is another successful example of a dedicated window model.

The success of the window model lies largely in its blend of specialist expertise and global capabilities. A specialist team brings strategic focus and commitment to building a successful Islamic franchise, and also brings a set of technical capabilities (e.g., Shariah structuring) that is vital. Unlike the situation at firms using the product model, executives working under the window model are typically not expected to work on conventional business as well. Therefore, they have every incentive to ensure that the Shariah-compliant business grows. At the same time, specialist teams working under the window model are able to draw on the global infrastructure, capabilities, and reputation of the overall institution. This often provides a tremendous competitive advantage over fully Islamic banks, which (lacking scale) often do not have the same depth of technical infrastructure, functional support (e.g., marketing, legal, and compliance), and credibility in the marketplace. Another major strength of the window model is its ability to attract world-class talent and human resources. Professionals who are keen to work in Islamic finance but are uncomfortable working for lesser-known institutions take comfort in being able to work for a leading global giant while also focusing on their area of interest. From an employee perspective, working under a window model may seem like an ideal combination of conventional credibility and Islamic opportunity.

From a customer perspective, the branded window model conveys commitment and dedication to Islamic finance. One benefit of this is the signal of greater Shariah authenticity—customers take comfort from the fact that the bank has a Shariah committee and a set of specialist capabilities that are apparent in the distinct branding. Another benefit is that customers feel that their preference for Islamic products and services will be understood and respected throughout the banking relationship, from the account-opening experience to the day-to-day service received through branches and other channels. By establishing Islamic brands, institutions that pursue a window model put forth a promise of service that is sensitive to Shariah-compliant customers' needs. At the same time, customers may question the Shariah authenticity of the window model, fearing that the commingling of Islamic and conventional funds on a single balance sheet may be an ethical compromise. Without a separate balance sheet, the mixing of funds is unavoidable.

Despite its substantial strengths, the window model also has significant drawbacks that—unless they are adequately addressed—can curtail the business's growth potential over time. A number of the issues associated with the window model can be broadly classified as organizational or business design challenges. On the one hand, the Islamic business requires sufficient autonomy to develop and pursue a growth strategy tailored to the Shariah-compliant sector. At the same time, however, the Islamic business must be sufficiently integrated into the overall institution to ensure that all parts of the organization reinforce one another and contribute to one another's success. Operationally, meeting both of these goals can prove to be a substantial challenge.

Table 12.1 provides an overview of some of the business design challenges that may arise under the window model, highlighting key questions that require resolution.

At first glance, a number of the questions outlined in Table 12.1 may seem straightforward. In practice, however, they can be highly challenging, especially in large organizations with complex systems and many decision makers at various levels of the institution (e.g., country, regional, and global). In the realm of financial reporting, for example, one may assume that addressing the allocation of distribution costs in order to assess the profitability of the Islamic business should be simple enough. In practice, however, a great many judgment calls need to be made regarding line items of cost, and the decisions are hardly easy.

Customer relationship management offers another set of complex questions. Often, the same customer will use both Islamic and

T A B L E   12.1

Key Business Design Challenges Related to the Window Model

Area	Key Challenges/Questions
Accounting and financial reporting	How should revenues associated with Islamic products and services be allocated between the Islamic team and the distribution channels?
	How should distribution and overhead costs be allocated when assessing the profitability of the Islamic business?
Customer relationship management	Who manages the relationship with customers who use both Islamic and conventional products?
	How does the institution decide whether to offer a conventional product or the Islamic equivalent to a particular customer?
Brand building and public relations	How much of the overall branding budget should be allocated to the Islamic brand and how much to the conventional one?
	How much visibility should the Islamic business have in general PR campaigns?
Management reporting	Where in the organization (e.g., at the country, regional, or global level) should the Islamic business report?
	Which functions require specialist Islamic expertise and which do not?

conventional products. In such cases, should the relationship be managed by an Islamic specialist, a conventional relationship manager, or both? When new products are offered to the customer, should the products be Islamic or conventional? These matters can prove highly contentious, especially if the teams involved are working under different incentive systems.

When there is a distinct Islamic brand, questions inevitably arise as to when the Islamic brand should be emphasized and when the conventional one should be used. On a billboard or in an event sponsorship, for example, should the Islamic brand appear at all? If so, how frequently should it be used? In media relations, what is the relative position of the Islamic business line in the overall story? With media outlets that specifically focus on Islamic finance, how should the links to the conventional business be discussed?

Most sensitive of all may be the questions of reporting lines for the management team. Islamic specialists will need to interact with their conventional counterparts at numerous levels, including the business line, the country, the region, and globally. What the nature of the interaction should be and where decision rights should lie are delicate matters. More fundamental is the question of which functions require specialist expertise in the first place—for example, the technology function may not need an Islamic team, but if there is no such team, who will be responsible for the technology projects needed to account for Shariah-compliant products? The good news is that global financial institutions may well be accustomed to managing such organizational complexities. At the same time, however, adding an Islamic layer on top of an already complex matrix reporting structure is no small feat.

Subsidiary Model

The final core model pursued by conventional institutions is the creation of a distinct Islamic *subsidiary*. The subsidiary may draw on the parent's brand, but it is established as a separate institution. As a distinct legal entity, it has its own governance processes (for example, a board of directors) and independent standing. The subsidiary model has become the norm in Malaysia, where leading conventional banks such as Maybank and CIMB have established distinct entities for their Islamic banking businesses. Though they draw on their parents' infrastructure, Maybank Islamic and CIMB Islamic are legally separate entities.

Creating a subsidiary has its costs. First, there are the direct costs of incorporation—setting up the entity, registering it, obtaining a license, and so on. As these are financial services institutions, minimum capital requirements and other central bank rules would govern how large an initial investment is needed. On an ongoing basis, administrative and governance costs associated with a legal entity recur—the costs of reporting, auditing, maintaining a separate board, and so on. Furthermore—and potentially far more extensive—there are the costs associated with building a full range of organizational capabilities. Since subsidiaries can often draw upon the parent's infrastructure through service-level agreements and contracts, the extent to which they build out their own capabilities can vary greatly. Nonetheless, one would expect the investment required for a subsidiary to be greater than that of a window, since corporate expenses are required above and beyond the core commercial capabilities.

There are, however, important benefits of the subsidiary model. The main motivation for creating such entities (particularly in

Malaysia) has been Shariah authenticity. Bank Negara Malaysia, the country's central bank, has led a migration away from the window model to a subsidiary approach. From a Shariah perspective, creating subsidiaries should prevent the commingling of Islamic and conventional funds, ensuring that Shariah-compliant deposits are used for Shariah-compliant financing and that Shariah-compliant financing comes from Shariah-compliant sources. This addresses an important concern of Shariah scholars (and some customers), who saw the window model as a necessary step for the industry but problematic because of the commingling issue. Bank Negara's stance in favor of subsidiaries may set a trend for other regulators to adopt similar measures, putting regulatory pressure on the window model.

Another benefit of creating subsidiaries may be the stand-alone value of the subsidiary within the broader portfolio of the institution. One challenge that global banks often face is that their fastest-growing and most profitable businesses are embedded in the overall operations of the bank and therefore are not valued separately. It may be, on certain occasions, that the sum of the value of the conventional bank and that of the Islamic bank is greater than the value of a single financial services entity. In addition, having a distinct Islamic entity makes it possible for the institution to attract Shariah-compliant investors at the subsidiary level, unlocking additional value for the parent company.

Finally, the requirement (in the case of an independently operated subsidiary) that the subsidiary develop the full range of organizational capabilities can in fact be a source of advantage under certain circumstances. As discussed earlier, the business design and organizational challenges of the window model can be complex, and can threaten to limit an institution's potential to win Islamic business. In such cases, the window's operating model can become a hindrance to its growth. Subsidiaries, however, can potentially avoid such issues because of their singular focus and high degree of autonomy. The presence of minority shareholders at the subsidiary level, while introducing some governance complexities, can also lead to greater autonomy for the subsidiary. A genuinely arms-length relationship can protect the subsidiary's independent interests as it pursues its expansion strategy. At the management level, there can be significant value in having a full set of competencies that are dedicated to the Islamic finance business, especially if the volume of business justifies such investment. As we shall now discuss, fully capturing the Islamic opportunity may often require a range of capabilities that go well beyond the technical matters of Shariah structuring.

THE ISLAMIC FINANCE CAPABILITIES SPECTRUM

Building a winning Islamic finance business requires capabilities along a number of dimensions. Shariah structuring and product development are a core capability, without which the venture cannot operate. However, there are other skills that are also needed if the institution is to plan and execute the business successfully. Figure 12.2 provides an illustration of the "capabilities spectrum" needed for success in Islamic financial services.

A key set of capabilities relates to a business's overall strategy and proposition design. Leaders of the business need a clear sense of their competitive positioning in the marketplace—who their competitors are, how the competitive landscape may evolve, and what can make their own products and services stand out. They need to understand the customer's mindset, and especially the mindset of customers who are Shariah-inclined. Only then can they develop a differentiated overall proposition that optimally captures the market opportunity and draws on the institution's core strengths.

Strategy and proposition design issues may be very different in the context of an Islamic offering from what they are for a conventional one, even within the same institution. For example, a global bank may find itself competing with a set of local Islamic banks for Shariah-compliant business, whereas it has long been used to competing with other global banks for conventional customers. In markets where there has been little or no Islamic banking to date, the strategy may be to tap into customer pools that are currently underserved and

F I G U R E   12.2

The "Capabilities Spectrum" Required for Success in Islamic Finance

Strategy and Proposition Design	Structuring and Product Development	Distribution and Customer Experience
• Competitive positioning • Customer insight and understanding • Overall proposition	• Shariah structuring • Design of benefits and features • Pricing and bundling strategies	• Marketing approach • Sales and delivery channels • Ongoing service and support

hardly engaged with the banking sector. The team responsible for corporate strategy needs to be sufficiently attuned to the strategic context of Islamic financial services in its markets to craft an approach that is suited to the situation. Often an institution is well served by having a specialist team addressing matters of strategy for the Islamic business. However, if strategy development is done by the same team that covers conventional strategy, it is critical that the relevant information and data on the Shariah-compliant landscape are adequately obtained and considered.

The next set of capabilities is skills associated with structuring and product development. Within this realm lies the complex role of Shariah structuring—the challenges of which are rich and many. Shariah structuring requires a deep base of specialized knowledge that most bankers do not customarily have. Therefore, Islamic financial institutions and windows of conventional ones need to build internal Shariah teams that can support the business units in developing products and structuring transactions. These Shariah teams (who are full-time staff members of the institution) work under the guidance of the scholars on the Shariah committee (who, in contrast, are part-time advisors). The skill set required combines Shariah understanding with legal and regulatory insight, structuring expertise, and an understanding of tax considerations. Leaders of Shariah functions therefore often have formal training in both secular law and Islamic jurisprudence. For example, two successive heads of HSBC Amanah's internal Shariah team held degrees from both Harvard Law School and the International Islamic University in Pakistan.[6] The blend of such skills is rare and highly sought-after.

The product development process, if it is to be optimized, must include a number of considerations in addition to Shariah matters. The features and benefits of the product or service must be both competitive and tailored to the needs of the target customer base. Matters of pricing and bundling (combining multiple products into a single proposition) are also important decisions in the design process. Simply assuming that the same features and benefits that worked for a conventional product will work for an Islamic one can be a major mistake and may mean that the institution misses out on opportunities specific to the Shariah-compliant segment of the market. It is, however, a mistake that is commonly made in institutions that do not develop specialist expertise across the full capabilities spectrum.

A third key set of capabilities pertains to distribution and the customer experience. This domain is often overlooked (especially by firms using the product and window models), but it can be absolutely critical to a business's success or failure. The marketing approach for Shariah-compliant products often needs to differ from conventional campaigns in order to reflect Shariah authenticity and values. Heavy promotion of personal loans for consumption, for example, may rightly be criticized as being inconsistent with Islamic perspectives on limiting the use of debt for such purposes. Instead, the promotion of financing products related to education, home ownership, and other productive ends may find better reception and be viewed as more appropriate.

It is also essential that the sales and service channels responsible for distributing Islamic products have an adequate level of product and Shariah knowledge. In a conventional branch or call center, it may be impossible or highly impractical to train all personnel on the details of Islamic products. There does, however, need to be some level of expertise in every branch or call center so that questions on these products can be routed to individuals who are competent to address them. Conventional institutions offering Islamic products can expect that at least some customers will probe them on their Shariah credentials and authenticity, asking tough questions like, "What makes this Islamic home financing any different from your conventional mortgage?" One deadly mistake is to have nobody available who can answer such questions. Another—perhaps more deadly—mistake would be for the salesperson to provide an answer that is inaccurate or shallow, and thereby lose the customer's confidence forever.

To illustrate the importance of the full capabilities spectrum, consider the example of launching an Islamic *mudaraba*-based savings account for retail customers. Customarily, such an account would involve a profit-sharing mechanism by which the bank provides a return to depositors based on its overall performance. From a Shariah perspective, there should theoretically also be the possibility of a loss (although central bank guarantees of deposits may make this inapplicable in practice). One might assume that developing, launching, and distributing such a product should be no more complex than carrying out the equivalent process for a conventional savings account. A closer look, however, reveals complexities and nuances across the entire capabilities spectrum.

At the strategy and proposition design stage, it is necessary to consider the competitive landscape and what Islamic savings accounts are being offered by other institutions. In some markets, *mudaraba* savings accounts are common; in others, they are rare and relatively unfamiliar. Thus, introducing the product may require a greater or lesser degree of customer education, and the positioning of the product—whether it is positioned as a breakthrough or as a staple product—will depend on how new the concept is to the marketplace. To assess the likely returns that the product will provide, it is necessary to look at the historical performance and profit-sharing policies. Customarily, the profit-sharing amount for a particular month is announced after the month is over, since it needs to be based on the institution's performance. Strategists and product developers would need to collect historical data and consider likely profit rates going forward based on patterns from the past.

At the structuring and product development stage, the profit-sharing formulas and mechanics need to be carefully thought through. Too small a profit share may disappoint and drive away customers; too generous a profit share may unnecessarily raise an institution's cost of funds. For institutions operating under a product or window model, there is also the delicate question of how the rate of return on an Islamic savings account should compare with that on a conventional account. If the two rates are consistently identical, observers will question the Shariah authenticity of the Islamic account and wonder whether the account is truly linked to the bank's performance. If the Islamic rate is consistently higher, conventional bankers may view this as "cannibalizing" conventional customers and raising the bank's overall cost of funds in the process. If Islamic rates are consistently lower, Islamic customers may feel slighted. Hence, there are no easy answers.

Unique complexities continue into the distribution and customer experience stage. Sales representatives need to be trained to address the unfamiliar process by which profit rates are not known until the end of the month and are paid out based on average daily balances for the period. In the case of a conventional product, a sales representative will rarely be asked about historical interest rates; with an Islamic product, this is a common (and understandable) question. Beyond the initial sale, ongoing support may be needed to address questions about the profit share and other matters that may arise over time. Also, the announcement of profit rates provides a monthly opportunity to communicate with the customer—a chance to build trust, enhance the brand, and perhaps even cross-sell a few products. Thus, a broad set of capabilities, spanning beyond the core area of Shariah structuring and product development, poses a challenge but also introduces many opportunities.

SHAPING THE ENVIRONMENT

For breakthrough success in Islamic finance, leading institutions may often need to play a role in shaping the broader environment in which they operate. While this applies to conventional financial services as well, it is a far more pressing need in the Islamic financial services sector. This is because Islamic finance is a more recent phenomenon, and thus developing an environment conducive for its success is often required.

Figure 12.3 illustrates four broad areas in which leading Islamic institutions shape their environment to enable success.

In most Muslim markets, customer awareness of Islamic finance remains relatively low. Indonesia, with the world's largest Muslim population, is a prime example. Despite its massive customer base, it is estimated that less than 5 percent of total banking assets are Islamic.[7] One major reason for this is believed to be a relatively low level of awareness of Islamic finance, its offerings, and its viability. Even in markets where Islamic finance is present, questions about these matters may be prevalent. Addressing them through public campaigns, media interviews, and the like can therefore be very important for enabling Islamic finance to succeed in the marketplace.

Another essential dimension in which Islamic financial institutions need to shape their environments is regulatory enablement. As discussed in Chapter 3, regulatory enablement is essential if Islamic

FIGURE   12.3

Leading Islamic Financial Institutions Actively Shape Their Environments

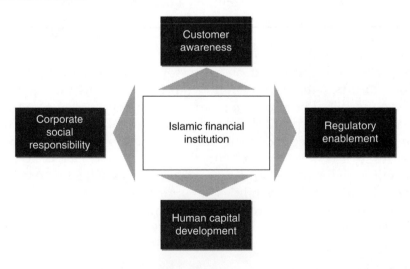

financial institutions are to compete with their conventional counterparts. Changes in tax laws, stamp duty policies, and other aspects of financial regulation are typically required. While a minimal level of enablement is needed just to maintain parity with conventional finance, more supportive regulation can help Islamic financial institutions structure themselves in more authentic and compelling ways. Institutions that are leaders in their markets (or aspire to become them) often play formal and informal roles in advising regulators, providing comments on policy recommendations, and helping to suggest government initiatives. The government of the United Kingdom, for example, has established a number of advisory bodies on which leaders from the industry serve and provide their counsel to the appropriate regulators.[8]

Third, leading institutions play a role in fostering human capital development for the industry. This is achieved through participating in training seminars, supporting research initiatives involving students and young professionals, and supporting programs at universities. Harvard University, for example, has had a pioneering Islamic finance research project since 1995. Its corporate sponsors to date have included the Abu Dhabi Islamic Bank, Bahrain-based Arcapita, Kuwait Finance House, HSBC Amanah, and other leading institutions.[9] In addition to producing research, holding seminars, and developing intellectual capital, the project has also inspired a number of Harvard alumni to pursue careers in Islamic finance. Many more young professionals have been developed at well-established training centers such as the London-based Institute of Islamic Banking and Insurance,[10] the Center for Islamic Finance at the Bahrain Institute of Banking and Finance,[11] and the Malaysia-based International Centre for Education in Islamic Finance (INCEIF). INCEIF enjoys the support of Malaysia's central bank and is chaired by its current governor, Dr. Tan Sri Dato' Zeti Akhtar Aziz.[12] Such initiatives are vital for developing a long-term talent pool for Islamic finance made up of professionals who are able to view the sector from a principle-based and holistic perspective rather than seeking to always imitate conventional finance.

Fourth, leading Islamic financial institutions are expected to undertake meaningful corporate social responsibility (CSR) initiatives. Part of this is a standard expectation of all financial institutions, especially in a postcrisis era in which the public trust in banks has suffered significantly. In addition to this basic level of CSR required, however, customers will often expect an Islamic institution to be especially responsible and charitable. Since responsibility and the support of good causes is part of the Islamic value system, one would expect Shariah-compliant institutions to be at least as responsible as their conventional competitors, and perhaps even more responsible given their espoused values. In 2009, the business journal *Dinar Standard* launched a survey to benchmark CSR in the Islamic finance sector, the results of which may motivate an increased level of CSR activity among Shariah-compliant financial institutions.[13]

Illustration: BIBD's "Wish Campaign"

Bank Islam Brunei Darussalam (BIBD), Brunei's largest Islamic bank, provides an instructive example of influencing the environment in its "Wish Campaign." The campaign, launched in 2009, is an innovative blend of awareness building, marketing, and CSR. In the campaign, which is open to BIBD account holders, customers are asked to submit a wish stating what they plan to do with the prize funds if they should receive them. The submission form forces entrants to think about their financial objectives in a structured way. A panel of judges reviews the submissions and chooses winners based on standard criteria. As shown in the Figure 12.4, Wish Campaign helps BIBD shape its environment in a number of ways consistent with its values.

F I G U R E   12.4

BIBD's Wish Campaign Shapes the Environment in a Number of Ways

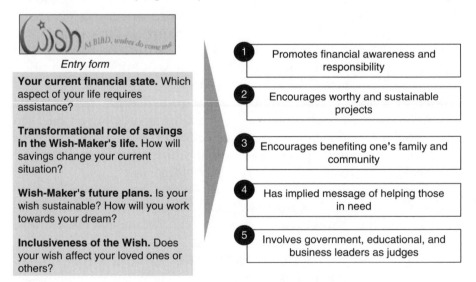

Source: BIBD Web site, http://bibdwish.com/index.php, and research team analysis, 2009.

The form itself encourages financial awareness and responsibility by requiring the entrant to think through his financial state and future plans. Implied in this requirement is that the wish should have a concrete and long-term impact on the entrant's financial well-being. The form also encourages the entrant to make "inclusive" and "sustainable" wishes, both of which enforce BIBD's brand positioning as values-based and community-focused. Setting this up as a contest gives entrants an incentive to craft the most worthy wish with the greatest social impact. By assessing the entrant's "financial state," the form implies that it seeks (at least in part) to help customers who may be in financial need because of extraordinary circumstances. Finally, the judges of the contest include an official from the Ministry of Culture, Youth, and Sports, two senior university officials, a Shariah scholar, two business leaders, and BIBD's own CEO. This deepens the bank's relationships with each of these sectors and builds on its goodwill with decision makers throughout the country.

BIBD's Wish Campaign is an example of a well-considered initiative that reflects the bank's values, raises customer awareness, and builds goodwill with external stakeholders. It is likely to help both BIBD and the community it serves.

KEY LESSONS

- Conventional institutions employ *three core business models* in offering Islamic financial services: the product, window, and subsidiary models.

- Each model has its *relative benefits and drawbacks*, with the optimal model for any given institution being dependent on that institution's unique circumstances.

- For a winning Islamic finance proposition, institutions need skills along *a full capabilities spectrum*—Shariah structuring and product development skills alone are not enough.

- Leading Islamic financial institutions play a role in *shaping their environments*, helping to create the conditions for their success.

CONCLUSION

Embracing Change

Our exploration of Gulf capital and Islamic finance is nearly completed. In Part I, we provided a background for and overview of these new global players, reviewing their origins, their evolution to date, and the current landscape. In Part II, we discussed key trends that are shaping the development of Gulf capital and Islamic finance, highlighting key shifts in the strategies and behaviors of these actors on the world stage. In Part III, we explored the implications of our analysis for a range of stakeholders and firms: companies and advisors seeking to attract Gulf capital, principal investors in global capital markets, regulators overseeing capital flows from the region, and financial services institutions seeking to tap into Islamic finance as a growth opportunity.

In closing, we share a handful of observations pertaining to ongoing change and ever-shifting global and regional markets. Our concluding thoughts seek to frame the rise of Gulf capital and Islamic finance in the broader context of a changing world, and to highlight key areas of ongoing evolution. We aim to highlight a few broad questions that are of fundamental relevance to Gulf capital and Islamic finance and will need to be addressed in the years ahead. Effectively anticipating, recognizing, and adapting to change will remain, in our view, the core challenge both for Gulf investors and

Islamic financial institutions and for global firms that wish to incorporate these global players into their corporate and investment strategies.

THE BIGGER PICTURE: TOWARD A MULTIPOLAR WORLD

This book has explored Gulf capital and Islamic finance as key phenomena shaping international markets, and has discussed them largely as stand-alone global trends. Doing so has enabled us to review Gulf capital and Islamic finance in greater depth and with a significant level of detail. It is, however, pivotal to note that the rise of these global players—and the shifts in their behavior and outlook—is linked to broader economic and financial trends. The Gulf and Islamic finance do not operate in isolation; they are shaped by the world around them, and they interact with global markets in increasingly interdependent ways.

The economic forces that have enabled Gulf surpluses have also brought clout to other resource-endowed economies, such as Russia, and other savings-oriented economies, such as China. The growth of Islamic finance, while outpacing that of conventional finance in the Gulf, nonetheless owes much of its expansion to the underlying favorable economics of the Gulf Cooperation Council (GCC) region (and of other key Muslim markets) and to social trends supporting a more assertive Muslim identity. Gulf investors' increased affinity for alternative investments reflects a broader trend among large institutional investors (including university endowments, for example) toward private equity and direct investments. The Gulf's enhanced focus on investing in emerging markets is also inherently linked to a general shift seen among the world's institutional investors and to the realities of how emerging markets have become increasingly attractive destinations for capital. Increased disclosure and transparency are requirements not only for Gulf-based institutions, but also for investors worldwide as regimes tighten their requirements in order to monitor capital flows closely because of security and tax-related concerns. All these trends, though not exclusive to the Gulf, manifest themselves in a unique way in the GCC context.

For global firms and international stakeholders, the rise of the Gulf and of Islamic finance may perhaps best be understood as part of a shift toward an increasingly multipolar world. In recent years, the topography of global markets has, for a number of fundamental reasons, been migrating toward a more multipolar financial system. Increased collaboration and coordination within the European Union (EU) has (as least to some degree) made the EU a sizable and cohesive economic superpower. The "BRIC" economies of Brazil, Russia, India, and China have become increasingly meaningful economic actors, with China and India being especially important to the global flow of goods, services, and capital. A global financial crisis and worldwide recession have highlighted the vulnerability of the world's most developed economies, leading regulators to fundamentally question their approach to supervision and institutions to recraft their long-term geographic investment allocations. Underpinning all this is the fact that firms are increasingly global, with commercial and financial exposure to a broad range of markets through direct business and through their networks of customers, suppliers, and partners. Within these currents of change, the rise of Gulf capital and Islamic finance are two waves contributing to broader shifts in the tide.

The implications for global firms of a multipolar financial world are profound. Companies and funds that are seeking to raise capital must look not only at the preferences of New York and London, but also at the appetites of Beijing, Abu Dhabi, Riyadh, and Doha. Principals that are making global investments can draw insights not only from the analysis and commentary of Organisation for Economic Co-operation and Development (OECD)–based economists, but also from the activities and evolving preferences of Middle Eastern and Asian investors. Regulators monitoring capital markets must recognize the increasingly central roles of non-OECD players and adapt their supervisory strategies accordingly.

Gulf Capital and Islamic Finance has given you an understanding of these phenomena and a perspective on their evolution. This is an essential step in developing strategies that incorporate these new global players effectively. As you continue to explore Gulf capital and Islamic finance, however, viewing them in isolation may not be enough. It is also important that you appreciate the linkages between these phenomena and other trends that are shaping the global financial system. In fact, the inherent linkages between Gulf capital, Islamic finance, and other developments only affirm the status of Gulf capital and Islamic finance as genuinely global players. As their actions in the world have real impact on financial markets, what happens internationally necessarily shapes these two phenomena.

THE NUANCES OF GULF CAPITAL

In much of our commentary, we have spoken of "Gulf capital" in the aggregate. This has allowed us to assess its overall background and evolution, ongoing trends, and implications for external counterparties and stakeholders. Indeed, Gulf capital has manifested itself as a singular phenomenon with the constituent institutions and markets that make up the GCC having common patterns of behavior. As we close our analysis, however, it's worth remembering that Gulf capital is by no means a monolith. The diverse landscape that we presented in Chapter 2 and revisited throughout the book is crucial in appreciating that different types of Gulf-based institutions have different objectives, approaches, and portfolios, and therefore a robust segmentation is needed to understand them.

At the market level, it is also worthwhile to note that the economies of the GCC, while they continue to have much in common, diverge meaningfully along a number of key economic indicators. Figure C.1 illustrates a "barbell" clustering of the region based on salient economic attributes.

The UAE, Qatar, and Kuwait, identified as "surplus-enabled states" in our framework, collectively enjoyed a GDP per capita of $51,000 and a surplus per capita of more than $10,000 in the year 2008. Their small population base—about 8 million across all three countries—enables them to focus a large share of their income on international investments. As we have observed throughout the book, many of the most prominent

FIGURE C.1

GCC Markets May Be Seen as Being Clustered like a Barbell

Note: 2008 data used; GDP expressed in purchasing power parity.
Source: *CIA World Factbook*, 2009; research team analysis.

institutions leading the evolution of Gulf capital hail from these countries, and these institutions have driven the bulk of the high-profile and groundbreaking transactions that we've discussed.

Saudi Arabia, as the "core market" of the GCC, is a cluster in and of itself. With roughly two-thirds of the region's population and half its overall GDP, Saudi Arabia is the dominant market from the perspective of commercial activity within the region. Its large population—estimated at 29 million—and large territory demand significant domestic investment, job creation, and ongoing infrastructure enhancements. While the country has historically had sizable surpluses (about $5,500 per person in 2008), volatility in global oil markets can bring price levels close to Saudi Arabia's breakeven point, and the Kingdom has experienced deficits before in previous oil busts. As we have discussed, Saudi Arabia has been marked by traditionally conservative institutional investments complemented by a wide range of private institutions and business families.

Bahrain and Oman make up a third cluster, dubbed "real economies" in our framework. With a relatively modest GDP per capita of $23,000 and minimal surpluses, both of these countries have been engaged in active diversification strategies for their economies. Bahrain, a longstanding financial services hub of the region, has developed significant manufacturing and industrial capabilities to complement its services backbone. Oman is a diversified economy, with services making up the bulk of its activity.[1] Outward investment flows from these two countries are nonetheless meaningful (Bahrain is home to a number of key investment houses) and often strategic to support the countries' development strategies.

The barbell clustering of Gulf economies is an important nuance for understanding the sources, objectives, and behavior of Gulf capital. As global energy markets evolve, the barbell structuring may become even more pronounced as oil- and gas-based windfalls remain modest outside the surplus-enabled states. We can expect the GCC countries to continue to have a great deal in common, but these differences in economic structures will shape their outward investment volume and strategies.

DEFINING MOMENTS AHEAD

We live in rapidly changing times, marked by compressed business cycles and fast-moving international trends. Looking back, we can see the rise of Gulf capital and Islamic finance as new global players. Looking ahead, we see a number of defining moments on the horizon that can profoundly shape the course that these global players will take and the role that they may play in international finance.

Within the Gulf, a pressing imperative in the period ahead will be job creation for the millions of GCC nationals who are coming of age—roughly half the population of the GCC is under 20 years old.[2] As unprecedented numbers of Gulf nationals enter the workforce, the need to utilize this human capital (ideally in high-value sectors) will be a central theme for the region's decision makers. The "jobs imperative" will be a key driver of decisions cutting across all sectors: budget priorities, capital allocation, project initiation, skill development, economic policy, commercial law, employment law, and so on. Gulf capital—and particularly public-sector vehicles—can be expected to find itself increasingly influenced by a pervasive regional initiative to create employment.

A related (and highly delicate) question involves the balance between fostering local industries and enhancing the free flow of investments. Over the past decade, ongoing deregulation has been a consistent theme in the GCC and a key component of its increased market attractiveness. The rise of free zones has brought in world-class firms, and the ongoing reform of onshore ownership laws has made the region more accessible to global companies that can bring expertise to the Gulf. As boom times wane and domestic pressures rise, however, leaders' ability to maintain this trend of deregulation may face greater challenges. On the one hand, there is widespread acknowledgment that freer markets can enhance GCC competitiveness in the long run. At the same time, pressures to protect and grow local firms are real—especially as the private sector is expected to put more and more locals to work. Key test cases for this balance include whether and how Saudi Arabia introduces foreign ownership allowances in some of its new economic cities, and how the Kuwaiti parliament develops its stance on intervention in local capital markets and on joint ventures between foreign companies and state-owned enterprises.

Third, the evolution of Gulf governance models toward more participatory approaches will provide a number of key decision points. As discussed earlier in this book, private-sector governance models have become more participatory as a new generation of leaders has emerged and conglomerates are increasingly drawing on public markets and external sources of capital. In the public sector, participatory governance at the municipal level (through local elections) has taken root in the Gulf, and parliaments (particularly those of Kuwait and Bahrain) are playing increasingly vocal roles in decision making. In Kuwait, the parliament has been able to rock the government and block a high-profile joint venture with a multinational company. If the trend toward greater participation continues, state-linked investment vehicles may find themselves with a broader set of stakeholders—a change that could have a real impact on investment priorities and strategies.

At the multilateral level, there are also pivotal decisions to be made. The GCC union has proved to be important and valuable for enhancing political and trade ties within the region, as well as facilitating the flow of people and businesses. Further economic and monetary integration appears highly challenging, however, because of the barbell dynamics of GCC economies and other factors. The Organization of the Petroleum Exporting Companies (OPEC) remains a key platform for the Gulf to use to exercise global influence—as the organization evolves and the energy sector broadens, the integrity and importance of OPEC will continue to affect how much clout the Gulf states wield globally. Multilateral agreements like the Santiago Principles for sovereign wealth funds (discussed in Chapter 8), if they can take root and find acceptance, may be another platform for Gulf influence and proactive engagement of the international community.

The Islamic finance sector, as we discussed in Chapter 3, is at a critical juncture. The sector has continued to gain market share and is a sizable component of financial services in the Gulf and in certain other markets as well. By all accounts, Islamic finance has proven its viability. To advance further, however, the sector needs to address a perceived tension between authenticity and market share, and must also demonstrate genuine differentiation in the eyes of many potential customers. Another key challenge is for the industry to demonstrate an ability to (in the spirit of its focus on real assets) stimulate genuine economic development in the markets that it serves. The global financial crisis and the ensuing redesign of global financial regulation have provided an unprecedented opportunity for the sector to articulate and demonstrate the relevance of its core principles. A key question will be whether Islamic finance is able to effectively show the broader financial system its applicability and thereby strengthen its posture in international finance.

ENGAGING NEW GLOBAL PLAYERS

In recent years, Gulf capital and Islamic finance have influenced global markets in ways that few people would have expected. Companies raising capital—and the firms that serve them—are finding it increasingly important to incorporate the Gulf into their global fund-raising strategies. Principal investors find themselves encountering GCC-based institutions as sources of capital, competitors for attractive assets, and integral parts of exit strategies from portfolio companies. Banks and other financial services institutions clamor to serve Gulf clients. In addition, they see Islamic finance capabilities as essential for being a truly global firm and for serving key clients in the GCC and beyond. This book has given you tools and perspectives to understand the origins, trends, and implications of Gulf capital and Islamic finance for capital markets worldwide.

Your next encounter with Gulf capital and Islamic finance may be across the table, negotiating a transaction. Or you may find yourself marketing to a GCC-based or Shariah-compliant institution that is interested in your products and services. Alternatively, your work may not directly engage with the Gulf, but the actions of Gulf entities will influence your corporate strategy and investment outlook. Regardless of whether you actively engage with Gulf capital and Islamic finance, if your work involves capital markets, you cannot afford to ignore them. You've gotten to know two new global players—chances are that you will soon meet them again.

NOTES

INTRODUCTION

1. Yahoo! Finance, 2006 data.
2. BP, "Statistical Review of World Energy 2007."
3. Diana Farrell and Susan Lund, "Windfall in the Gulf: Big Bucks, Bigger Plans," *Milken Institute Review*, Second Quarter 2008.
4. Investcorp corporate Web site: www.investcorp.com/; accessed August 13, 2009.
5. Farrell and Lund, "Windfall in the Gulf."
6. IMF and *The Economist*, 2005 data; accessed 2006.
7. Gillian Tett, "Islamic Bonds Used to buy 007's Wheels," *Financial Times*, March 16, 2007, www.ft.com/cms/s/ 7461bd9c-d40a-11db-83d5-000b5df10621.html.
8. "Qatar," *CIA World Factbook*, (www.cia.gov/library/ publications/the-world-factbook/geos/qa.html, last accessed August 2009).
9. Qatar National Bank, 2006.
10. Farrell and Lund, "Windfall in the Gulf."
11. Aamir Rehman and S. Nazim Ali, "Breakthrough Ideas for 2008—Islamic Finance: The New Global Player," *Harvard Business Review*, February 2008.
12. Farrell and Lund, "Windfall in the Gulf."
13. Ibid.
14. Ibrahim Warde's book *Islamic Finance in the Global Economy* has been a seminal contribution in discussing the evolution of Islamic finance and its impact on international economies.
15. Julio Rotemberg, *The Dubai Ports World Debacle and its Aftermath* (Boston: Harvard Business School Publishing, 2006).
16. Emily Thornton and Stanley Reed, "Who's Afraid of Mideast Money?" *BusinessWeek,* January 10, 2008.

17. Andrew England and Javier Blas, "Saudis Set Aside $800m for Foreign Food," *Financial Times*, April 14, 2009, www.ft.com/cms/s/0/59a9da3a-2920-11de-bc5e-00144feabdc0.html?nclick_check=1.

18. The "accessible market" excludes Iran, which (at the time of this writing) is inaccessible to most global financial institutions.

19. Lorenzo Totaro, "Vatican Says Islamic Finance May Help Western Banks in Crisis," Bloomberg.com, www.bloomberg.com/apps/news?pid=20601092&sid=aOsOLE8uiNOg&refer=italy.

20. "Four Seasons Agrees to Gates, Alwaleed Buyout Bid," Reuters.com, February 12, 2007, www.reuters.com/article/businessNews/idUSWNAS052320070212.

21. Sundeep Tucker and Roula Khalaf, "Qatar Fund Spurned Wall Street," *Financial Times*, September 25, 2008, www.ft.com/cms/s/0/0d5a391e-8a9b-11dd-a76a-0000779fd18c.html.

22. Qatar National Bank, 2006.

23. MSCI, research team analysis, 2007.

24. "Kuwait to Invest $720 million in IPO of China's ICBC," Yahoo! Singapore, September 24, 2006, sg.biz.yahoo.com/060924/3/43mep.html; last accessed May 18, 2007.

25. Gulf African Bank Web site, www.gulfafricanbank.com/Home/About-Us; accessed May 2009.

26. Bank Islam Malaysia Web site, www.bankislam.com.my/bimb_pdf%5Cshareholding_structure.pdf; accessed May 2009.

27. Islamic Bank of Asia corporate Web site, www.islamicbankasia.com/about/factsheet/Pages/default.aspx; accessed May 2009.

28. The term *conventional finance* is used in contrast to *Islamic finance* to describe prevailing financial practices that do not comply with the Shariah.

29. Aamir Rehman, "Chasing Exchanges: Borse Dubai, the QIA, and OMX," December 2007, rehmaninstitute.wordpress.com/2007/12/06/chasing-exchanges-borse-dubai-the-qia-and-omx/.

30. Aamir Rehman, "Advantaged Airlines: Gulf Carriers' Competitive Positioning," rehmaninstitute.wordpress.com/2008/07/15/advantaged-airlines-gulf-carriers-competitive-positioning/.

CHAPTER 1

1. Quoted by Prince Amr bin Mohammad Al Faisal, PBS *Frontline*, 2003.

2. This anecdote, told to me by a leading Gulf executive, has been paraphrased and sanitized to protect the identities of the parties involved.

3. Diana Farrell and Susan Lund, "Windfall in the Gulf: Big Bucks, Bigger Plans," *Milken Institute Review*, Second Quarter 2008.

4. "A Country Study: United Arab Emirates," Library of Congress, January 1993, lcweb2.loc.gov/cgi-bin/query/r?frd/cstdy:@field(DOCID+ae0052) or lcweb2.loc.gov/frd/cs/aetoc.html; last accessed February 8, 2009.

5. Qur'an, 14:37. Author translation.

6. "Migrating Worlds—Yemeni Hadhramis in Southeast Asia," www.buzzle.com/editorials/1-11-2006-86065.asp.

7. Stanley Reed, Dexter Roberts, and Nandini Lakshman, "The New Silk Road," *BusinessWeek*, November 6, 2008, www.businessweek.com/magazine/content/08_46/b41080 46852388.htm?chan=globalbiz_europe+index+page_top+stories.

8. New Silk Route corporate Web site, nsrpartners.com/index.html; accessed May 12, 2009.

9. David Clingingsmith, Asim Ijaz Khwaja, and Michael Kremer have undertaken important research on the impact of the Hajj on the attitudes of pilgrims—in particular, as related to religious tolerance; ksgaccman.harvard.edu/publications/Search_Faculty.asp?PersonID=72

10. Aamir Rehman, "The 'Hajj Economy' and Gulf Competitiveness," December 24, 2008, rehmaninstitute.wordpress.com/2008/12/24/the-hajj-economy-and-gulf-competitiveness-fostering-and-leveraging-capabilities/.

11. For in-depth background on the economies of the Gulf, see Chapter 4 of *Dubai & Co.*

12. Farrell and Lund, "Windfall in the Gulf."

13. *CIA World Factbook*, 2006, and author analysis.

14. US Treasury Direct, www.treasurydirect.gov/NP/BPDLogin?application=np, and US Census Bureau,

Population Division, www.census.gov/popest/estimates
.html; last updated April 25, 2009; accessed May 2009.

15. Farrell and Lund, "Windfall in the Gulf."

16. Ibid.

17. Ibid.

18. "Saudi Arabia Expects $16b Budget Deficit," Reuters,
December 22, 2008, www.gulfnews.com/Business/
Economy/10269427.html.

19. Yahoo! Finance, accessed May 12, 2009.

20. *CIA World Factbook*, February 2009.

21. Ibid.

22. Ibid.

23. For further discussion of economic diversification in the
region, see Chapters 2 and 4 of *Dubai & Co.*

24. "World Economic Outlook Update: Global Economic Slump
Challenges Policies," IMF, January 28, 2009, www.imf.
org/external/pubs/ft/weo/2009/update/01/index.htm;
last accessed March 10, 2009.

25. For a detailed profile of each Gulf state, see Chapter 4 of
Dubai & Co.

26. "World Economic Outlook Update."

27. BP, "Statistical Review of World Energy 2006."

28. WSJ.com, online.wsj.com/public/page/news-oil-gold-
commodities.html; accessed May 24, 2009.

29. US Department of Energy Web site; www.oe.energy.gov/;
accessed June 2009.

30. US Department of Energy Web site, apps1.eere.energy.gov/
news/news_detail.cfm/news_id=12509; accessed June
2009.

31. US Department of Energy Web site, www.energy.gov/
organization/dr_steven_chu.htm.

32. For insights into the phenomenon of speculative boom-
and-bust cycles, see John Kenneth Galbraith's classic work
A Short History of Financial Euphoria. (New York: Penguin,
1994).

33. BP, "Statistical Review of World Energy 2007."

34. BP, "Statistical Review of World Energy 2006."

35. Brad Setser and Rachel Ziemba, "GCC Sovereign Funds: Reversal of Fortune," Working Paper, Council on Foreign Relations, January 2009.

36. For more on "Gulf-style democracy," see Chapter 4 of *Dubai & Co.*

CHAPTER 2

1. This anecdote was told to me anonymously by a senior Gulf-based investment professional in 2009.

2. Sovereign Wealth Fund Institute, Global Fund Rankings, January 2009.

3. Diane Farrell, Susan Lund, Eva Gerlemann, and Peter Seeburger, "The New Power Brokers: How Oil, Asia, Hedge Funds, and Private Equity Are Shaping Global Capital Markets," McKinsey Global Institute, October 2007, p. 52.

4. Zawya, "Wealth Funds in the UAE Lead Way with Transparency," March 3, 2009.

5. MoneyWorks, "Challenges of Asset Management in the GCC," October 2007, p. 6.

6. Profile excerpted from *Dubai & Co.*

7. "Sovereign Wealth Funds," *Economist*, May 24, 2007, www.economist.com/finance/displaystory.cfm?story_id= 9230598.

8. "Money and Mystery: Adia Unveils Its Secrets," *Euromoney*, 2006, www.euromoney.com/Article/1018077/Article.html

9. IFSL Research, "Sovereign Wealth Funds 2009," March 2009.

10. Ibid.

11. Richard Vietor and Nicole Forrest, "Saudi Arabia: Modern Reform, Ensuring Stability," Harvard Business School case, February 2009.

12. Farrell et al, "The New Power Brokers," p. 54; William Miracky et al., "Assessing the Risks: The Behaviours of Sovereign Wealth Funds in the Global Economy," Monitor Group, June 2008; Brad Setser and Rachel Ziemba, "Understanding the New Financial Superpower—the Management of GCC Official Foreign Assets," December 2007.

13. "Barclay's Foreign Investors Raise Stake to 16%," *Times Online*, July 18, 2008.

14. Sovereign Wealth Fund Institute, QIA profile; accessed 2009.

15. "The Impact of the Global Financial Crisis on Sovereign Wealth Funds," *Khaleej Times*, Knowledge@Wharton, March 11, 2009.

16. Ibid.

17. Zawya, "Kuwait Sovereign Fund Head Urges Coordination," April 5, 2009.

18. Rawi Abdelal and Irina Tarsis, "Mubadala: Forging Development in Abu Dhabi," Harvard Business School case, January 2009.

19. SDIF Historical Review, www.sidf.gov.sa/english/4/Historical/index.htm; accessed June 2009.

20. Ziemba, RGE Monitor, June 2008.

21. Abdelal and Tarsis, "Mubadala: Forging Development in Abu Dhabi."

22. Mark Mulligan and James Drummond, "Santander Offloads Cepsa Stake to MidEast Group," *Financial Times Online*, March 31, 2009.

23. "Abu Dhabi's IPIC to Buy Debt-Laden Nova Chemicals," Reuters, February 23, 2009.

24. Miracky et al., "Assessing the Risks," p. 80.

25. Ziemba, RGE Monitor, June 2008.

26. Abdelal and Tarsis, "Mubadala: Forging Development in Abu Dhabi."

27. Mubadala Web site, www.mubadala.ae/en/media/press-releases/ratings-agencies-assign-aa-to-mubadala.html; accessed June 2009.

28. Andrew England, "Abu Dhabi Flexes International Dealmaking Muscle," *Financial Times Online*, March 24, 2009.

29. William Miracky et al., "Sovereign Wealth Fund Investment Behavior: Analysis of Sovereign Wealth Fund Investment Behavior during Q3 2008," Monitor Group, December 2008, p. 17.

30. Abdelal and Tarsis, "Mubadala: Forging Development in Abu Dhabi."

31. Zawya, "GCC Private Wealth Reserves over $1.5 Trillion," November 1, 2008.

32. Farrell et al, "The New Power Brokers," p. 52.

33. Ibid.

34. IMF, 2007 estimates, www.imf.org/external/country/ SAU/index.htm.

35. *CIA World Factbook*, 2008.

36. For more information on regulatory barriers to market entry by international firms, see Chapter 5 of *Dubai & Co.*

37. IMF, 2007 estimates, www.imf.org/external/country/ SAU/index.htm.

38. "Special Report: The World's 50 Richest Arabs, Profile of Nasser Al Kharafi," *Arabian Business*, December 2008.

39. "Profile: Al Khair National for Stocks and Real Estate Co.," GulfBase, March 2009.

40. "DIFC Opens Up to Family-Run Businesses," *Trade Arabia*, September 2, 2008.

41. "Special Report: The World's 50 Richest Arabs," *Arabian Business*, December 2008, www.arabianbusiness.com/richlist.

42. "Santander, Spain's biggest bank, on Tuesday agreed to sell its 32.5 per cent stake in oil refiner Cepsa to the International Petroleum Investment Company (Ipic) of Abu Dhabi for about €2.8bn ($3.8bn). The sale, following a year of intermittent negotiations, represents the divestment of the Spanish bank's last remaining substantial equity holding. Unión Fenosa, the Spanish electricity group, will sell its 5 per cent stake in Cepsa as part of the same deal." This article can be found at: www.ft.com/cms/s/0/ 400cdba8-1dd7-11de-830b-00144feabdc0,_i_email=y.html.

43. Investcorp corporate Web site, www.investcorp.com/; accessed August 2009.

44. Abdelal and Tarsis, "Mubadala: Forging Development in Abu Dhabi."

45. Investcorp corporate Web site, www.investcorp.com/ Template1a.aspx?pageid=IR2.6.

46. Markaz Research, "GCC Equity Funds," February 2009, Appendix 9.

47. Ibid.

48. Johanna Symmons, "MENA on Track to Be the New BRIC," *Wealth Bulletin*, March 10, 2008.

49. Gulf Venture Capital Association, "Private Equity and Venture Capital in the Middle East," 2008 Annual Report.

50. Ibid.

51. Alf Yad Web site, www.alfyad.ae/; accessed June 2009.

52. Gulf Venture Capital Association, "Private Equity and Venture Capital in the Middle East."

53. Ibid.

CHAPTER 3

1. Lorenzo Totaro, "Vatican Says Islamic Finance May Help Western Banks Crises," Bloomberg.com, March 4, 2009, www.bloomberg.com/apps/news?pid=20601092&sid=aOs OLE8uiNOg&refer=italy.

2. This incident is paraphrased from an experience in 2008.

3. Aamir Rehman and Nazim Ali, "Islamic Finance: The New Global Player," *Harvard Business Review*, February 2008.

4. The term *conventional* is used to describe prevailing financial practices that do not conform to the Shariah.

5. Important reference works on Islamic finance include the works of Prof. Mahmoud El-Gamal, Prof. Ibrahim Warde, and Justice Taqi Usmani. For insight into the broader economic principles underpinning Islamic finance, seminal works include the writings of Dr. M. Umer Chapra and Prof. Nejatullah Siddiqui.

6. The term *Shariah* is derived from the same root as the word *path*, reflecting the view of Shariah as the path prescribed by God.

7. The title *shaykh* traces its origins to the term used for elders in traditional tribal societies. Over time, the term also came to be applied to scholars and intellectuals. Today, it is additionally used for royalty and other dignitaries, particularly in the Gulf.

8. The principles that follow have been articulated by the author, who is not a specialist in Islamic law. They are presented as a basic framework for reference in understanding the ethics behind Islamic financial services.

9. For more on the concept of *riba*, see Prof. Mahmoud El-Gamal's work *A Basic Guide to Contemporary Islamic Banking and Finance* (Houston: Rice University, 2000).

10. El-Gamal, *A Basic Guide to Contemporary Islamic Banking and Finance.*

11. Ann Pettifor, presentation at the MASIC Investment Forum, Riyadh, January 2009.

12. Differing views regarding the sale of debt are the reason why many Islamic debt offerings originated in Malaysia are not deemed to be Shariah-compliant by a majority of scholars globally.

13. Aamir Rehman, "The Relevance of Islamic Finance Principles to the Global Financial Crisis," presented at Harvard Law School, March 2009.

14. The two cases here reflect the spirit of the *murabaha* and *istisna'* modes of financing present in Islamic finance.

15. Qur'an, 2:275, translated by the author.

16. *Let's Make a Deal* profile at TV.com, www.tv.com/show/5457/summary.html; accessed July 2009.

17. Rehman, "Relevance of Islamic Finance Principles."

18. Tabung Haji corporate Web site, www.tabunghaji.gov.my/th/TH/THHajiMontaj.html.

19. *CIA World Factbook*, 2009.

20. Bank Islam Malaysia Web site, www.bankislam.com.my/bimb_pdf%5Cshareholding_structure.pdf; accessed July 2009.

21. Shariah Capital Web site, www.shariahcap.com/products.php; accessed July 2009.

22. For an in-depth discussion of *tawarruq*, see the proceeding of the Harvard Islamic Finance Program workshop on this topic: "Tawarruq: A Methodological Issue in Shari'a-Compliant Finance," February 2007 (brief report at ifptest.law.harvard.edu/ifphtml/ifpseminars/WorkshoponTawarruq.pdf).

23. I am indebted to Iqbal Khan, CEO of Fajr Capital and formerly founding CEO of HSBC Amanah, for his insight into this matter in particular and all aspects of Islamic finance more broadly.

24. I am grateful to the insights of my colleagues Rafe Haneef and Saud Hashimi regarding the need for incentive systems that reward Shariah authenticity.

25. Tax treatment is of negligible concern in the GCC today because of the minimal or absent taxation there.

26. Mohammed Amin and Tariq Hameed are to be thanked for sharing their insights regarding the United Kingdom's regulatory approach to Islamic finance.

CHAPTER 4

1. This anecdote is based on an incident reported by a member of the research team.

2. Diane Farrell, Susan Lund, Eva Gerlemann, and Peter Seeburger, "The New Power Brokers: How Oil, Asia, Hedge Funds, and Private Equity Are Shaping Global Capital Markets, McKinsey Global Institute, October 2007.

3. Forbes.com, "Crude Oil Prices 1861–2009," www.forbes .com/2005/11/01/oil-prices-1861-today-real-vs-nominal_flash.html; accessed August 2009.

4. GulfBase Daily Market Review, www.gulfbase.com/site/ interface/SpecialReport/m/3/Abu_Dhabi_Stock_Exchange_ 02-08-09.htm; accessed August 4, 2009.

5. Qatar Investment Authority, About Us,www.qia.qa/QIA/ about.html.

6. Yale University endowment annual report, 2006.

7. For a detailed discussion of staffing and organizational matters, see Chapter 7 of *Dubai & Co.*

8. "Money and Mystery: ADIA Unveils Its Secrets," *Euromoney*, 2006, www.euromoney.com/Article/1018077/ Article.html.

9. Emily Thornton and Stanley Reed, "Inside the Abu Dhabi Investment Authority," *BusinessWeek*, June 6, 2008.

10. Public Register, QFC Authority, accessed spring 2009.

11. Poppy Trowbridge and Amber Choudhury, "KKR Hires Former Saudi Ambassador Fraker as Adviser," Bloomberg .com, May 18, 2009.

12. "Carlyle Raises $500 Million for Mideast Fund," *New York Times Online*, March 9, 2009.

13. Dean Foster and H. Peyton Young, "The Hedge Fund Game: Incentives, Excess Returns, and Performance

Mimics," Nuffield College Economics Working Papers, March 2008.

14. Richard Teitelbaum, "Paulson Bucks Paulson as His Hedge Funds Score $1 Billion Gain," Bloomberg.com, December 2, 2008.

15. Philip Aldrick, "Sheikh Mansour Has Been Ahead of the Game on Barclays," Telegraph.co.uk, June 2, 2009, www.telegraph.co.uk/finance/comment/5431878/Sheikh-Mansour-has-been-ahead-of-the-game-on-Barclays.html.

16. Stanley Reed and Emily Thornton, "Meet the Master of Mideast Buyouts," *BusinesssWeek*, February 28, 2008, www.businessweek.com/magazine/content/08_10/b40740 68316530.htm.

17. Zawya Profile, Lubna Olayan, www.zawya.com/cm/officers_bio.cfm?id_officer=64107.

18. Milken Institute Global Conference 2009 Web site.

19. Thornton and Reed, "Inside the Abu Dhabi Investment Authority."

CHAPTER 5

1. Center for Muslim-Christian Understanding Web site, http:cmcu.georgetown.edu/about/; last accessed August 2009.

2. Harvard Law School Web site, www.law.harvard.edu/students/dean/resources/courseevals/ProfsN-Z.php; accessed August 2009.

3. Qatar Foundation, Education Division, Universities Web site www.qf.org.qa/output/page277.asp.

4. Emaar corporate Web site, www.emaar.com/International/usa/Index.asp.

5. Waleed Khalil Rasromani, "Financial Executives Foresee Weaker Correlation with Gulf Stock Markets," *Daily Star* (Egypt), July 12, 2006, www.dailystaregypt.com/article.aspx?ArticleID=2235.

6. Stanley Reed, "The New Middle East Oil Bonanza," *BusinessWeek*, March 13, 2006.

7. *CIA World Fact Book*, 2009.

8. J. E. Peterson, "The Emergence of the Nation-States in the Arabian Peninsula," *GeoJournal* 13, no. 3, October 1986.

9. William Miracky et al., "Assessing the Risks: The Behaviours of Sovereign Wealth Funds in the Global Economy," Monitor Group, June 2008, p. 5.

10. "The History of KAUST," KAUST Web site, www.kaust.edu .sa/about/history-of-kaust.aspx; last accessed August 2009.

11. Jon Leyne, "Dubai Ruler in Vast Charity Gift," BBC News, May 19, 2007.

12. Florence Eid, "The Other Face of Arab Wealth: Domestic Investment Opportunities," Passport Capital, Syrian Banking Conference, November 2008.

13. New York University, Abu Dhabi Campus Web site, nyuad.nyu.edu/about/index.html.

14. "Etisalat Denies Foreign Ownership Rumour," Reuters, October 25, 2007, www.arabianbusiness.com/502580-etisalat-denies-foreign-ownership-rumour; last accessed August 2009.

15. AME Info, "QSTP Unveiled as Qatar's Newest Beacon of Knowledge with Official Inauguration," March 19, 2009.

16. "RAK Free Trade Zone," UAE Free Zones Web site, www.uaefreezones.com/fz_ras_al_khaimah.html : last accessed September 2009.

17. "Saudi Arabia: Six New Cities to Change the Face of the Kingdom," Adnkronos International Web site, www .adnkronos.com/AKI/English/Business/?id= 1.0.1116763895; last accessed August 2009.

18. Shawkat Hammoudeh and Eisa Aleisa, "Dynamic Relationships among GCC Stock Markets and NYMEX Oil Futures," *Contemporary Economic Policy*, April 2009.

19. "GCC Market Cap Slumps $38bn in 10 Days," Zawya, June 28, 2009.

20. Khalil Hanware, "GCC Market Cap Breaches $1 Trillion Mark," *Arab News*, January 24, 2006.

21. David Ignatius, "Where's the Oil Money?" *Washington Post*, December 9, 2005, www.relocalize.net/node/1723.

22. AME Info, "GCC Market Capitalization Crossed $1 trillion Threshold to Constitute 20% of the Market Capitalization of All Emerging Markets," February 21, 2006.

23. Rasromani, "Financial Executives Foresee Weaker Correlation."

24. Mushtak Parker, "Saudi Banking and Industrialization," *Arab News*, December 6, 2006, www.arabnews.com/? page=15&section=0&article=89608&d=10&m=5&y=2007.

25. Reuters, "Gulf Markets 'Cannot Afford a Crash,'" *Gulf News*, April 3, 2006, archive.gulfnews.com/articles/ 06/03/04/10022969.html.

26. Jia Lynn Yang, "Saudi Arabia's Stock Collapse," *Fortune*, January 17, 2007, money.cnn.com/magazines/fortune/ fortune_archive/2006/12/11/8395382/index.htm.

27. Investment Company Institute, "Half of American Households Own Equities," 2002, www.ici.org/ shareholders/dec/02_news_equity_ownership.html.

28. Bloomberg data and analysis by research team.

29. Bloomberg, Dubai Financial Market, April 1, 2007– September 1, 2008.

30. Bloomberg, Dow Jones Industrial Average, March 2, 2007–October 12, 2007.

31. Merrill Lynch, "Global Economic Decoupling Gathers Pace but It's a Marathon, Not a Sprint," June 8, 2007.

32. Bloomberg Web site, www.bloomberg.com/?b=0&Intro= intro3; last accessed August 2009.

33. David Pais, "Remember $150 Oil?" *Indian Express*, April 13, 2009.

34. Margaret Coker and Chip Cummins, "Financial Storm Hits Gulf," *Wall Street Journal*, October 27, 2008.

35. Bloomberg, Saudi Tadawul All Share Index, November 27–December 24, 2007, and January 15, 2008–January 22, 2008.

36. Peter Cooper, "My 2008 forecasts, right globally, wrong locally," blog entry on December 30, 2008, arabianmoney .net/2008/12/, retrieved on September 16, 2009.

37. AME Info, "Investors Bewildered by GCC Stock Market Crash, March 14, 2006.

38. "Gateway to Growth," World Finance Web site, www .worldfinance.com/special-reports/; last accessed August 2009.

39. Eid, "The Other Face of Arab Wealth."

40. Zawya, "Markets Need to Pull In Fervent Foreign Investors," May 9, 2009.
41. APS Diplomat Recorder, "GCC Common Market Becomes a Reality, January 5, 2008.
42. SHUAA Capital, "The Easing of Foreign Ownership Limits—Step 1," Strategy Note, April 28, 2008.
43. Ibid.
44. Pier Terblanche, "Restrictions on Foreign Ownership of UAE Companies Reviewed," International Law Office, June 15, 2009.
45. Ibid.
46. "Etisalat Wins License for 2nd Mobile," *Arab News*, August 10, 2004.
47. "Saudi Telecom Bags Bahrain's 3rd License for $230m," *Arabian Business*, January 22, 2009.
48. "Etisalat Revives Zain Hopes as Vivendi Stalls," *Euroweek*, July 25, 2009.
49. Saudi Telecom Investor Relations Presentation, Ownership Summary, May 2009, www.londonstockexchange.com/ companies-and-advisors/products-and-services/ capital-markets-events/past-capital-markets-days/ saudi-arabia/stc.pdf.
50. "DP World in Landmark IPO," *Arabian Business*, October 21, 2007.
51. "Saudi Arabia's Inma Bank Launches $2.8bn IPO," *Gulf News*, April 7, 2008.
52. "IPO Watch—Enthusiasm Remains," Zawya, February 2008.
53. Mahmoud Haddad and Sam Hakim, "Irrational Exuberance on the Saudi Stock Exchange," Equity and Economic Development Conference Paper, March 2008
54. Rebecca Bundlun, "GCC Equity Fund Assets Down 46%," *Arabian Business*, February 2, 2009.
55. Markaz Research, "GCC Equity Funds," February 2009.
56. Ibid., Appendix 9.
57. Haddad and Hakim, "Irrational Exuberance on the Saudi Stock Exchange."
58. "Markets Need to Pull In Fervent Foreign Investors."
59. Tom Healy, quoted in ibid.

60. Ayah el Said and Rachel Ziemba, "What Role Could Bonds Have in the Quest for New Sources of Finance in the GCC?" *RGE Monitor*, March 6, 2009.

61. Cambridge University Gulf Research Meeting, Workshop Summary, grcevent.net/cambridge/index.php?page=workshop&wname=1.

62. Ibid.

63. "GCC Debt Market Prospects Brighten," Zawya, June 8, 2009.

64. Ibid.

65. Said and Ziemba, "What Role Could Bonds Have?"

66. "Reality Check for Gulf Capital Markets," *Middle East Economic Digest*, October 27, 2008.

67. "Regional Stock Markets: Reality Bites," *Middle East Economic Digest*, March 20, 2006.

68. Coker and Cummins, "Financial Storm Hits Gulf."

69. Global Investment House, "GCC Macroeconomics: Changing Paradigms," Strategy Paper, January 2009.

70. "GCC Expected to Slip into Recession in 2009: NBK," *Arab Times*, April 5, 2009.

71. Coker and Cummins, "Financial Storm Hits Gulf."

72. Ibid.

73. "Central Bank May Buy Part of 2nd Dubai Bond," *Khaleej Times*, July 16, 2009.

74. Global Investment House, "GCC Macroeconomics."

75. Ibid.

76. John C. Bogle, *Little Book of Common Sense Investing* (Hoboken, N.J.: John Wiley & Sons, 2007).

CHAPTER 6

1. "Buck House Can't Accommodate King Abdullah's Entourage," *First Post*, October 20, 2007, www.thefirstpost.co.uk/9371,life,the-people-page&usg=__QnyyUN2tJ-qtFDDVQktpvoYuIBw=&h=270&w=360&sz=45&hl=en&start=3&tbnid=U6oCSDT2jXLpZM:&tbnh=91&tbnw=121&prev=/images%3Fq%3Dabdullah%2Bbuckingham%

2Bpalace%26gbv%3D2%26hl%3Den; last accessed September 2009.

2. "Saudi King Arrives in China to Discuss Energy," *China Daily*, www.chinadaily.com.cn/english/doc/2006-01/23/content_514686.htm; last accessed August 2009.

3. Khalil Hanware and K. S. Ramkumar, "Saudi Arabia-India Investment Gets Immense Boost," *Arab News*, December 14, 2007, www.arabnews.com/?page=15&section=0&article=104658&d=29&m=5&y=2008.

4. "Aramco in $5bn China Deal," *Arab News*, March 31, 2007, www.saudi-us-relations.org/articles/2007/ioi/070401-china-deal.html.

5. Hanware and Ramkumar, "Saudi Arabia-India Investment Gets Immense Boost."

6. Huang Fuhui and Li Zhen, "China-Saudi Strategic Friendship Deepens with Frequent High-Level Visits," Xinhua, February 9, 2009, news.xinhuanet.com/english/2009-02/09/content_10787335.htm.

7. Aamir Rehman, *Dubai & Co.* (New York: McGraw-Hill, 2007), p. 222.

8. Gene Carlson, "U.S. Cautiously Welcomes Arab Investment Boom," *Ludington Daily News*, March 24, 1975, news.google.com/newspapers?id=-DgKAAAAIBAJ&sjid=JEoDAAAAIBAJ&pg=7235,5759864&dq=arab+investment; last accessed September 2009.

9. Ibid.

10. Investcorp Web site, www.investcorp.com/Template1a.aspx?pageid=OB6.0; last accessed September 2009.

11. "Emerging Financial & Economic Trends," *Arab Insight* 2, no. 2, Summer 2008, www.arabinsight.org/aiarticles/189.pdf.

12. "Ratification of the Convention on the OECD," Organisation for Economic Co-operation and Development Web site, www.oecd.org/document/58/0,3343,en_2649_201185_1889402_1_1_1_1,00.html; last accessed September 2009.

13. "Leadership for the 21st Century," Harvard Business School Centennial Global Business Summit, October 12–14, 2008, www.hbs.edu/centennial/businesssummit/leadership/leadership-for-the-21st-century.html

14. "China Is No.1 Exporter," *Straits Times*, August 26, 2009, www.straitstimes.com/Breaking%2BNews/Money/Story/STIStory_421446.html; last accessed September 2009.

15. "Kuwait May Invest $720 m in ICBC IPO," *Financial Express*, September 25, 2006, www.financialexpress.com/news/kuwait-may-invest-720-m-in-icbc-ipo/178644/; last accessed September 2009.

16. Rawi Abdelal, Ayesha Khan, and Tarun Khanna, "Where Oil-Rich Nations Are Placing Their Bets," *Harvard Business Review*, September 2008.

17. Afshin Molavi, "The New Silk Road," *Washington Post*, April 9, 2007, www.washingtonpost.com/wp-dyn/content/article/2007/04/08/AR2007040800923.html.

18. New Silk Route corporate Web site, nsrpartners.com/team_investment_professionals.html; accessed September 2009.

19. Nick Godt, "BRIC countries Seek More Clout at Summit," *Market Watch*, January 16, 2009, www.marketwatch.com/story/bric-countries-seek-more-clout-at-summit; last accessed September 2009.

20. Marcos Aguiar et al., "The 2009 BCG 100 New Global Challengers: How Companies from Rapidly Developing Economies Are Contending for Global Leadership," January 2009, www.bcg.com/publications/files/The_2009_BCG_100_New_Global_Challengers_Jan_2009.pdf; last accessed September 2009.

21. "China-Africa Development Fund," Sovereign Wealth Fund Institute, March 18, 2009, www.swfinstitute.org/fund/cad.php.

22. UNCTAD, "South-South Investment," UNCTAD.org Home, March 18, 2009, www.unctad.org/Templates/Page.asp?intItemID=3972&lang=1.

23. Malaysian government Web site, www.mm2h.gov.my/; accessed September 2009.

24. Speech by the chancellor of the exchequer, the Rt. Hon. Gordon Brown, MP, at the Islamic Finance and Trade Conference, London, www.hm-treasury.gov.uk/speech_chex_130606.htm.

25. William Miracky et al., "Assessing the Risks: The Behaviors of Sovereign Wealth Funds in the Global Economy," Monitor Group, June 2008.

26. Ibrahim Warde, "Islamic Finance After September 11: Toward Arab-Malaysian Integration," In National Bureau of Asian Research, *Islamic Finance in Southeast Asia*, March 2008, www.nbr.org/downloads/pdfs/ETA/IF_PR_Mar08.pdf.

27. Ibid.

28. Andrew England and Javier Blas, "Saudis Set Aside $800m to Secure Overseas Food," *Financial Times*, April 15, 2009.

29. Abdelal et al., "Where Oil Rich Nations Are Placing Their Bets."

30. Ibid.

31. Ibrahim Warde, *Islamic Finance in the Global Economy*, 2nd ed. (Edinburgh, UK: Edinburgh University Press, February 15, 2009.

32. Abdelal et al., "Where Oil-Rich Nations Are Placing Their Bets."

33. "Egyptian Bank May Buy Stake in Damac," *Business Intelligence Middle East*, March 14, 2009, www.bi-me.com/main.php?id=31226&t=1&c=34&cg=4.

34. Rafi-uddin Shikoh and Maria Zain, "Malaysia, Turkey & Saudi Arabia Driving Increased Intra-OIC Trade," *DinarStandard*, May 28, 2008, www.dinarstandard.com/intraoic/intraoic052708.html.

35. Carolyn Lim and E-ling Liaw, "Middle Easterners Flock to Malaysia," *Wall Street Journal*, November 22, 2006.

36. "Temper Tantrums," *Economist*, February 5, 2009, www.economist.com/world/europe/displaystory.cfm?story_id=13059789&fsrc=rss.

37. "Turkish Economy Looks East to Counter Global Slowdown," *DinarStandard*, February 12, 2009, www.dinarstandard.com/intraoic/TurkEcon020809.htm.

38. "Abraaj Capital and BMA Capital Launch Largest Ever Pakistan Focused USD 300 million Private Equity Fund," AME Info, June 1, 2006, www.ameinfo.com/87701.html.

CHAPTER 7

1. HSBC Amanah marketing video, 2002.

2. Abdulrahman Al-Hamidi, "Banking Sector Issues in Saudi Arabia," Bank for International Settlements Web site,

www.bis.org/publ/bppdf/bispap28v.pdf; last accessed January 2007.

3. "A Country Study: Bahrain," Library of Congress, 1993.

4. HSBC presentation, Euromoney Conference, 2007.

5. "Winning Back Hearts and Minds," *Asiamoney*, December 2002, and company Web sites.

6. Khalil Hamware, "You Can Bank on It: Islamic Finance Is the Fastest Growing Phenomenon," *Arab News*, March 23, 2009; and Lahem al Nasser, "The National Commercial Bank and Islamic Banking," *Asharq Alawsat*, September 15, 2008.

7. Mubaseher.info, "GCC Banks to Be Shariah-Compliant before 2015—Study," March 15, 2009.

8. As Oman currently has no Islamic banks, its banking market skews the GCC average for Islamic market share downward.

9. Shaikh Taqi Usmani, *Principles of Shariah Governing Islamic Investment Funds*, www.accountancy.com.pk.

10. Ibid.

11. Faizal Ahmed Manjoo. "Comments of Muhammad al-Bashir Muhammad al-Amine on Reviewing the Concept of Shares: Towards a Dynamic Legal Perspective" islamiccenter.kaau .edu.sa/7iecon/Ahdath/Con06/_pdf/Vol2/33%20Comment %20by%20Bashir%20Al%20Amin.pdf; retrieved April 15, 2009.

12. Islamic Financial Information Service data and research team analysis.

13. Shariah Capital, "Products & Partnerships," www .shariahcap.com/products.php; retrieved August 17, 2009.

14. Ernst & Young, "Islamic Funds and Investment Report," 2008.

15. Islamic Financial Information Service, "Islamic Funds Database," site.securities.com/ifis/; retrieved March 31, 2009.

16. "KSA– SABIC Prefers Islamic Finance for Fundings," MENAFN—Arab News, March 7, 2008, www.menafn .com/qn_news_story_s.asp?StoryId=1093202625; retrieved April 26, 2009.

17. "Islamic Project Finance: Saudi Innovation," *International Financial Law Review*, January 2007, www.iflr.com/Article/1977384/Saudi-innovation.html; retrieved April 1, 2009.

18. "Executive News 200[7], *Islamic*Finance.*de*, issue 20, www.islamicfinance.de/files/islamicfinance20.pdf; retrieved April 12, 2009.

19. Khalil Hanware, "Etisalat IPO Fetches Record SR51 Billion," *Arab News*, November 1, 2004, www.arabnews.com/?page=6&section=0&article=53757&d=1&m=11&y=2004; retrieved March 20, 2009.

20. "Huge investor interest," *Africa Analysis* 462, no. 11, January 2005, Ethnic NewsWatch (ENW) database, Document ID: 812386101; retrieved March 21, 2009.

21. "SAMBA Announce the Coverage of 55.5% of Retial Shares Offered in the IPO," Kingdom Holding Company Press Release, July 17, 2007, www.kingdom.com.sa/en/MC_PR_NewsDetails.asp?p=1&z=22&ID=57, retrieved on September 16, 2009.

22. "East Cameron Gas Sukuk: A New Sukuk Innovation Comes to Market," Bemo Securitisation SAL, June 19, 2006, www.securitization.net/pdf/content/BSEC_19Jun06.pdf; retrieved March 15, 2009.

23. Standard & Poor's, "Islamic Finance Outlook 2009," 2009.

CHAPTER 8

1. Janet Lowe, *Warren Buffett Speaks: Wit and Wisdom from the World's Greatest Investor* (Hoboken, N.J.: John Wiley & Sons, 2007).

2. Robert G. Hagstrom, *The Warren Buffett Way*, 2nd ed. (Hoboken, N.J.: John Wiley & Sons, 2005).

3. Berkshire Hathaway Web site, www.berkshirehathaway.com/meet01/visitguide.pdf; accessed August 2009.

4. Yahoo! finance, finance.yahoo.com/q/ks?s=BRK-A; accessed August 2009.

5. "SAMBA Announce the Coverage of 55.5% of Retial Shares Offered in the IPO," Kingdom Holding Company Press Release, July 17, 2007, www.kingdom.com.sa/en/MC

_PR_NewsDetails.asp?p=1&z=22&ID=57, retrieved on September 16, 2009.

6. "Mubadala Development Assigned 'AA/A-1+' Long- and Short-Term Ratings; Outlook Stable," AME Info, September 16, 2008, www.ameinfo.com/168883.html; accessed August 2009.

7. Fidelity Investment Web site, personal.fidelity.com/products/products_overview.shtml.cvsr?bar=p; accessed August 2009.

8. Investcorp Web site, www.investcorp.com/; accessed August 2009. Abraaj Capital Web site, www.abraaj.com/english/index.aspx/; accessed August 2009. Arcapita Web site, www.arcapita.com/terms.html/; accessed August 2009.

9. Investcorp Web site; accessed August 2009.

10. "Prosperity Is the Issue," *International Financial Law Review* Web site, September 1, 2008, www.iflr.com/Article/2017791/Prosperity-is-the-issue.html; last accessed August 18, 2009.

11. Peralte C. Paul and Shelia M. Poole, "Branching Out, with Limits," *Atlanta Journal Constitution*, July 30, 2006.

12. "Abu Dhabi-Owned Mubadala Takes AMD Stake," CNBC.com, November 16, 2007, www.cnbc.com/id/21830959.

13. Gillian Tett, "Islamic Bonds Used to Buy 007's Wheels," *Financial Times*, March 16, 2007, www.ft.com/cms/s/7461bd9c-d40a-11db-83d5-000b5df10621.html.

14. AMD corporate Web site, www.amd.com/us-en/0,,3715_15966,00.html; accessed August 2009.

15. "ADIA 'Is Not a Political Tool,'" Zawya.com, March 19, 2008, www.zawya.com/story.cfm/sidZAWYA20080319105415; accessed August 2009.

16. UAE Embassy Web site, www.uae-embassy.org/embassy/ambassador-yousef-al-otaiba; accessed August 2009.

17. "Generally Accepted Principles and Practices (GAPP)—*Santiago Principles*," International Working Group of Sovereign Wealth Funds, October 2008, www.iwg-swf.org/pubs/eng/santiagoprinciples.pdf: accessed September 2009.

18. Sovereign Wealth Funds Institute, Linaburg-Maduell Transparency Index, updated January 2009.

CHAPTER 9

1. Emily Thornton and Stanley Reed, "Inside the Abu Dhabi Investment Authority," *BusinessWeek,* June 6, 2008.

2. "P&I/Watson Wyatt World 500: The World's Largest Managers," *Pensions & Investments* Web site, October 1, 2007, www.pionline.com/apps/pbcs.dll/article?AID=/20071001/CHART/70927004/-1/DataPresentationStore; last accessed September 2009.

3. Stanley Reed, "Dubai's High-Profile Money Man," *BusinessWeek*, March 27, 2007.

4. "Mubadala to Take 7.5%, $1.35 Billion Stake in the Carlyle Group; Investment Company Commits Additional $500 Million to Carlyle Fund," Carlyle Group Web site, September 20, 2007, www.carlyleassetmgmt.com/media%20room/news%20archive/2007/item9873.html; last accessed September 2009.

5. "Kuwait May Invest $720 M in ICBC IPO," *Financial Express*, www.financialexpress.com/news/kuwait-may-invest-720-m-in-icbc-ipo/178644/; last accessed September 2009.

6. "Board of Directors," SABB Web site, www.sabb.com/About%20SABB/Profile/Board%20of%20Directors/Board_of_Directors_en.shtml; last accessed September 2009.

7. Arcapita Web site, www.arcapita.com/contact/contact.html; last accessed September 2009; and Unicorn Capital Web site, www.unicorncapital.com.tr/english/index.html; last accessed September 2009.

8. "Assessing the Risks: The Behaviors of Sovereign Wealth Funds in the Global Economy," Monitor Group. December 17, 2008.

9. Government of Abu Dhabi, *The Abu Dhabi Economic Vision 2030*, www.abudhabi.ae/egovPoolPortal_WAR/appmanager/ADeGP/Citizen?_nfpb=true&_pageLabel=p_citizen_homepage_hidenav&did=131654&lang=en; last accessed September 2009.

10. Yahya Al-Nawawi, *Al-Nawawi's Forty Hadith* (Cambridge, UK: Islamic Texts Society, 1997).

11. In Arabic, the expression runs as follows: "*Ma al-Islam? Teeb al-kalaam wa 'it'aam al-t'aam.*"

12. "Abu Dhabi-Owned Mubadala Takes AMD Stake," CNBC.com, November 16, 2007, www.cnbc.com/ id/21830959.

13. "GE to Open Technology Center at Qatar Science and Technology Park," *Qatar Foundation News*, December 2005, www.qstp.org.qa/output/page1633.asp.

14. Ibid.

15. "GE in the Middle East," GE Web site, www.ge.com/mea/ factsheet_me.html; last accessed September 2009.

16. M. A. Ramady and Mourad Mansour. "The Impact of Saudi Arabia's WTO Accession on Selected Economic Sectors and Domestic Economic Reforms," *World Review of Entrepreneurship, Management and Sustainable Development* 2, no. 3 (2006), 189–199.

17. Poppy Trowbridge and Amber Choudhury, "KKR Hires Former Saudi Ambassador Fraker as Adviser," Bloomberg.com, May 18, 2009.

18. "Carlyle Raises $500 Million for Mideast Fund," *New York Times* online, March 9, 2009.

CHAPTER 10

1. Emily Thornton and Stanley Reed, "Who's Afraid of Mideast Money?" *BusinessWeek*, January 10, 2008.

2. Louise Armitstead, "Bid Fever as Qataris Raid LSE and OMX," *Sunday Times* (London), September 20, 2007.

3. "NASDAQ and Borse Dubai Hammer Out OMX Pact; QIA Takes 20% Stake in LSE," Finextra, September 20, 2007.

4. NASDAQ-OMX Group Investor Relations Overview, http://ir.nasdaq.com/.

5. Louise Armitstead, "Gulf Deal Will Make London Stock Exchange 'Bid Proof,'" *Sunday Times* (London), October 21, 2007.

6. Ibid.

7. London Stock Exchange Group Plc, Bloomberg, September 1–November 16, 2007.

8. Zain, Milestones, www.zain.com/muse/obj/lang.default/ portal.view/content/About%20us/Overview/Milestones.

9. CPI Financial, "The UAE Telecoms Sector: A 'Du-opoly'?" *Alternative Investments Report*, July 6, 2008.

10. Fatima El Saadani, "Etisalat Wins Third License," *Business Today Egypt*, August 2006.

11. Zawya, "Etisalat Wins Third License," August 2006.

12. Ebru Tuncay, "Turkey the Winner in Gulf's Investment Hunt," Abraaj Capital New Archive, September 1, 2008.

13. Ibid.

14. Ibid.

15. Metin Demirsar, "Special Report, Turkey: Outsiders Pile In," *FDI Magazine*, August 1, 2006.

16. Zawya, "NCB Pays $1bn for Turkiye Finans Stake," July 18, 2007.

17. HSBC, "Turkey's Finance Sector Finds Profit in Participation," September 29, 2008, www.hsbcnet.com/country/tr/turkiye_finans.html.

18. Preqin Private Equity Intelligence, "Sovereign Wealth Fund Activity in Private Equity and Private Real Estate," WSG Annual Meeting, September 12, 2008.

19. Henry Sender, "Deep Well: How a Gulf Petro-State Invests Its Oil Riches," *Wall Street Journal*, August 24, 2007.

20. Norton Rose LLP, "Sovereign Wealth Funds and the Global Private Equity Landscape Survey," June 2008.

21. Helia Ebrahimi and Philip Aldrick, "Financer Amanda Staveley Misses Mega Payout," *Telegraph* (London), June 23, 2009.

22. James Quinn, "Barclays Offloads Fund Management Business BGI to BlackRock for $13.5bn," *Telegraph* (London), June 12, 2009.

23. KKR press release, September 18, 2008, www.kkr.com/releasedetail.cfm?ReleaseID=338847.

24. EFG-Hermes News, "ADIA Accumulates an 8 Per Cent Stake in EFG-Hermes Holding," May 21, 2007, www.efg-hermes.com/English/NewsDetails.aspx?NID=67&h=h1.

25. The Carlyle Group News, "Mubadala to Take 7.5%, $1.35bn Stake in the Carlyle Group," September 20, 2007, www.carlyleassetmgmt.com/media%20room/news%20archive/2007/item9873.html.

26. Gregory White of TH Lee Partners, quoted in Thornton and Reed, "Who's Afraid of Mideast Money?"
27. Carol Matlack, "How Long Can Middle East Airlines Keep Buying?" *BusinessWeek*, June 16, 2009.
28. Madelene Pearson, "Virgin Blue May Seek Middle East Investor, Australian Reports," Bloomberg, July 20, 2009.
29. "Porsche Shares Up on Qatar Deal," BBC News Online, August 14, 2009.
30. "Abu Dhabi Lifeline for Citigroup," BBC News, November 27, 2007.
31. Eman Goma, "Kuwait: No Plan to Sell Off Merrill Lynch, Citigroup Stakes," *ArabianBusiness.com*, September 6, 2009.
32. "Abu Dhabi Makes $2.5bn by Selling Stake in Barclays," *LiveMint.com* (& *The Wall Street Journal*), June 2, 2009.

CHAPTER 11

1. Lee M. Cohn, "Agency to Check Arab Investment," *St. Petersburg (Florida) Times*, March 7, 1975, http://news.google.com/newspapers?id=C_8NAAAAIBAJ&sjid=qXkDAAAAIBAJ&pg=7188,5808182&dq=arab+investment; accessed August 2009.
2. "Lockheed Confirms It Turned Down $100 Million Arab Investment Offer," *Los Angeles Times*, December 2, 1974, http://pqasb.pqarchiver.com/latimes/access/601190242.html?dids=601190242:601190242&FMT=ABS&FMTS=ABS:AI&type=historic&date=Dec+02%2C+1974&author=&pub=Los+Angeles+Times&desc=Lockheed+Confirms+It+Turned+Down+%24100+Million+Arab+Investment+Offer&pqatl=google; accessed August 2009.
3. Julio J. Rotemberg, "The Dubai Ports World Debacle and Its Aftermath," Harvard Business School case, August 29, 2007.
4. Fredrik Erixon, "World Trade and Trade Policy: New Impetus for Liberalization or Drift to Protectionism?" conference paper, KAS-SWP conference on Global Governance in the Era of Financial Crises, Berlin, March 19, 2009, www.ecipe.org/people/fredrik-erixon/other-publications/KAS%20SWP%20paper%20March%202009.pdf.

5. Jaime Ros, *Development Theory and Economics of Growth* (Ann Arbor: University of Michigan Press, 2001), p. 187.

6. Sean Glynn and Alan Booth, *Modern Britain: An Economic and Social History* (London and New York: Routledge, 1996), p. 254.

7. David Bender and Larry Ponemon, "Binding Corporate Rules for Cross-Border Data Transfer," *Rutgers Journal of Law & Urban Policy* 3, no. 2 (2006), pp. 154–171; "App Remover for Removing Etisalat's 'Registration' Application on BlackBerry Smartphones," BlackBerry security notice on official Web site, http://na.blackberry. com/eng/ataglance/security/regappremover.jsp; last accessed August 2009.

8. David Tallman, "Financial Institutions and the Safe Harbor Agreement: Securing Cross-Border Financial Data Flows," *Law and Policy in International Business*, Spring 2003, http://findarticles.com/p/articles/mi_qa3791/is_200304/a i_n9192493/.

9. *The 9/11 Commission Report* (New York and London: WW Norton & Company, 2004), p. 231.

10. "Background Note: Saudi Arabia," U.S. Department of State, January 2009, www.state.gov/r/pa/ei/bgn/ 3584.htm; last accessed August 2009. M. Ghazanfar Ali Khan, "Security Beefed Up: Riyadh on High Alert," *Arab News*, April 23, 2004, www.arabnews.com/?page= 1&section=0&article=43649&d=23&m=4&y=2004; "Saudi Arabia in the War on Terror," Voice of America, May 31, 2006, www.voanews.com/english/archive/2006-05/ SaudiArabia2006-05-31-voa31.cfm.

11. Yaroslav Trofimov, "U.S. Navy Fleet's Mideast Home Is Facing Rise in Sectarian Strife," *The Wall Street Journal*, June 22, 2009, http://online.wsj.com/article/SB124545647884133003.html.

12. Emily Thornton and Stanley Reed, "Who's Afraid of Mideast Money?" *BusinessWeek*, January 10, 2008, www.businessweek.com/magazine/content/08_03/ b4067042272294.htm; accessed August 2009.

13. "Principles of the Trading System," World Trade Organization, www.wto.org/english/thewto_e/whatis_e/ tif_e/fact2_e.htm#nondiscrimination; accessed August 2009.

14. For a detailed discussion regarding post-WTO deregulation in the GCC, see Chapter 3 of *Dubai & Co.*

15. Rotemberg, "The Dubai Ports World Debacle."

16. Ibid.

17. James K. Jackson, "The Committee on Foreign Investment in the United States (CFIUS)," *CRS Report for Congress*, Congressional Research Service, April 8, 2008, www.fas.org/sgp/crs/natsec/RL33388.pdf.

18. Rotemberg, "The Dubai Ports World Debacle."

19. C. J. Karamargin, "Kolbe: Real Ports Issue Is Container Inspection," *Arizona Daily Star*, March 9, 2006, www.azstarnet.com/sn/byauthor/119282.

20. Rotemberg, "The Dubai Ports World Debacle."

21. Martin Crutsinger, "US Postpones Free Trade Talks with UAE," *San Francisco Chronicle*, March 10, 2006, www.sfgate.com/cgi-.

22. Shakir Husain, "Informal US-UAE Trade Talks to Go On," *Gulf News*, March 12, 2007, http://archive.gulfnews.com/articles/07/03/12/10110486.html.

23. Jackson, "The Committee on Foreign Investment in the United States (CFIUS)."

24. Rotemberg, "The Dubai Ports World Debacle."

25. David Ellis and Tami Luhby, "Government: U.S. Needs Foreign Cash," CNNMoney.com, March 5, 2008, http://money.cnn.com/2008/03/05/news/companies/swf/index.htm?section=money_latest.

26. William Miracky et al., "Assessing the Risks: The Behaviors of Sovereign Wealth Funds in the Global Economy," Monitor Group, June 2008, http://www.monitor.com/Portals/0/MonitorContent/documents/Monitor_SWF_report_final.pdf.

27. "Chinese President's Visit Boosts Ties with Saudi Arabia, GCC," Xinhua Net, February 11, 2009, http://news.xinhuanet.com/english/2009-02/11/content_10803765.htm.

28. Ibid.

29. "Europe's Capital of Islamic Finance," UK Trade & Investment Services, April 30, 2007, www.ukinvest.gov.uk/Financial-services/4003968/en-GB.html.

30. "Singapore Issues Islamic Banking Norms," MENAFN.com, August 5, 2009, www.menafn.com/qn_news_story_s.asp? StoryId=1093247845.

31. Emma Vandore, "Crisis Widens Appeal of Islamic Finance," Associated Press, January 6, 2009, www.finalcall.com/ artman/publish/article_5526.shtml.

32. Jeff Casale, "Lawsuit Arguing AIG Bailout Is Unconstitutional Can Proceed," *Business Insurance*, June 4, 2009, www .businessinsurance.com/article/20090604/NEWS/906049983; Catherine Herridge, "AIG Bailout Promotes Shariah Law, Lawsuit Claims," FoxNews.com, December 22, 2008, www.foxnews.com/story/0,2933,471004,00.html.

33. Michael Silva, "Islamic Banking Remarks," *Law and Business Review of the Americas* 12 (2006), pp. 201–214, 203.

34. Aamir Rehman, "Gulf Investors Exert New Control," *Financial Times*, December 18, 2007, www.ft.com/cms/ s/0/cf446b26-ad0b-11dc-b51b-0000779fd2ac.html.

35. *Middle East Economic Survey*, January 2009.

36. Miracky et al., "Assessing the Risks."

37. "Lockheed Confirms It Turned Down $100 Million Arab Investment Offer."

38. International Working Group of Sovereign Wealth Funds Web site, www.iwg-swf.org/pubs/gapplist.htm; accessed August 2009.

CHAPTER 12

1. Gillian Tett, "Islamic Bonds Used to buy 007's Wheels," *Financial Times*, March 16, 2007, www.ft.com/cms/s/ 7461bd9c-d40a-11db-83d5-000b5df10621.html.

2. Deutsche Bank press release, January 11, 2009, www. deutsche-bank.de/presse/en/content/press_releases_ 2009_4287.htm?month=7&dbiquery=null%3Aislamic.

3. Deutsche Bank press release, January 27, 2009, www .deutsche-bank.de/presse/en/content/press_releases_ 4305.htm?month=2&dbiquery=null%3Aislamic.

4. Morgan Stanley press release, April 24, 2007, www .morganstanley.com/about/press/articles/4797.html.

5. HSBC Amanah Graduate Program brochure, www.hsbc.com/ 1/PA_1_1_S5/content/amanah/assets/html/hsbc_amanah_i nternational_development_programme.pdf.

6. The executives referred to here—Kamal Mian and Mansoor Shakil—are former colleagues of the author.

7. Katrina Nicholas, "Islamic Finance Key to Asian Recovery, Kuwait Finance House Says," *Jakarta Globe,* July 29, 2009, http://thejakartaglobe.com/business/islamic-finance-key- to-asian-recovery-kuwait-finance-house-says/320942; last accessed August 2009.

8. Michael Ainley et al., "Islamic Finance in the UK: Regulation and Challenges," Financial Services Authority presentation, November 2007, slide 10.

9. Harvard Islamic Finance Project Web site, http://ifptest .law.harvard.edu/ifphtml/index.php?module=sponsors; last accessed August 2009.

10. Institute of Islamic Banking and Insurance Web site, www.islamic-banking.com/contact_us.aspx; last accessed August 2009.

11. Bahrain Institute of Banking and Finance Web site, www .bibf.com.bh/content/index.htm/; accessed August 2009.

12. INCEIF Web site, www.inceif.org/discover/inceif_fact_ sheet/inceif_fact_sheet.php; last accessed August 2009.

13. "First Ever Islamic Finance Social Responsibility Survey Launched," Zawya.com, June 21, 2009, www.zawya.com/ story.cfm/sidZAWYA20090623055920; last accessed August 18, 2009.

CONCLUSION

1. "Oman," *CIA World Factbook,* 2009, www.cia.gov/library/ publications/the-world-factbook/geos/mu.html; last accessed September 2009.

2. ACNielsen, cited in *RetailME,* November 2006.

INDEX

Page numbers followed by a *t* refer to tables; those followed by an *f* refer to figures.

ABOUT THE AUTHOR

Aamir A. Rehman is an expert in global corporate strategy and the Gulf region. He is a managing director at Fajr Capital Limited, a principal investment firm focused on emerging markets. Previously, Mr. Rehman was global head of strategy for HSBC Amanah, the worldwide Islamic finance business unit of the HSBC Group. Prior to HSBC, he was a consultant with the Boston Consulting Group.

Mr. Rehman is the author of *Dubai & Co.: Global Strategies for Doing Business in the Gulf States* (McGraw-Hill, 2007), a groundbreaking work on corporate strategy in the GCC region. *Dubai & Co.* has been sold worldwide, with two Chinese-language editions published in 2008. Mr. Rehman's research and commentary have been featured in media outlets worldwide, including the *Financial Times*, the *Wall Street Journal*, and the *Harvard Business Review.*

Mr. Rehman is an adjunct scholar at the Middle East Institute, a nonpartisan Washington, DC, institution. He holds a bachelor's degree from Harvard College, a master's degree from Harvard University, and an MBA from the Harvard Business School. A native of Staten Island, New York, he and his wife split their time between New York City and the Gulf region.

Mr. Rehman may be reached at aamir.rehman@rehmaninstitute.com. For additional information go to www.rehmaninstitute.com.